INDIGENOUS POPULATION AND SOCIAL EXCLUSION

INDIGENOUS POPULATION AND SOCIAL EXCLUSION

Edited by

Dr. Anjuli Chandra

M.Sc., Ph.D (Anthropology)
Assistant Professor cum Assistant Director
Centre for Study of Social Exclusion &
Inlcusive Policy (CSSEIP)
Gandhigram Rural Institute - Deemed University
(Re-Accredited by NAAC with 'A' Grade)
Gandhigram - 624302
Dindigul
Tamil Nadu (INDIA)

D P H

DISCOVERY PUBLISHING HOUSE PVT. LTD.

NEW DELHI-110 002

Published by:
Tilak Wasan
DISCOVERY PUBLISHING HOUSE PVT. LTD.
4383/4B, Ansari Road, Darya Ganj
New Delhi-110 002 (India)
Phone : +91-11-23279245, 43596064-65
Fax : +91-11-23253475
E-mail : discoverypublishinghouse@gmail.com
sales@discoverypublishinggroup.com
parul.wasan@gmail.com
web : www.discoverypublishinggroup.com

***First Edition:* 2014**

ISBN: 978-93-5056-478-3

Indigenous Population and Social Exclusion

Printed at:
Aditi Fine Art Press
Delhi

Preface

Indigenous people worldwide stand between 300-500 million. They constitute 80 per cent of the world's cultural and biological diversity and occupy 20 per cent of the world's land surface. The indigenous communities throughout the world are of extensive diversity as peoples and communities, but there is one thing in common – they all share a history of injustice. Indigenous peoples have been exploited, tortured, enslaved and killed. The United Nations Special Rapporteur to the Sub-Commission on Prevention of Discrimination and Protection of Minorities defines indigenous communities, people and nations as: Those which having a historical continuity with pre-invasion and pre-colonial societies that developed on their territories, consider themselves distinct from other sectors of societies now prevailing in those territories, or parts of them. They form at present non-dominant sectors of society and are determined to preserve, develop and transmit to future generations their ancestral territories, and their ethnic identity, as the basis of their continued existence as people, in accordance with their own cultural patterns, social institutions and legal systems.

The term Social Exclusion has been defined by the Department for International Development (DFID), Government of United Kingdom as "a process by which certain groups are systematically disadvantaged, because they are discriminated against on the basis of their ethnicity, race, religion, sexual orientation, caste, descent, gender, age, disability, HIV status, migrant status or where they live". Though, the term Social exclusion evolved in 1960s, the prevalence of exclusive practices occurred since the time immemorial. In India, Dalit, tribals, women, minorities and more recently population ageing, differently-able, people with HIV, transgenders etc. are considered socially excluded references for policy intervention.

Adivasis/Tribal are the indigenous people of India, who have a unique culture, identity and autonomy. However, the Indian state did not recognise their indigenous status, neglected them in terms of development and denied their rights and justice. It is well known that the tribal peoples have a symbiotic relationship with the nature which includes their land and forests. But Permanent Settlement Act, 1793 introduced by British in India alienated them from their own forest. Since then, at an alarming rate, they have been losing their land and livelihood to extractive industries which will destabilize their habitats. As a result, they have been rendered landless, homeless, foodless, jobless and sadly enough, cultureless, leaving them with only a bleak future staring at them. They have increasingly been the victims of a model of development which benefits a certain class of people. It is a matter of fact that since India gain independence millions of tribal peoples has lost their land and livelihood to large scale industries and mega dams development projects. Studies have pointed out that around 40 per cent of people displaced by projects belong to tribal communities though they account for only 8 per cent of total population of the country.

At this juncture, the present book on *'Indigenous Population and Social Exclusion in India'* provides all the scholars, academicians and social scientists working in the field of social exclusion, an insight to understand the issues of social exclusion among the indigenous people in India and also highlight the imperatives needed for their positive inclusive development.

Editor

Acknowledgements

It is a great opportunity for me to acknowledge all those who helped me throughout my academic endeavor of this edited volume. First of all, I would like to pay my humblest reverence to the Almighty God whose unseen but felt power strengthen me and blessed me for the completion of this book.

In the series, I would like to express my humblest gratitude to Dr. SM. Ramasamy, honorable Vice Chancellor, GRI, Gandhi gram and Dr. N. Narayansamy, Registrar, GRI, Gandhigram for their continuous encouragement and guidance.

Next, I would like to express my heartfelt thanks to all the contributors of this edited volume for giving the modified and corrected versions of their full papers and sharing their experiences and knowledge about indigenous population in India for the success of the book.

I would like to thank Dr. C. Ramanujam, Coordinator and Associate Professor cum Deputy Director, CSSEIP, GRI, Gandhi gram; Dr. A. Mani; Dr. P. A. Sam Velladhurai, Assistant Professors cum Assistant Directors, and Dr. V. Thirukanni, Research Associate, CSSEIP, GRI, Gandhigram for their continuous support and fruitful advices to bring the book in the present form.

I would also like to thanks Discovery Publishing House Pvt. Ltd., New Delhi for the quick and timely publication of the book with professional fervor and perfection.

Last, but not the least I would like to acknowledge the support and care of my parents Dr. A. C. Srivastava, Mrs. Shakuntala Srivastava and my brothers Mr. Aashish Chandra and Mr. Amrish Chandra, in all the phases of my life.

Dr. Anjuli Chandra

Contents

SECTION-III
Indigenous Population
Extremism, Displacement and Education

SECTION – I

Indigenous Population

Multi Dimensionality of Social Exclusion

1

Introduction

*Dr. Anjuli Chandra

People who inhabited a land before it was conquered by colonial societies and who consider themselves distinct from the societies currently governing those territories are called indigenous peoples. In the pre-colonial period, indigenous peoples were called by various pejorative names – 'Black Barbarians' and 'White Barbarians' in China, or Mleccha in India. Indigenous peoples in Asia are now referred to officially by a number of designations – scheduled tribes or Adivasis in India, national minorities or minority nationalities in China and Vietnam (though those terms can also refer to other minorities like Muslims or Tibetans in China), hill tribes in Thailand. There are approximately 370 million indigenous people spanning 70 countries worldwide which embodies and nurtures 80 per cent of the world's cultural and biological diversity, and occupies 20 per cent of the world's land surface (Singh and Kaur, 2009). The indigenous peoples of the world are very diverse. They speak their own languages are largely self-sufficient and their economies are tightly bound to their intimate relationship with their land. Indigenous

* Assistant Professor cum Assistant Director, Centre for Study of Social Exclusion and Inclusive Policy, Gandhigram Rural Institute-Deemed University, Gandhigram - 624 302, Dindigul, Tamil Nadu.

peoples have historically faced social exclusion and marginalization. They are disproportionately represented among the poor and extremely poor, their levels of access to adequate health and education services are well below national averages, and they are especially vulnerable to the consequences of environmental degradation.

Social Exclusion refers to the complex processes that deny certain groups full participation in society. The term Social Exclusion has been defined by the Department for International Development (DFID), Government of United Kingdom as "a process by which certain groups are systematically disadvantaged, because they are discriminated against on the basis of their ethnicity, race, religion, sexual orientation, caste, descent, gender, age, disability, HIV status, migrant status or where they live". Though, the term social exclusion evolved in 1960s, the prevalence of exclusive practices occurred since the time immemorial. In India, Dalit, tribals, women, minorities and more recently population ageing, differently-able, people with HIV, transgenders etc., are considered socially excluded references for policy intervention. This edited volume however, focuses on the social exclusion of tribals or the indigenous people of India.

The United Nations Special Rapporteur to the Sub-Commission on Prevention of Discrimination and Protection of Minorities defines indigenous communities, people and nations as: Those which having a historical continuity with pre-invasion and pre-colonial societies that developed on their territories, consider themselves distinct from other sectors of societies now prevailing in those territories, or parts of them. They form at present non-dominant sectors of society and are determined to preserve, develop and transmit to future generations their ancestral territories, and their ethnic identity, as the basis of their continued existence as people, in accordance with their own cultural patterns, social institutions and legal systems.

The indigenous communities throughout the world are of extensive diversity as peoples and communities, but there is one thing in common – they all share a history of injustice. Indigenous peoples have been exploited, tortured, enslaved and killed. In many cases, they have been the victims of genocide. Indigenous peoples have historically faced social exclusion and marginalization. Colonialism and development are the twin processes responsible for their exclusion. Until colonization they were autonomous, self-sufficient, self-reliant and their economies are tightly bound to their intimate relationship with their land and forest. After colonization started from Western Europe to Northern and Southern America it directly affected the indigenous people throughout the world. Their autonomy was taken away from them, they became dependent on colonial administrators and their economy was shackled. During 1840s at the time of Gold Rush in California more than one lakh of Native Americans were uprooted, debased and killed by the colonialists. On the other hand, Apartheid *i.e.*, the South African Indigenous people are still facing racial residential discrimination while in Australia the indigenous people have not yet got recognition and are known as 'stolen generation'.

Indigenous Population in India

Adivasis are the indigenous people of India, who have a unique culture, identity and autonomy. However, the Indian state did not recognise their indigenous status, neglected them in terms of development and denied their rights and justice. Adivasis do not only depend on natural resources for their livelihood but their entire social, economic and political systems, including identity, autonomy and distinct culture are based on natural resources. They are not only consumers of the natural resources but also protectors and conservators of the same. They have their century-old comprehensive methods, rules and policies for preservation, protection and conservation of the forests. It is well known that the tribal peoples have a symbiotic relationship with their land and forests (Dash, 2002: 357). Their culture, world view and customary law are the product of their interaction with their land and forests (Krishnan, 2004: 48). Yet, at an alarming rate, they have been losing their land and livelihood to extractive industries which will only destabilised their habitats. As a result, they have been rendered landless, homeless, foodless, jobless and sadly enough, cultureless, leaving them with only a bleak future staring at them. They have increasingly been the victims of a model of development which benefits a certain class of people. It is a matter of fact that since India gain independence millions of tribal peoples has lost their land and livelihood to large scale industries and mega dams. Studies have pointed out that around 40 per cent of people displaced by projects belong to tribal communities though they account for only 8 per cent of total population of the country (Fernandes, 2008: 92).

Historically, they have been dispossessed of their lands, are in the centre of conflict for excess to valuable resources where they live. Conquest and colonization have attempted to steal their dignity and identity as well as fundamental rights of meaningful survival. History discloses that many tribal societies have been completely wiped off by either war, disease or by exploitation and cultural assimilation over these last centuries. The intellectual and cultural property rights of indigenous people are under threat. These includes their believes, knowledge (agricultural, technical, medicinal and ecological), movable and immovable cultural properties, customary laws, traditions, rights to flora and fauna, arts and artistic works and other forms of cultural expression, handed through the generations. The issue of cultural rights of indigenous people, the theme of the discussion, raises complex and difficult questions (Social Action, Vol. 60, No. 4).

Development as a Cause for Social Exclusion

Development has entered into our world with two accomplices: *(i)* modern science and *(ii)* colonialism. From science, development has inherited the belief that we go on increasing the 'power' of the human beings over the non-human cosmos; for the world has enough resources to meet not only the needs but also the greed of all humans. From colonialism, development has inherited the faith that those on the higher rungs of history have the right to shape the ways of life of those on the lower. And the 'tribes' of India, as history tells us, are the indigenous, sons of soil, autochthonous people of the land, who had been settled for long in different parts of the country before the Aryan-speaking people invaded Kabul and Indus valleys are the direct sufferers of this development and still facing the consequences of development. The so called civilized invaders slowly pushed the aboriginal or indigenous people of this land, to the forest outskirts and today the modern technologies are beyond their reach. The evolution of the strategy of tribal development as well as the beginning of their exclusion in Indian context can be perceived at four levels:

1. *Muslim Period:* During this period after the arrival of Mughals the tribal/indigenous people of India have been raided for the resources. The Muslim rulers not only conquered the geographical regions but also shackled the culture of these local autochthonous people. As a result they faced discrimination and exclusion in their own land and territory.
2. *British Period:* The credit of initiating the process of development, through railways and roadways in the inaccessible tribal regions goes to the British. Realising the extensive potentialities of natural resources in the tribal areas they started colonising the regions and exploited the natural resources. Along with the British many non-tribal people also entered into the region and thereby started disturbing the cultural and ecological milieu of the indigenous people. The colonial policy towards land and forest disturbed the life long bond of the tribals and engendered wide spread revolts like the Khond rebellion of 1846, Santal revolt of 1855, powerful movement of 1931 by the Eliangs and the Kuki rebellion (1917-19).
3. *Post- Independence Period:* To promote the integration of tribals with the rest of India, the Constitution provided special safeguards and facilities to this weaker section by way of 'protective discrimination'. It incorporates special clauses for creation of the Scheduled Tribes as well as Scheduled Areas for their intensive development. On the basis of Indo-US Operational Agreement. Community Development (CD) programme evolved on 2nd October 1952 as the first systematic programme on rural development. As the tribal areas needed special treatment, 43 Special Multipurpose Tribal Development (SMPT) Blocks

were launched in 1954. The Verrier Elwin Committee (1959) found that the programme did not yield desired results and the need of tribals did not reflect properly. Later on it was converted into Tribal Development Blocks (TDBs) and after that Tribal Sub-Plan came into existence.

4. *Post-Liberalization Period:* The exploitation and exclusion of indigenous people increases manifold after the period of liberalization. Due to coming of innumerable multinational companies and due to their dwellings again in the tribal areas, the exploitation of natural resources aggravated at an unprecedented rate. Once again they felt alienated in their own land and this time the consequences are more severe than during the British period. Therefore, continuous negligence, failure of inclusive development and exclusion, leads indigenous people towards the path of insurgency and extremism which according to our Prime Minister is the biggest internal threat for the country.

The present book is being divided into three sections and each section consists of six research articles, in all there are eighteen articles, including Introduction written by the editor. The first chapter, *'Introduction'*, highlights the meaning, international and national scenario of Indigenous population and the very process of social exclusion. The author asserted that colonialism and development are the twin processes responsible for the exclusion of indigenous population in India.

The second chapter titled, *'Plight of Paliya Tribe in Tamil Nadu'*, by Dr. M. P. Boraian, examines how far non-discrimination, under the UN declaration of Human Rights has been translated at the ground level, by focusing upon the Paliyas of Palani hills in Kodaikanal block, one of the 461 tribes in India and 36 tribes in Tamil Nadu. The author stated that in the course of their economic transactions such as offering manual labour, marketing farm yield, delivering forest produce, trading cattle, and making domestic purchases, they were largely exploited, indebted, abused and some persons were even bonded to the employers while the plight of those living in inaccessible settlements is pathetic and painful. The author therefore, concluded that the Paliyans are highly excluded due to their geographical limitations, economic deprivation and continuous displacement and ended the paper with suggestions for their uplift.

Next chapter titled, *'Social Exclusion and Inclusive Policies: A Methodological Issue in Studying Tribes of Assam'*, Dr. C. J. Sonowal asserted that investigating and measuring social exclusion has been a complex issue in methodological front. Thus, his paper is an attempt to delineate different perspective of looking at the process of social exclusion and to bring forward a widely acceptable model of investigation in the issue of social exclusion among tribes of India.

Chapter four, titled, *"Multi-Dimensional Exclusion of Muslim Nomads: The Gujjars Living at the Margins in Jammu and Kashmir"* by Dr. Farida Siddiqui started with the origin followed by elaborate discussion about the multidimensional exclusion of Gujjars life in education, economy, linguistic, specifically focusing on the exclusion of the Gujjar women. The paper ends with recommendations mainly focusing on educational measures for their inclusion.

Next chapter titled, *'Indigenous Population and Strategies for Inclusion with reference to Souria Paharia Tribe of Sahibganj, Jharkhand'*, by Mr. J. Nelson starts with definitions, major problems and inclusive governance for societal upliftment of tribes. The paper proceeds by discussing Millennium Development Goals, India's progress and its achievement through Evangelical Fellowship of India Commission on Relief (EFICOR). The author further described the details of Souria Paharia tribe's social, political, economic and cultural aspects and concluded the paper with some accomplishments by EFICOR provided to improve the quality of life of Sauria Paharia community.

'Indigenous Population of Irulas and Social Exclusion at Vasantham Nagar, Thiruppachur Village, Thiruvalluvar District: A Case Study', a combined paper by Prof. S. Antonysamy and Prof. A. Baskar Jayabalan, is an elaborate study on the life status of Irula tribal group. The authors described that the people live in the lower slopes of hills and forests and their prime occupation is collecting and selling honey and firewood. They pointed out that the Irulas get very low wages and work as bonded labourers. Their life is very pathetic living in houses with thatched roof and mud floor. The authors also narrated several socio-economic issues and problems faced by Irulas due to exploitation by non-tribal people in Vasantham Nagar. Finally, suggestions were given on how to improve the livelihood with the support from the government and introduction of new schemes to educate the youth and uplift the poor in society.

In the next chapter titled, *'Issues of Poverty among Indigenous Communities'* Dr. P. Anantharajkumar has discussed about the origin, understanding, identification and criteria of being indigenous. The author highlighted the common characteristics, key facts, distribution, rights, concerned issues and the alarming status of poverty among the indigenous communities. The author concluded that though the indigenous people make valuable contributions to world's heritage due to their traditional knowledge and their understanding of ecosystem management but they are also among the world's most vulnerable, marginalized and disadvantaged groups. Therefore, we must ensure that their voices are heard, their rights respected, and their well-being improved.

Next chapter entitled *'Historical Locks and Economic Deprivation of Indigenous Population: Evidence from Kerala'* by Mr. M. P. Saji discussed elaborately about the economic deprivation of indigenous population in Kerala and demonstrated through various graphs and charts that how they are facing alienation from their own land and forest; educational backwardness and also the affect of market economy on them.

'Determinants of Marriage and Natal Care among Tribal Communities in India', paper authored by Dr. A. K. Ravishankar informed us that early marriage was so high among the Indian tribal community and most of the tribal women preferred home for their child deliveries. The author further pointed out that a quite significant proportion of the child deliveries are carried out by untrained persons among these communities. Further he revealed the tribal conception for their home delivery in which they strongly believe that it is not necessary to visit the health facilities to deliver the child.

Chapter *'Right to Health and Tribal Communities in India: From a Social Exclusion Perspective'*, by Mr. Jobi Babu tries to throw light on the diverse health problems among the different target groups of tribal community in India and the exclusion of these underprivileged groups from the realm of better health facilities, their miseries due to the lack of accessibility, affordability and availability of health services etc., are emphasised. The paper also gives certain suggestions to improve the health conditions of the tribal people and there by improve the quality of life of tribal populace of India.

Another paper authored by Mr. K. Veeramani was on *'The Quest for Survival-Nebulous Future of Onge: Indigenous population of Andaman Nicobar Island'* who are one among the 75 Primitive Tribal Groups of India and had the least facilities and was dominated by ancient tribal believes in this advanced technological world. The paper gave ethnographic picture of this tribe living on the edge of extinction and also the reason for their decreasing population. The author ended the paper by pleading that the policies should be revamped according to the real met needs of all such Primitive Tribal Groups. The fate of their livelihood and destiny of forthcoming generations of these indigenous groups altered only by the collective efforts of all of the actors involved in it.

Last chapter of this section titled, *'Social Exclusion of Populations with Indigenous Knowledge is Crisis to the Nation'*, Mr. Ashok Das Gupta discussed elaborately about the meaning, classification and criticism of indigenous knowledge; indigenous knowledge holders; indigenous culture; challenges in front of indigenous culture; indigenous knowledge and folk life; indigenous rights and people. The author stated that social exclusion of indigenous communities is considered as a crisis to the Indian Nation with support from historical evidences and with three suitable examples, implications of Indigenous Knowledge Systems/Indigenous World View for all the time and all the humanity.

First chapter of the last section titled *'Insurgency in the State of Manipur from Ethnic Contest to Societal Exclusion'*, authored by Mr. Sonkhogin Haokip attempts to highlight the fact that 'Insurgency' in Manipur is the offshoot of ethnic contests reflected in the form of 'dominant ethnic groups *vs* non-dominant ethnic groups' where the former submerges and excludes the latter from social, political and economic advantages and concludes by saying that the strong and deep-rooted nexus between the Militants, Politician and Bureaucrats has eventually excluded people by and large, irrespective of the ethnic group they belong to, from social, political and economic advantages.

The chapter titled, *'Rise of Extremism in Adivasis (Tribal People) of Kerala: A Close Look on Muthanga Incident'* by Mr. N. Sumesh discussed about a mass struggle for land and life of the adivasis of Kerala and how the nature of agitation got an extremist character. The author asserted that the unexpected turn of events that led to the Muthanga tragedy was the culmination of the State's inaction on the Adivasis' just demands for a homeland. The State Government failed to keep its promise on the distribution of land to the landless Adivasis as a result hundreds of them 'encroached' upon the Muthanga wild life sanctuary on 5th January, 2003.

Next chapter entitled, *'Displaced Massai: A Study on an Ethnic Group in East Africa'* written by Fr. I. Sekar focuses on Massai tribe in East Africa who are well known for their cultural heritage and migration. The author argued that century's nomadic pastoralist turned to be bead workers, watchman in urban areas and small traders that are the consequences of civilization and deforestation. The study describes the richness of Massai tribe in East Africa, their struggle for survival and their contribution to the national tourism.

Next chapter in this section named *'Strategies to Overcome Barriers in Education of Maasai Girls in Kenya'* was jointly written by two research scholars named Mr. H. Magara Robinson Makori and Ms. Nyangwencha M. Jeridah. The authors said that these populations were nomadic in nature and tried to explain that how the girls were excluded from the educational system. They also gave a detailed account on the existence of gender discrimination in Kenya. Finally they mentioned suggestions to overcome the educational exclusion of Maasai Girls in Kenya specifically increasing their school enrolment, empowering the women and educating the entire community.

Another chapter titled, *'A Study on the Educational Status of Tribal children with special reference to Kuttakarai Village, Jawadhi Hills, Thiruvannamali District, Tamil Nadu'*, also a combined paper by Mr. F. Jayachandran and Dr. P. B. Shankar Narayanan which is an exhaustive study on the educational status of the tribal children. The universe of the study was tribal children aged between 6 to 14 years in Jawadhi hills block using survey method. It analysed the socio-economic reasons for illiteracy among the tribes and suggested that appropriate awareness programmes on importance of education, special attention by the teachers towards students, periodical check on quality of mid-day meals can increase the number of school-going children and thereby enhance the literacy rate.

The last chapter in the section named *"Education and Social Equity: With a Special Focus on Scheduled Castes and Scheduled Tribes in Elementary Education in India"* was authored by Mrs. C. Praba. The author compares the educational status of SC and ST and argued that though there are several commonalities in the experience and outcomes of social exclusion for both groups, there are also some critical differences in the ways in which it takes place that have led to somewhat different struggles for equal rights. The author has touched upon a few issues that have direct implications for educational equity and inclusion of both the groups.

In this way, the book comprises of total eighteen articles covering wide range of exclusion among the indigenous population in Indian context while two papers also throw some light on African Massai tribe's exclusion.

2

Plight of Paliya Tribe in Tamil Nadu

*Dr. M. P. Boraian

ABSTRACT

According to the International Labour Organization (ILO), there are about 5000 different groups of Indigenous and tribal people worldwide, totaling about 300 million people or 4.8 per cent of world's total population, living in more than 70 countries from the Arctic to Amazon and Australia. Nearly two thirds of these tribal people live in Asia. Scheduled Tribes comprising 67.8 million people constitute 8.2 per cent of India's population (2001). With 6.51 lakh tribals, Tamil Nadu accounts for one per cent of India's total tribal population. Under the Universal Declaration of Human Rights, the United Nations observes that nobody can be discriminated against on the basis of his or her race, colour, or ethnic background. This paper examines how far this has been translated at the ground level, by focusing upon one schedule tribe *viz.*, the Paliyas of Palani hills in Kodaikanal block, one of the 461 tribes in India and 36 tribes in Tamil Nadu State. The Paliya tribe struggle for their basic minimum needs and a minimum comfort more than any of their bottom rang counterparts such as the dalits, the

* Prof. and Head, Department of Extension Education and Co-ordinator, Centre for Disability and Development, Gandhigram Rural Institute (Deemed University), Gandhigram - 624 302, Dindigul District, Tamil Nadu.

poor and the destitute. The deficiency in their decent standard of life is pervasive across the vital sectors of human progress – food, clothing, shelter, drinking water, health, education, transportation, energy, livelihood assets, government certification of their living status, community of origin, land ownership, and dwelling places. They are concealed, discriminated, exploited, and neglected, both by the government, and the society. They live amidst the risk of eviction by the Estate owners, threats from Forest/Revenue officials, and the danger of fire, wild animals and occupational hazards. Illiteracy, drop out, early marriage, and elopements, are a commonality. The invasion of tribal settlements by the Law enforcers, on the apprehension of terrorist intrusion, causes greater hardship than protection, and their welfare inputs make the tribals more dependent. Intervention by the external agencies like the government, panchayats are more peripheral and perfunctory. NGOs' and Donor agencies' direct intervention projects encourage and enable the tribals to be independent, assertive of their rights and fight against forces of exploitation. This paper examines the ways and means of overcoming these constraints, and offers suggestions for their uplift.

Keywords: Tribes, Paliyan, Health care, Primitive Tribal Groups.

Introduction

According to the International Labour Organization (ILO), there are about 5000 different groups of indigenous and tribal people worldwide, totaling about 370 million people or 4.8 per cent of world's total population. Nearly two-thirds of these tribal people live in Asia. They are living in 72 countries from the Arctic regions to the Amason and Australia. Besides being the oldest people, they are often poor, live in remote or inhospitable lands, many of them cannot read or write and they generally suffer from social discrimination. Under the Universal Declaration of Human Rights, the United Nations says that nobody can be discriminated against on the basis of his or her race, colour or ethnic background. Scores of agreements put together by the UN also support equal rights for indigenous peoples.

Tribes in India

Scheduled tribes, comprising 84.3 million people, constitute 8.3 per cent of India's population. India houses 698 Scheduled Tribes and Orissa has the largest number of 68 Scheduled Tribes. Seventy five of the 698 scheduled tribes are identified as Primitive tribal groups as they are considered more backward than the other tribes. Scheduled Tribes are those who are notified as such by the President of India under Article 342 of the constitution. The first notification was issued in 1950. The President considers characteristics like the tribes' primitive traits, distinctive culture, shyness with the public at large, geographical isolation and social and economic backwardness before notifying them as a Scheduled Tribe.

Primitive Tribal Groups (PTGs) are Scheduled Tribes known for their declining or stagnant population, low levels of literacy, pre-agricultural technology, primarily belonging to the hunting and gathering stage and extreme backwardness. They were considered as special category for support for the first time in 1979. There are 25 lakh PTG populations, spread over 15 States and Union Territories, constituting 3.6 per cent of the tribal population. PTGs comprise 0.3 percentage of the country's population. PTGs have not benefited from government development activities and they face continuous threats of eviction from their homes and lands. One of the Nehruvian Panchasheel, spelt out in 1952 notes that the index of tribal development should be the quality of their life and not the money spent. Yet another principle cautions that tribal development should be undertaken without disturbing tribal social and cultural institutions. The National Policy for Tribals recognises that a majority of scheduled tribes continue to live below the poverty line, have poor literacy rates, suffer from malnutrition and diseases and are vulnerable to displacement.

Paliya Tribe in Tamil Nadu

Tamil Nadu houses a total of 6.51 lakh tribals, accounting for about one per cent of India's total tribal population. The paliya tribe is one of the 36 tribes in Tamil Nadu. Six of them are classified under Primitive Tribal Groups (PTGs). The paliya tribe has been concentrated in Coimbatore, Dindigul, Theni, Madurai, Virudhunagar and Tirunelveli districts in the Western Ghats bordering Kerala. Tribes in Tamil Nadu are categorised under five predominant economic activities *viz.*, *(i)* settled cultivators, *(ii)* shifting cultivators, *(iii)* pastoral people, *(iv)* artisans and *(v)* food gatherers (hunting, fishing and collection). A total of six tribes belong to the category of food gatherers *viz.*, *(i)* Irulas, *(ii)* Kurumbas, *(iii)* Mudugars, *(iv)* Malasars, *(v)* Paliyas and *(vi)* Uralis. The Paliya tribe inhabits the Lower Palani hills particularly in the lower region down Kodaikanal, a popular summer hill resort in India. Paliya tribe, says Hutton, is one of the ancient and primitive hill tribes of India, found in parts of the Western Ghats in Tamil Nadu. Thurston describes paliya tribe as a very backward caste who reside in small scattered parties around the jungle of the Upper Palani hills and in the Varushanad valley of Madurai district.

House in Exploitation

Plight of Paliya tribe in Tamil Nadu leads to concern since their condition in remote areas are alarming. The paliyas live in four types of habitations – in settlements in their own houses, in the houses provided by their employers, in the government provided free houses, or in scattered farmsteads located remotely. Tribes living in government provided free houses built by contractors, have their tale of woes, due to poor quality after a short period of construction. Encroachment of tribal houses and settlements by money lenders and traders from the plains is another dimension of the problem. Tribal families comfortably living in the employer – provided houses located within the plantation premises, face the risk of religious conversion. Those living in crowded shelters provided by their Hindu employers are subjected to exploitation and near bondage. Employers in both the cases strive to channelise the benefits of government programmes as a benefactor, filter them wherever possible or scuttle them altogether, with the intent of maintaining their dependency level. The employers also utilise the opportunity to exploit the tribal children of these families, by engaging them in work along with their parents and carefully avoiding their schooling, for obvious reasons. Both categories of the employers keep the activists and NGOs at bay, by preventing their access to the tribals. Further, every source of their livelihood brought them burdens. In the course of their economic transactions such as offering manual labour, marketing farm yield, delivering forest produce, trading cattle, and making domestic purchases, they were largely dependent, exploited, indebted, abused, and some persons were even bonded to the employers.

Distance is Darkness

Life in the tribal settlements located near roadside is better than their counterparts hold up in the interior forests. The latter are devoid of connectivity, free housing, drinking water facilities, education of children, access to health care facilities, benefits of government schemes, voluntary social services, employment opportunities, mobility, interaction with non-tribals and exposure to the external world. Roadside or nearby settlers have all these in abundance and have lesser hardship. The plight of those living in inaccessible settlements is pathetic and painful. Superstition, ignorance, illiteracy, poverty, unemployment, exploitation, and bondage constitute the characteristics of tribals housed in remote habitations. Tribals located in scattered and far-flung settlements lack their bare minimum necessities of life such as adequate food, protected shelter, drinking water, health care, electricity and primary education. Bondage, poverty, landlessness, lack of subsidiary activities, economic exploitation, superstition, and ignorance make their livelihood base very slender and their life sub human. Longer the distance from the main land, greater the darkness in their lives. Huts raised by the tribals with a bundle of poles and bunch of wild grass are highly prone to rains, wind and the wild lives. Huts perched on sloppy tracks of hills witness seepage of rain water cutting across the huts, drenching all the inmates at night. Adults are awake the whole night, holding the main poles of their hut from being blown away during heavy winds.

Displacement Prone Tribe

The paliya tribals are highly vulnerable to displacement. Wild animals and forest fire forcibly evict tribal families *en masse* from their existing settlements. Coffee estate owners, who suspect an imminent threat to their economic interests from government or NGOs, through the tribals living close by, indulge in violence to clear them out. Lands are largely owned by estate owners and rich farmers. Tribals invariably toil as workers. Wherever the tribals cultivate in tiny plots, the forest officials promptly evacuate them or exploit them. Collection of minor forest produce, permitted by the government, is disallowed and disturbed by the forest officials. Traders from near and far, procure these produces for paltry sums. Spells of rain deprives them of their farm labour or minor forest produce collection. Tribals cultivating the bits and pieces of land are a few and far between. With lack of mobility, exposure, social interaction and awareness, these tribals do not live their life fully. The vast span of life of these tribals is spent in an enduring struggle for subsistence, subjugation, superstition and exploitation.

Basic Needs

Food is taken by the tribals twice a day and they ignore their lunch while at work. Ration shops do not extend the best of their services to the tribals. Tribals are shuttled by ration shop salesmen wherever possible, and tribals in certain settlements, report that they are overcharged in the name of transportation cost. Many a times, they forego their work and wages in the process of collecting their ration. People in remote settlements especially the aged and children, find it difficult to frequent the ration shops. Drinking water is a problem for tribals settled in upland areas. Women and children fetch water from private estates with fear. Climbing up with a filled pot on the narrow, muddy, steep pathways during winter poses a serious problem especially to the pregnant and aged women. Coffee estate owners use this opportunity for exploiting the tribals living nearby. During summer, the tribals both men and women traverse additional distance, in search of water. Often, they are forced to forego their work as the employers insist on their punctual or early entry in their estates.

Healthcare

Basic health care is a luxury for tribals living in interior settlements, nor do they seriously care for their health, until it becomes fatal. Staff from nearby Health centres chooses the easy way, giving priority to their personal convenience rather than the agony of patients. A sick person, when he turns serious, has to inevitably await his death, unless the local adults take him on a *dolly,* a bed sheet wrapped up on the edge of two poles. When all the adults are away for work and there is no one to carry the serious person, women and children around the sick person simply watch him dying. Electricity is not available in most of the interior settlements. Burning of firewood in the evenings while cooking their meal, provide them with light. During winter, they have a mini bonfire at the centre of their houses, which drives away the chilling cold and provides them with the required warmth. In the process, they inhale excessive smoke which affects their lungs and lead to tuberculosis. All the family members cuddle around this fire which keeps burning throughout night. During summer too, they sleep outside their huts around the burning firewood in order to frighten away the wild animals.

Life in Transition

The Paliya tribe of the Lower Palani hills in Tamil Nadu has been on the threshold of transition, witnessing both progress and problems in the process. Shift in their dwelling places from stone houses to huts and colony houses in settlements, transition from hunting/food gathering stage to plantation labour stage, and growing external contacts have enabled them to extricate from their primitive life in deep forests and live closer to the mainlanders. In due course, they have cemented their cultural base, stabilised their social structure and streamlined their economic life. Together with their men folk, the Paliya women performed most of the economic activities collectively in wage employment, livestock rearing, and farming and to a limited extent, in minor forest produce collection too. The men and women shared most of the domestic responsibilities such as gathering forest-based food, fetching drinking water, collecting firewood and fodder, purchasing the essential goods, mobilising building materials for house construction and looking after their domestic affairs.

Government and NGOs

Development programmes sponsored by the Government and Non-government Organizations delivered an array of benefits to the tribal families in the economic, educational and health spheres. But in the process of availing these programmes from the government, people faced problems like payment of bribe to the officials, delay in the sanctioning of loans and diversion of benefits to non-tribals. Bribery was alien to their culture and hence the tribals conferred the officials and inferior status than the Paliya tribe. At this juncture, the NGOs have been perceived by the tribals as a shield of protection, source of hope and a means of support. The non-tribals in the neighbourhood on the contrary, were disgruntled about the concessions extended to the tribals and they attempted to corner the benefits reserved for the triabls. In spite of these hurdles and hardships, the tribals continued to repose faith in both the Government and NGOs for redressing their problems, since there were no better alternatives.

Status of Paliya Women

The status of women in the Pailya tribe was encouraging. They commanded equality of status with men and practiced no sex preference or gender discrimination. They enjoyed absolute independence in choosing their partners and availed the freedom of successive marriages with the persons of their choice. Further, the women played an equal role in the process of decision-making on all vital family matters and freely moved out from their settlements for purchasing essential domestic requirements and participating in important social events. The husband and wife collectively decided on matters such as the marriage of sons and daughters, number of children they should have, purchase of valuables, education of children, place of employment, undergoing family planning and borrowal for domestic needs. The women were thus better placed in the Paliya tribe. The major problems confronting women included early marriage, post-delivery problems, health complaints after tubectomy and a host of general health complaints, including sexually transmitted diseases (STD). Two out of every ten persons suffered from STD and two thirds of the infected were women. Heavy work burden, denial of wage employment during pregnancy, low wage rate and sex abuse were the prime botherations of women employed in the coffee plantations. Many women lived with their problems, some longed for salvation but only a few strived for solution. The study revealed that the problems of the tribal women emanated more from outside than from their fellow tribe. They were more external and environmental than internal and socio-cultural. The women suffered those problems more because they were born as women than because they belonged to a tribe employed in the coffee plantation.

Plight of Tribals in Plantations

Summary of Case studies based on the response of heads of two tribal households on their living and working conditions in the plantation premises are capsulized here. Serial marriages *i.e.,* many wives to the father, many husbands to the mother in succession, besides their own successive marriage, and caring for children born to different pairs of spouses marked the social life of the Paliya tribe. Drinking water was scarce during summer and its procurement became equally strenuous during winter. They lived on two meals a day. Gruel was common, gravy was occasional and meat was rare. Comfortable sleep was a luxury for them. Devoid of their own dwelling place, ration card, voting rights, registration in health/school registers or the benefits of any development programme, these tribals did not have an identity of their own and have been battling for fulfilling their basic needs. Their prime needs include adequate food, a leak-proof shelter, potable water and basic health care. Working life-long under a single master, living within his premises, these families struggled both at the work-site and at the mater's residence, from dawn to dusk without any fixed working hours. Employment outside the plantation was strictly prohibited and their external mobility was systematically shadowed. They never received wages in cash. All advances paid by the master for their health care, dress, purchase of durable, festivals, pilgrimage and the like were adjusted against their wages. Their domestic purchases were rationed and the place of purchase too was restricted. Pending advances with their employers was a perennial phenomenon. Every active male Paliya worker carried a price of Rs. 3, 000 to 4,000, which is collected from the new employer and remitted to the present employer while circumstances warrant his shifting. The higher amount of Rs. 4,000 is paid only to a hard working Paliya tribe, upon detailed enquiries by the prospective employer from his fellow workers. Such movements were restricted earlier but have been gradually relaxed in the recent years. Perennially indebted, perpetually bonded and permanently exploited, the Paliya tribe silently bears the burnt of deprivation, exploitation, abuse and the consequent anguish. On the whole, the life of these Paliya families settled down in the farm houses and clusters is agonizing and their salvation rests equally with them as also with others.

Need of Paliyas

Government and NGOs have to do far more than what they have done to the tribals so far. The life of tribals will undergo transformation by providing them with the following support:

1. Provision of around two acres of land to each family from government lands for cultivation.
2. Required minimum area for housing all the displaced families with free house site patta.
3. Construction of free houses for all the homeless and those families living in huts.
4. Relocation of all the tribal families, living in houses provided by the employers within their premises, by constructing free houses away from their erstwhile location.
5. Strict enforcement of minimum wages to the tribal workers employed in plantations, cultivation operations, construction works and other activities.
6. Forming a cooperative for minor forest produce collecting tribals by relaxing the restrictions and offering them reasonable prices.
7. Centralising the projects of all NGOs aimed at tribal welfare, through a tribal co-ordination council, comprising NGOs, government, tribal representatives, banks, cooperatives, school, and an independent institution with a clean record of social service.
8. Entrusting the responsibility of implementing the entire field based tribal welfare programmes of the government to specially recruited development workers, preferably drawn from among the committed youth belonging to the target groups, as also activists chosen from among the local NGOs in the project area.
9. Delivery of ration goods to the tribals periodically at the doorsteps of tribal settlements on fixed days when they do not go for work in a week or month.

10. Conduct a fresh enumeration of all the tribals living in the settlements, employer premises and scattered farm houses and provide them with essential government documents such as ration card, voter identity, community certificate, and house site patta wherever not provided.

3

Social Exclusion and Inclusive Policies
A Methodological Issue in Studying Tribes of Assam

*Dr. C. J. Sonowal

ABSTRACT

Despite its origin in western domain, the concept of social exclusion has gained wide spread popularity in India across varied academic spheres. Discourse and discussion on this issue goes beyond the grip of western paradigms and its parochial models and course of investigations are in vogue in India. Measuring and investigating social exclusion remains a challenge to social scientists due to its subjective nature, relative components and varied socio-political arrangement across space and time. The vicious cycle and interrelation between distributional and relational aspects of social exclusion makes the issue even complicated. Tribal societies across the world exhibit relative aloofness, difference in life ways and world views, contrasting meaning of development in relation to non-tribal counterpart. The issue of exclusion of these population groups comes in to being when the idea of inclusion of them in to the national communities at par is taken as an ideological task. Being a historical, it is quite difficult to reconstruct tribal socio-political domain in timeline which is very much

* Associate Professor, Centre for Study of Social Exclusion and Inclusive Policies, Tata Institute of Social Sciences, Sion-Trombay Road, Deonar, Mumbai 400 088, Maharashtra.

crucial to understand the process and impact of social exclusion among the tribal groups. Assam is one of the eight states situated in the north east region of India. The tribal people in this region are categorically different from their tribal counterparts of the country in physical, socio-cultural and political history. This article tries to delineate different perspective of looking at the process of social exclusion and specific issues of the same to investigate and understand the process in a holistic manner.

Keywords: Disadvantage, Relational, Distributional, Social Policy.

Introduction

Social Exclusion Defined

The term social inclusion was originated in French social policy in the 1970s. The idea of Social exclusion is primarily based on the understanding what social inclusion is. Luhmann (1990: 34) defines the concept of inclusion as a mechanism of encompassing of the entire population in the performances of the individual function systems. Definitions of social exclusion range from little more than a re-naming of poverty (Burchardt *et al.* 1999: 228) to more broad based concepts based on a lack of, or inability to participate in society, for example, exclusion from goods and services, labour market, land resources and social security (Rodgers 1995: 46-7).

Different Perspectives of Looking at Social Exclusion

Silver (1994) distinguished three paradigms of social exclusion. In the 'solidarity paradigm' dominant in France, exclusion is the rupture of the social bond between the individual and society that is cultural and moral. The poor, unemployed and ethnic minorities are defined as outsiders. A 'specialization paradigm', dominant in the US is determined by individual liberalism where it is perceived that individuals are able to move across boundaries of social differentiation and economic divisions of labour. It also emphasises the contractual exchange of rights and obligations. In this paradigm, exclusion reflects discrimination, the drawing of group distinctions that denies individuals full access to or participation in exchange or interaction. The 'monopoly paradigm' which is influential in Britain and many Northern European countries, views the social order as coercive and imposed through hierarchical power relation. Exclusion here is defined as a consequence of the formation of group monopolies.

The term 'disadvantage' has been widely used for conceptualization of 'social exclusion'. Disadvantage refers to curtailment of opportunities and life chances of individuals and groups in a given society. Sociologists have paid greater attention to 'identity-based forms of disadvantage'. Such disadvantage reflects the cultural devaluation of groups and categories of people in a society. Caste, ethnicity and religion are examples of such group identities. Social exclusion may also be seen as an institutionalized form of inequality, the failure of a society to extend to all sections of its population, the economic resources and social recognition which they need in order to participate fully in the collective life of the community. Besides these, social exclusion and inclusion can be seen as a simultaneous process. An individual or a society may be included in one desired area but may be excluded in another important area.

The Universal Characters of Exclusion may be summarised as follows:

(i) Inability to participate effectively in economic, social, political and cultural life.

(ii) Distance and alienation from a so called mainstream society.

(iii) Isolation from major societal mechanisms which produce or distribute social resources.

The concept of social exclusion is intimately related to two aspects namely; *(i)* 'distributional' and *(ii)* 'relational' (Room, 1994). When the distributional aspect is more related to economic aspects, the relational aspect is social in nature. But these two are not mutually exclusive. Rather, they are mostly interrelated. If we take social problems like infant mortality, education, literacy etc., as indicators of social exclusion, we see the distributional factors like income (cash) play a part here, especially in market economy. This is because; facilities available to avail such benefits or services are not easily accessible to them who do not have money to buy them. Simultaneously, adequate income also does not always assure the accessibility to such goods and services due to certain social factors – the relational aspects of social exclusion.

The issues like ownership, control, participation and access in relation to valued resources and socio-cultural activities are based on relational aspects (social relations and structure of society) which determine the distribution of wealth and income in a given society. Unequal income structure again influences such social relations. While solidarity and cohesion remains the central focus of social exclusion discourse there has been a paradigm shift of solidarity in welfare states. Even in states like India, where social entities like caste, tribe and religions communities have strong relations in forming a social and political web of the country, one can see the increasing dominance of market related phenomena playing vital role in inclusion and exclusion of people. Perception of solidarity as a moral concept constitutive for social cohesion and solidarity in a community has been gradually displaced by a concept of solidarity which focuses on the inclusion of people in the labour market. This is because, inclusion has been reflected and conceived as the opportunity and extent of people's participation in labour market and employment domain as earners, producers and thereby capable purchaser of available valued goods and services which ultimately rise the standard of living resulting in capability to participate in socio-political domain – a criterion of social inclusion.

Social exclusion as a concept can be seen in multidimensional perspectives. Most dominant perspectives are economic, social and political in nature. The economic dimension of exclusion is concerned with the issues like:

(i) Income.

(ii) Production.

(iii) Access to goods and services.

Economic activities are important in the discourse of social exclusion because they are socially related to the issue of 'recognition'. A person who is unemployed, who does not produce and who is out of labour market involvement is denied of recognition as a person having social worth, thereby denying social status and full social citizenship (Sen, 1975:5). Thus, where recognition is absent, the person is excluded one. Three main aspects of social exclusion thus have surfaced from these interactions of social dimension, are:

(i) Access to social services such as health care education.

(ii) Access to the labour market (with different nature of jobs).

(iii) The opportunity for social participation and the effect of denial to such opportunities.

The political dimension of social exclusion can also be seen in terms of rights a person as individual or a group member of certain category can or cannot enjoy or avail. The human and political rights to which a free citizen is entitled to, can be as follows:

(i) Civil rights – freedom of expression, rules of law, or right to justice.

(ii) Political rights – right to participate in the exercise of political power.

(iii) Socio-economic rights – personal security and quality of opportunity, right to minimum health care and to unemployment benefits etc.

Indicators of Social Exclusion

The components of social exclusion are not unidirectional in their indicative characters. Thus, instead of using a composite index, individual accounts of these components are more relevant in assessing or measuring social exclusion. Such indicators may be summarised, for example, as follows:

(i) Depth of poverty and income inequality is a relevant indicator because individuals or groups at the bottom of an income pyramid are usually excluded from benefits of growth and access to education, health and a decent livelihood, etc. The gap between the two extremes in terms of enjoying social goods and services is also very wide.

(ii) Indicators of access to public goods and services like access to education and health etc.

(iii) Indicators of access to the labour market and especially to the 'good' segment of the labour market.

(iv) Indicators of social participation – membership in certain organizations, representation capacity, attendance in certain social gatherings, decision-making bodies.

(v) Personal security.

(vi) Rule of law.

(vii) Freedom of expression,

(viii) Political participation.

(ix) Equal opportunity.

Tribal Situation in Assam

Tribal population constitutes around 13 per cent of the total population of the state of Assam. The tribal population in the state is basically consists of Mongoloid physical features. The traditional culture and life-ways of the tribal people of this region are very much different from the dominant pan-Indian culture. The influence of Hinduism on tribal societies of this region was almost non-existence till the later part of 18th century. The influence of Christianity was also very limited among the plains tribal groups of the state of Assam. The major tribal groups of Assam are the Bodo, Mising, Sonowal Kachari, Deori, Dimasa, Tiwa, Rabha and the Karbi. The Bodos are the largest tribal population in the state followed by the Misings and the Sonowal Kacharis. Except the tribal people living in Karbi Anglong and North Cachar Hills, all other tribal groups are usually settled in plains of the Brahmaputra and other river valleys of the state. Cultivation of rice and other garden crops are the main economic pursuits of the tribes. They usually practice wet rice cultivation. Besides selling their agro-products, the tribal people are hardly seen in business and other entrepreneurial activities within their traditional domains.

Acceptance of Vaishnavism by the tribal people is a late phenomenon compared to many other local communities in the state. The liberal (or deliberate) religious preachers allowed the tribal followers of Vaishnavism (and Hinduism) to continue their age-old traditions to certain extent parallel to the new religion. Parochialised legends were made popular among tribal groups to relate them directly or indirectly with the Kshatriya groups of Epic age of Pan-Indian stature. One side of the tribal cosmology was also modified or re-written to adjust the Hindu mythological link to the tribal groups of remotely placed of this region.

Inclusion of tribal world in to the pan-Indian domain was not followed by required progress in social relation and economic pursuits. Tribal people remained in archaic position. In some cases religion also hindered accepting modern elements like education, healthcare services, employment, labour and employment venture or non-traditional nature. Colonial rule came in the wake of devastating Burmese invasion and consequent anarchy and social and political disintegration in the entire plains of Brahmaputra valley. Total lawlessness, lack of administration and massive forced displacement due to Burmese invasion occurred by the first quarter of 19th century. In the event of lack of definite policy on land and forest relation, the British administration was free to apply all its autocratic administrative policies in the state. Vast tracts of land masses were given away to the tea planters virtually at no tax, forest were declared as state property and reserved without considering local people's dependence on them.

Colonial land revenue and land allocation policies restricted most of the tribal groups to their limited access to land and forest resources. Increased taxation on land and other resources, lack of commercial activities to generate cash income, spread of opium consumption had far reaching influence on local communities and more so on tribal communities due to their non- compatibility with new livelihood requirements. The tribal people also experienced the detrimental effect of massive wave of immigration from East Bengal towards the last part of colonial rule. In most cases local people were outnumbered and had to retreat to remote places.

The socio-economic development plans of post-independent India could not satisfy the tribal people's expectation. Some of them continue their pre-independent assertion during post-independent period for better administration. The state government has awarded autonomous council status to most of these tribal groups. But since its inception, lots of controversies have been around regarding the way of formation, working pattern and opportunities of tribal people's active and meaningful participation. The state is backward in terms of industrial and infra-structure development along with stagnation in primary sector development like agriculture and allied production.[1]

Investigating Social Exclusion: The Process and Outcome

Based on foregoing discussion we can draw a line of investigation to understand and unearth the process of social exclusion, inclusive processes and the outcome of these dynamics among the tribal groups of Assam. It is worth mentioning here that such lines of investigation may emerge as a model for further investigation among most of the tribal groups in the country because the tribal history across the world is mostly resemble each other in certain important issues. Encompassing the different perspectives of looking at the process of social exclusion and inclusive policies the lines of investigation are arranged in a tabular representation as follows. The first

1. For Detailed Information Please refer to "Quest for Identity, Autonomy and Development: The Contemporary Trends in Ethnic and Tribal Assertion in Assam", (Ed) C. J. Sonowal, Akansha Publishing House, New Delhi, 2010.

Table 3.1: Perspectives, Components and Context of the Study

Perspectives	Components of Investigation	Context of Investigation in Specific Areas
Social Policy Tradition	Equal/unequal interaction and treatment of tribal groups in relation to their non-tribal counterpart.	Historical and contemporary accounts of social, political, economic and cultural relations and the mechanism and extent of assimilation of tribal groups with other communities in the region. These may include: ***Social relation indicators*** Marital relation, mutual co-operation in community work, participating/observing cultural festivals, rituals, knowledge sharing etc. ***Political relations*** Hostile or friendly relations, mutual co-operation in maintaining ethnic boundaries, political relations mandates followed by tribal people under non-tribal rulers, taxes paid, labour and services rendered etc. ***Economic relations*** Barter and exchange of goods and services with non-tribal groups, tribal people as labourer, producer and consumers, interdependence between communities on these bases. ***Assimilation*** Extent of non-traditional ways of life, economic pursuits, ideology and political structure etc., along with its detailed process.
	Equal opportunity of tribal groups in their interaction with resources and in extracting societal benefits	Historical and contemporary accounts of rights and power relations of tribal groups in terms of valued resources, especially during the colonial and post-colonial period. These nay include:

Contd...

Perspectives	Components of Investigation	Context of Investigation in Specific Areas
Social Policy Tradition		Maintaining of territorial boundary of tribal people, nature and extent of Tribal people's control over land, forest and other natural and valued resources. Authority to clear forest for economic purposes at their own will, taxation if any, control over tribal land by state and other administrative entities, land distribution and redistribution, land holding pattern and forest land utilisation in pre-colonial, colonial and post colonial period. Forest Acts and tribal people's access to land and forest, nature and extent of their dependency on forest and land resources.
Poverty as a phenomenon of Social Exclusion	Nature and extent of participation in terms of social interaction and resource enhancement/utilisation etc.	Economic pursuits of tribal people through space and time, dependence and interdependence on tribal and non-tribal counterparts. Access to and interest and necessity for labour market, employment situation of tribal people and their skill level as employability, availability of opportunities to labour and employment – like vicinity to urban centres, presence of indusiry, enterprises to absorb tribal labourer and any relational aspect of distribution of such opportunities.
	What constituting the 'inability factor among tribal groups that deter them from full participation in society?	A detailed account of relational aspects influencing the 'inability' factors among tribes. This may include: Lack of access to land and forest, employment, labour, sources of income, identity related problems in accessing opportunity like: healthcare, education etc.
	Exclusion from goods and services.	Detailed accounts of availability of valued goods and services to the tribal people, affordability factors of such goods and services like: Healthcare facilities, educational institutes, roads and transport, food and shelter, water supply and irrigation and power, agricultural and allied services etc. Whether there are relational aspects restricting tribal people from their easy and fare access to these opportunities.

Contd...

Perspectives	Components of Investigation	Context of Investigation in Specific Areas
Denial of certain vital necessities	Exclusion from labour market	Available opportunity to enter in to the labour market, skill enhancement, employability of tribal people which includes existence/non-existence of Industry, extensive farm and other primary sector development, skill and resource development to fit into the requirement of these sectors.
	Exclusion from land	Detailed account of land relations of tribal people through history, state intervention, land and resource alienation due to state sponsored activities and policies etc.
	Exclusion from social securities	Nature and extent of contact with immigrants, essential and deliberate state sponsored one causing threat to the very existence of tribal groups in space and time in retaining their unique identity and dignity.
Policy/Process of social inclusion of tribal groups	Inherent ideology of inclusive policy/process	A detailed analysis, through pre-colonial, colonial and post-colonial stages, of the deliberate or non-deliberate process of inclusion of tribal groups in to the dominant society or ideology in terms of political, social, religious, economic and cultural aspects) along with the objective and expectation of the both groups.
	The actor or the decider of inclusion	Whether those inclusion processes are voluntary, informed and explained for the part of tribal groups, or are they attached with vested interest of certain entities like: Religious leaders, social reformers, political leaders, state and state as creator.
Characters of inclusive policy	Respect for all human rights	A detailed account of social, political, cultural and economic position and dignity of tribal groups included in the non-traditional domain – their expectation *vs* their experiences in all aspects of life before and after such inclusion by: Identifying basic human rights and their manifestation in such interactions How much tribal cultures and religious identities and uniqueness have been accepted with equal status and respects.
	Acceptance of Cultural and religious diversity of lesser groups	
	Guaranteed Social justice	

Contd...

Perspectives	Components of Investigation	Context of Investigation in Specific Areas
	Respects for needs of Vulnerable and disadvantaged	Account of equal treatment or discrimination in terms of social relations, distribution and redistribution of benefits and opportunities. Whether special care taken to fulfill the special needs of disadvantaged groups.
Solidarity as inclusive policy	Nature and extent of political rights to claim their share in society	How far tribal groups can represent or express themselves as a distinct and dignified population or similar and equal to non-tribal counterparts within the larger social fabric under solidarity paradigm. Besides constitutionally given safeguard, how tribal people can assert and eke out their claim of share of social and political benefits and dues shares within this larger framework so as to make themselves compatible with their non-tribal counterparts.
	Social accountability of the actor of social inclusion	How far the social, political and religious leaders and responsible entities exhibit their accountability towards tribal groups whose unique ways of life has been dismantled.
Solidarity (inclusion) as cultural and moral bond	Cultural and moral bond between tribal world and the non-tribal social entity (including social creators) or the universe	Investigate how tribal societies are linked with non-tribal societies throughout history till contemporary time through cultural and moral interaction and mutual respects etc.
	Exclusion or differential treatment or position tribal people as the Causes of rupture in moral and cultural bond.	Causes of dissent or ethnic differentials among the groups and the extent of conflicting elements causing rupture in cultural and moral bond.
		Causes of clash of interest and expectation. Account of tribal people's sacrifice of their traditional life ways for so called regional and national identity formation and development etc. The gap or differentials in give and take relations, *i.e.*, non-compliance of dominant groups towards equal treatment and distribution of social goods for tribal people.

Contd...

Perspectives	Components of Investigation	Context of Investigation in Specific Areas
Solidarity as economic contract	As economic usefulness of division of labour among people	Inclusion or exclusion of tribal groups on the basis of (or lack of) resourcefulness, employability, skill enhancement, potential benefits in labour market etc. A detailed trend of tribal people's involvement in labour market and economic activities in dominant market and economy structure, nature and extent of their involvement liken engagement in dignified and respectful jobs, secured jobs, precarious jobs etc.
Mechanical and organic solidarity and social Exclusion	Possibility of upward mobility based on organic mechanical entity to emphasise contractual exchange of rights and obligations: Across social differentiations. Economic division of labour.	An investigation in to the possibility or hindrance of upward mobility of tribal people for being attached to a certain identity like tribe. Any distinction in such mobility when identified as a member of tribe or an individual without concerning such affiliation. Consider if economic status and division of labour plays any role.
Exclusion as imposition of social order	Looking at social order as a forcefully imposed entity by some powerful social creators.	If there is any normative social order to be followed by tribal people while interacting with or treading through the domain of their counterparts. What are the bases of such social order and how does it affect tribal people's life-ways.
	As a result of long standing co-operative/ symbiotic outcome of interaction between the tribal groups and the outside world.	Restriction in participating in decision-making activities, in social activities like festivals, rituals, socio-political events, economic activities of greater benefits and importance etc.
	Locate/identifying the actor and/or the mechanism of social 'identity construction, and 're-construction' creating a disadvantaged group in society.	Detailed account of mechanism and extent of constructing and re-constructing social identity of certain social groups (here tribes) allotting lesser value in terms of social worth, dignity, political and economic potentiality etc. Locating the entities responsible for such identity construction.
	Process of devaluation of culture of certain group of people.	A detailed account of affect of such devaluation of certain group of people in social interaction.

Contd...

Perspectives	Components of Investigation	Context of Investigation in Specific Areas
Excluded as Disadvantaged group	Construction and re-construction of beliefs, values, Attitudes and behaviour pattern towards a certain group of people of lesser worth by social creators and dominant groups	
	Ways of creating a group of people of lesser worth affects people leading towards a disadvantaged position	
Exclusion as Institutional Failure	Success/failure of Government to provide institutionally arranged or managed aspects like Social recognition, economic resources, political access etc., to a certain section of people	How far the government and administration is able to provide constitutionally assured safeguard and benefits of development and welfare to the tribal people considering the relational aspects involved in it.
Issue of self-determination	Ability/inability of (say tribal people) to define/decide/determine the concept of 'Right' and 'Fair' etc., which are utilised to govern them.	The extent of self-determination of tribal groups in terms of deciding their right ways (for development, welfare, life-ways etc.,) and fair treatment in social and political interaction with others. Assertion for political autonomy, tribal state and greater power and authority to decide their own 'good' and 'fair' lines of development.
Exclusion from Market economy	As buyers who are lack of purchasing power (lack of employment/income/ money)	A detailed account of inclusion of tribal people in market economy (new solidarity in new welfare states) when they have and do not have: *(i)* Purchasing power *(ii)* Asset to sell or capacity to produce valuable commodities, *(iii)* Economic domain conforming the dominant Market structure and requirement. The impact of such inclusion or exclusion on social and political world of contemporary tribal groups.
	As producer or seller who neither have assets any capability to produce market-able assets	
	As both buyer and seller or producer who does not conform or who usually do not accept the value of existing market system	

column of the Table 3.1 incorporates the different perspectives of looking or investigating social exclusion and inclusion among the tribes. The next column deals with the components of investigations, that is, the determinants or variables on the basis of which social exclusion might occur in tribal society. The final column encompasses the context of investigation in Specific areas with detailed explanation.

Data Required

Both primary and secondary data are relevant for such sort of study. Secondary data sources will consist of:

(i) Historical accounts.

(ii) Literature related to ethnic groups encompassing their social, religious and political aspects and interaction with surrounding communities.

(iii) Use of archival sources for documents related to political, administrative and economic aspects.

(iv) Local level publication and vernacular accounts.

(v) Data from census organization, employment exchanges, labour organizations, land records, forest department records, local bodies like Gram Panchayats and tribal autonomous councils, ITDP and tribal welfare agencies etc.

Primary data can be collected from:

(i) Social and political elite among the selected tribal groups.

(ii) The leaders/office bearers of organizations among the selected tribal groups.

(iii) Firsthand information from field investigation regarding various development activities, facilities and welfare provisions available to the selected tribal groups and their access to them.

(iv) Nature and extent of tribal people's participation in decision making process regarding their development and welfare, the role of autonomous councils, Tribal Sanghas etc.

(v) Traditional folk literatures can be used to retrieve the historical events as tribal populations devoid of written records.

Conclusion

Investigating and measuring social exclusion has been a complex issue in methodological front. When the issue is deliberated widely among almost all sections of social scientists, preparing and handling tools to measure social exclusion is equally difficult. The issue always carries two opposite poles – the exclusion and inclusion. Moreover, being a relative term it is always difficult to ascertain at what point a particular population can be seen as excluded. Thus owing to its relative variations across different entities, a universally accepted tool for investigation and measurement of social exclusion is difficult to derive at. In this context understanding the process and nature of social exclusion and inclusion has been given a priority in this paper and a process and impact indication are tried to establish. It is hoped that such investigation might bring forward a widely acceptable model of investigation in the issue of social exclusion among tribes of India.

REFERENCES

Burchardt Tania, Grand Julian Le, Piachaud David (1999), 'Social Exclusion in Britain 1991-95'. *Social Policy and Administration*, 33(3): 227-244.

Luhman Niklas (1990), *Political Theory in the Welfare State*. Berlin, New York: Walter de Gruyter.

Rodgers Gerry (1995), 'What is Special about a Social Exclusion Approach?' In G Rodgers, C Gore, JB Figueredo (Eds.): *Social Exclusion: Rhetoric, Reality and Responses*. Geneva: International Labour Organization, pp. 46-47.

Room, G. (1994), 'Social Exclusion: Towards an Analytical and Operational Framework' Ajit Bhalla and Frederic Lapeyre (cf) in *Development and Change*, Vol. 28 (1997), 413-433.

Sen, A. K. (1975), *Employment, Technology and Development*. Oxford: Clarendon Press.

Silver H (1994), *Social Exclusion and Social Solidarity: Three Paradigms*, Geneva: IILS, Discussion papers No. 69, 1994.

4

Multi-Dimensional Exclusion of Muslim Nomads

The Gujjars Living at the Margins in Jammu and Kashmir

*Dr. Farida Siddiqui

ABSTRACT

Spread throughout Jammu and Kashmir, Gujjars, the nomadic Muslim tribe, are mainly goatherds and shepherds who belong to the same ethnic stock better known as Gujars or Gurjars in the rest of India. Always on the move the Gujjars of Jammu and Kashmir, lead a socio-economically excluded life in the high altitude meadows of the State. The Gujjars comprising almost twenty per cent of Kashmir's population have been the victims of multi-faceted exclusion since ages due to the nomadic unsettled life steeped in their tradition. They are deprived of the very basic and essential basic services such as drinking water, electricity, dispensaries and ration cards. Due to their inherent tendency towards their profession adopted by their forefathers their children do not have access to education which is a major basis for the high rate of unemployment and low per capita income for them. In this paper an attempt has been made to highlight the issues of environment friendly Gujjars who live in every nook of Jammu and Kashmir and lead their lives in exclusion trapped in vicious circle of poverty.

Keywords: Exclusion, Per Capita Income, Vicious Circle of Poverty, Inclusion.

---

* Associate Professor, Centre for the Study of Social Exclusion and Inclusive Policy, Maulana Azad National Urdu University, Hyderabad, faridajsiddiqui@gmail.com

Origin and Evolution of Gujjars in Jammu and Kashmir

The word Gujar is believed to have been derived from the Sanskrit word *gurjara* which is explained in Sanskrit Dictionary, *Shakabada1181,* as Gur+jar: 'Gur' means 'enemy' and 'jar' means 'destroyer'.[1]

Although the origin of the *Gujars* is not known in India but it is believed that the Gurjar clan entered into India about the time of the Huna invasions of northern India (Bhandarkar, and Ramakrishna 1989). They were foreign immigrants, possibly a branch of Hephthalites (White Huns) (Smith and Arthur, 1999). It is, generally, believed that these people migrated to India before 6th century A. D., from Central Asia and settled in Gujarat and Rajasthan. They are believed to be the descendants of the ancient *Yuchis* or *Kushans*. General Cunningham and A. H. Bingley consider the Gurjars as descendants of Tocharians of Indo-Scythian stock (Parvez Dewan, 2004).

Gujars have also been hypothesised to be descended from the nomadic Khazar tribes with links to Central Asia (Ajay Singh Rawat, 1993). Some others claim that the Gurjar caste is related to the Chechens and the Georgians, and argue that Georgia earlier was traditionally called as *'Gujaristan'* (Gorjestan) (Stephen M. Lyon, 2007). However, there is little evidence for such claims as the word *'Georgia'* is derived from the Arabic and Persian word *Gurj*, and not Gujar or Gurjar (Curtis and Glenn E. 2004).

The historians opine that in the IX and X centuries A. D., the greater part of Rajasthan was called by the name of *Gurjara Desa* (Country of the Gujjars) (R. P. Khatana, 1995). According to Scholars such as Baij Nath Puri, Mount Abu (ancient Arbuda Mountain) region of present day Rajasthan had been abode of the Gurjars during medieval period (Warikoo K, 2000). The association of the Gujars with the mountain is noticed in many inscriptions and epigraphs including *Tilakamanjari of Dhanpala* (Sudarúana Úarmâ 2002). These Gujars migrated from Arbuda mountain region as early as sixth century A. D., they set up one or more principalities in Rajasthan and Gujarat. Whole or a larger part of Rajasthan and Gujarat had been long known as *Gurjaratra* (country ruled or protected by the Gurjars) or *Gurjarabhumi* (land of the Gurjars) for centuries prior to Mughal period (Majumdar, Achut and Dighe, 1977). During Aurangzeb regime some of them accepted Islam as their Religion. During 7th century, a devastating drought occurred in Rajasthan and Gujarat and some of the *Gujjars* migrated to the Shiwalik hills *i.e.,* the outer Himachal Pradesh, Uttar Pradesh, Haryana and other Himalayan areas (Warikoo, 2000).

According to a study conducted by Tribal Research and Cultural Foundation in 2009, the word 'Gujjar' has a Central Asian Turkic origin, written in romanized Turkish as *Göçer*. Study claimed that according to the new research, the Gurjjar race "remained one of the most vibrant identities of Central Asia in BC era and later ruled over many princely states in northern India for hundreds of years. According to Cunningham, the noted explorer,

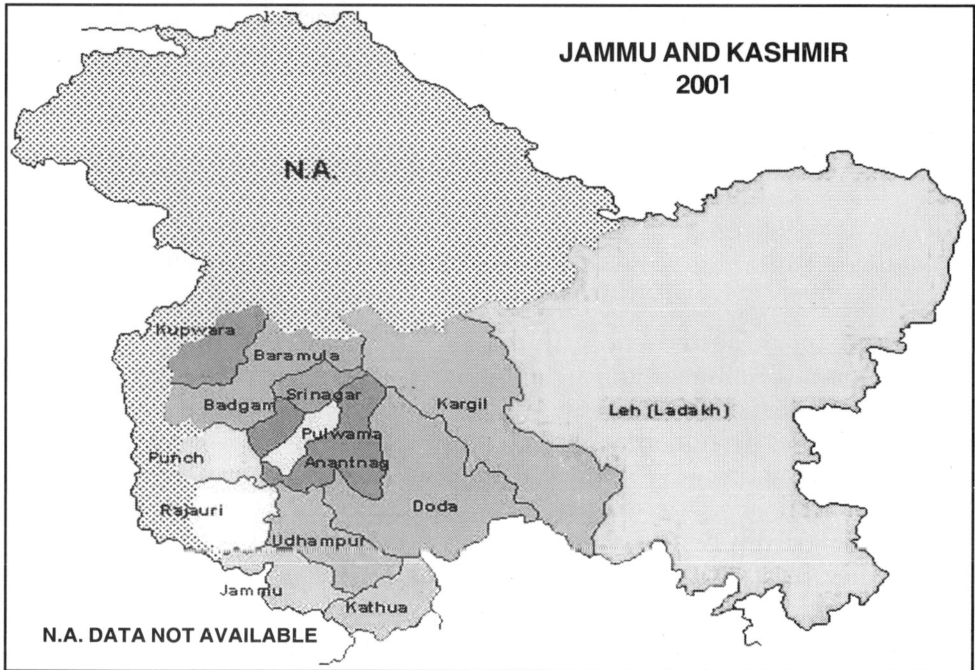

the Gujjars are prominently present in every part of the north western India from the Indus to Ganges and from Hazara mountains to the peninsular Gujarat. In Jammu and Kashmir, numerically they are the third largest ethnic group and are spread throughout Jammu and Kashmir.

Nomadic Gujjars and Migration: The Historical Perspective

The Jammu and Kashmir Gujjars have no authentic historical record of their migration. It is difficult to ascertain with exactness the essential features of their migration to the hills of Jammu and Kashmir. The assumption is that the main reasons of their migration were persistent drought, insufficient grazing facilities in their original lands, increase in their population, political or religious persecution in the plains of Punjab by invaders from the west (Warikoo, 2000). R. P. Khatana, quoting Jermey Page in his Paper 'Dilemma of the Gujjars in Jammu and Kashmir' writes:

"They entered by one route or another to seek refuge, in these hills. At times of invasions and persecutions, the flow of refugees from the Punjab plains into the Kashmir hills increased. It can be assumed that the members of a clan or caste fled in scattered groups and established themselves in one place or the other. Later on over the years or decades the word had spread in favour of a particular locality which was considered congenial place for them". [2]

The Gujars congregated in the localities where there were favourable opportunities (warikoo, 2000). The Census Report of 1941 explains the advent of Gujjars into Jammu and Kashmir in the following words:

"The migration of a part of the tribe to the territories now known as Jammu and Kashmir State is attributed to the outbreak of a serious famine in the regions inhabited by the tribe, now known as Rajputana, Gujerat and Kathiawar. The exact period has not been fixed but it is known as the Satahsiya famine. It is stated that some parts of the migrating tribes moved to the Punjab whilst others moved further north to the areas now known as Kaghan, Swat, Hazara, Kashmir and Gilgit. The Gujjars now living in the State are parts of two separate migrations, one direct from the Gurjara tribes of Rajputana, Gujerat and Kathiawar, the other and later migration from the Gujjar tribes settled in the Punjab".

The Gujjar families now living in Rajouri, Reasi, Jammu, Poonch, Udhampur and Kathua regions claim their ancestry from the Gujarat district of Punjab (Pakistan) having migrated to these hills after the outbreak of a serious famine. They settled along the Mughal imperial road leading to Srinagar via Rajouri and Pir Panjal Pass. The Gujjars of Jammu and Kashmir claim that their ancestors had entered the territories of Kashmir in 1539-42 A. D. Others claim that their ancestors entered Kashmir in about 1127-1154 A. D., when Bajay Singh was the ruler of the area beyond the Pir Panjal. It is believed that Gujars migrated to Jammu and Kashmir from Gujarat (via Rajasthan) and Hazara district of North West Frontier of Pakistan (NWFP) (Kapoor, Raha, and Kapoor S (1994).

Population, Sex Ratio and Religious Affiliation of Nomadic Gujjars

Out of twelve (12) Scheduled Tribes, Gujjar is the most populous tribe having a population of 763,806, thus forming 69.1 per cent of the total ST population in the state of Jammu and Kashmir. At the district level, Gujjar have the highest concentration in Punch and Rajauri districts, followed by Anantnag, Udhampur and Doda districts in the Valley.

Table 4.1: Population of Gujjars

Year	Population (Lakh)
1961	2.15
1971	3.49
1981	4.69
1991	5.71
2001	7.63

Source: Census of India 1961,71,81,91.

Table 4.2 shows that the overall sex ratio of ST population in the state is 910 females per 1000 males, which is lower than the national average (978) for the total ST population. Whereas in case of Gujjars of the state, it is 908 females per 1000 males which is lower than both the state as well as national average. The sex ratio among the STs in the age group 0-6 years is (973) and (979) for all India and Jammu and Kashmir respectively.

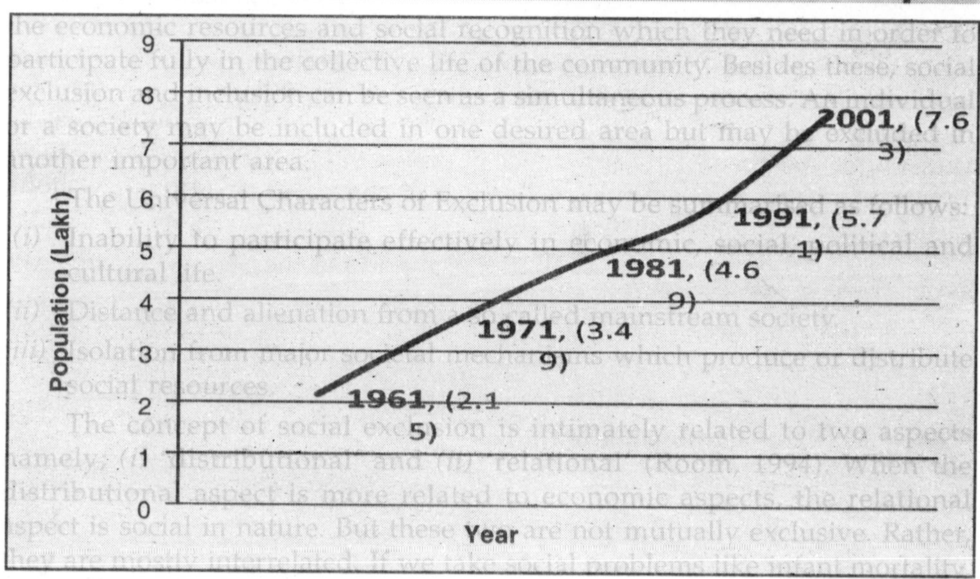

Fig. 4.1:

Table 4.2: Sex Ratio of Gujjars

Age Group	All STs (India)	All STs (J&K)	Gujjar
All ages	978	910	908
0-6 years	973	979	985

Source: Census of India, 2001.

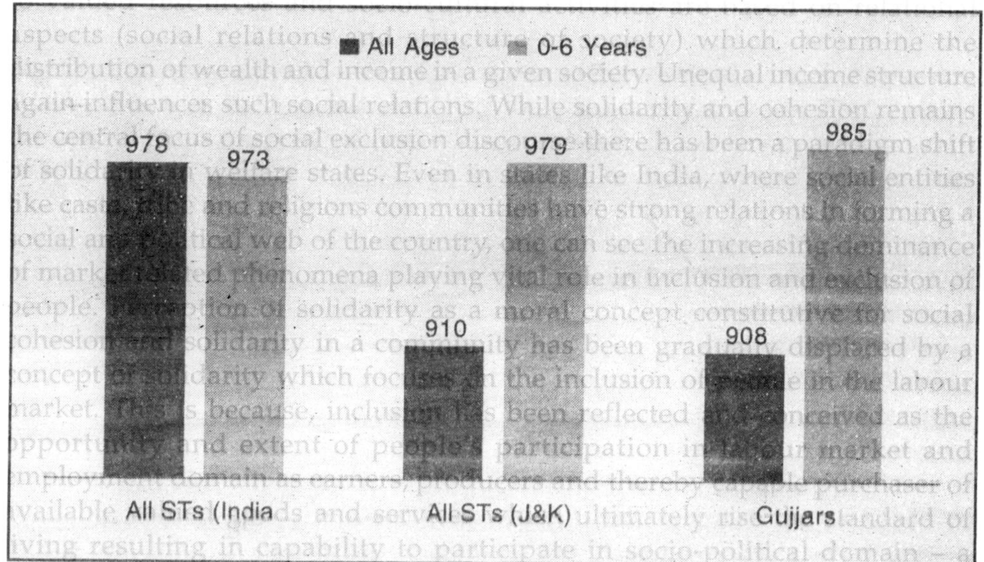

Fig. 4.2:

In case of Gujjars it is 985 at per 1000 Men, which is higher than both the national as well state average. This trend shows that the socio-cultural factors are in favor of girl child among the gujjars. The higher sex ratio for the 0-6 age group is particularly an indication that the easy availability of sex selection procedures and the unethical practice of pre-birth sex selection are not being practiced by gujjars in Jammu and Kashmir as compared to all STs population of the country and as well as the state.

Islam is the predominant religion of the STs of the State of Jammu and Kashmir. According to 2001 census, 86.3 per cent Gujjars are the followers of Islam in the state. Buddhist and Hindu tribes constitute 9.3 per cent and 4.3 per cent respectively. Among the major tribes, 99.3 per cent population of Gujjars living in Kashmir Valley profess Islam (Census 2001). (Table 4.3)

Table 4.3: Religious Affiliation of Gujjars

Religions	Population (%)
Islam	86.3
Budh	9.3
Hindu	4.3

Source: Census of India, 2001.

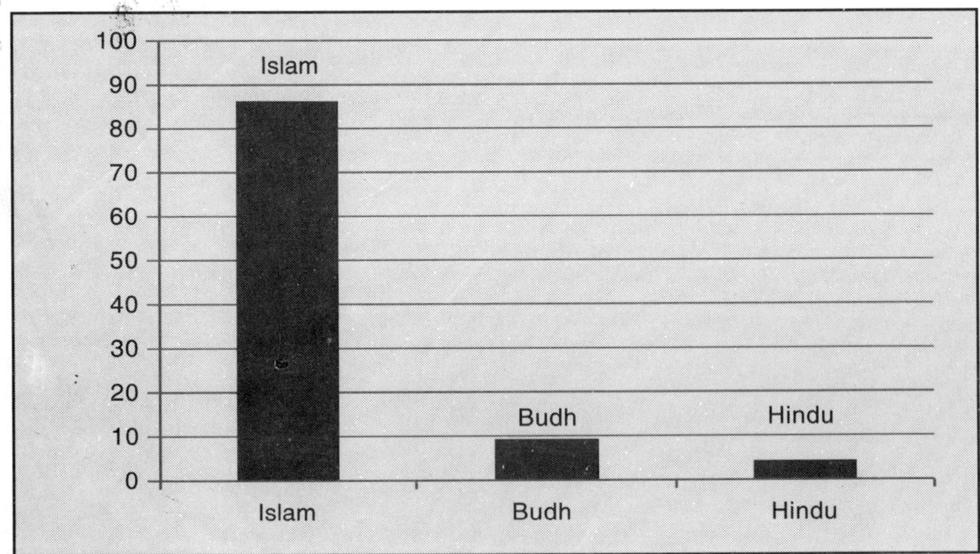

Fig. 4.3:

Multi-Dimensional Exclusion of Gujjars in Jammu and Kashmir

The Gujjars comprising almost twenty per cent of Kashmir's population have been the victims of multi-faceted exclusion since ages. Due to their unsettled nomadic life steeped into their tradition they are always deprived of the very basic and essential basic services such as: drinking water, electricity, dispensaries and ration cards. Due to their inherent tendency towards their profession adopted by their forefathers their children do not have access to education which then becomes a major basis for the high rate of unemployment and low per capita income for them. The environment friendly Gujjars who live in every nook of Kashmir leading their lives trapped in vicious circle of poverty face multi-dimensional exclusion in the state:

Educational Exclusion of Gujjars

Due to the nomadic nature of Life, the Gujjars' children do not have access to Schools or Colleges. As a result their literacy level has been observed as very low as compared to other STs in the state of Jammu and Kashmir. The census 2001 figures depict that less than half (44%) of total 3.2 lakh tribal children in the age group of 5-14 years attend school in the state. Around 1.4 lakh (56%) children do not attend school at all. Table 4.4 indicates that at the individual level, Purigpa, Balti and Bot have between 74-78 per cent children in the corresponding age group go to school whereas Gujjar community has only 38.5 per cent school going children in the state.

Table 4.4: Percentage of School Going Children in Jammu and Kashmir (in The Age Group 5-14 Years)

Categories	Percentage
All STs	44
Gujjar	**38.5**
Balti	74.7
Purigpa	74.2
Bot	78.2

Source: Census of India, 2001.

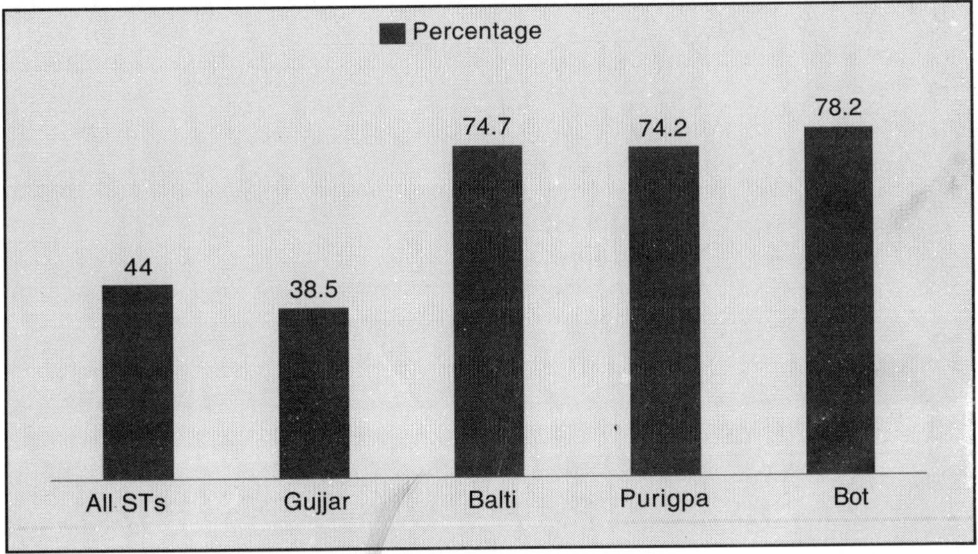

Fig. 4.4:

The overall literacy rate of the STs is 37.5 per cent in the state at 2001 census. This is much lower than the national average of 47.1 per cent aggregated for all STs. Male and female literacy rates (31.7% and 20.4%) are much below if compared to those recorded by all STs at the state level 37.5 per cent and 25.5 per cent respectively.

Table 4.5: Literacy Rate of Gujjars

Literacy Rate	All STs	Gujjar
Persons	37.5	31.7
Females	25.5	20.4

Source: Census of India, 2001

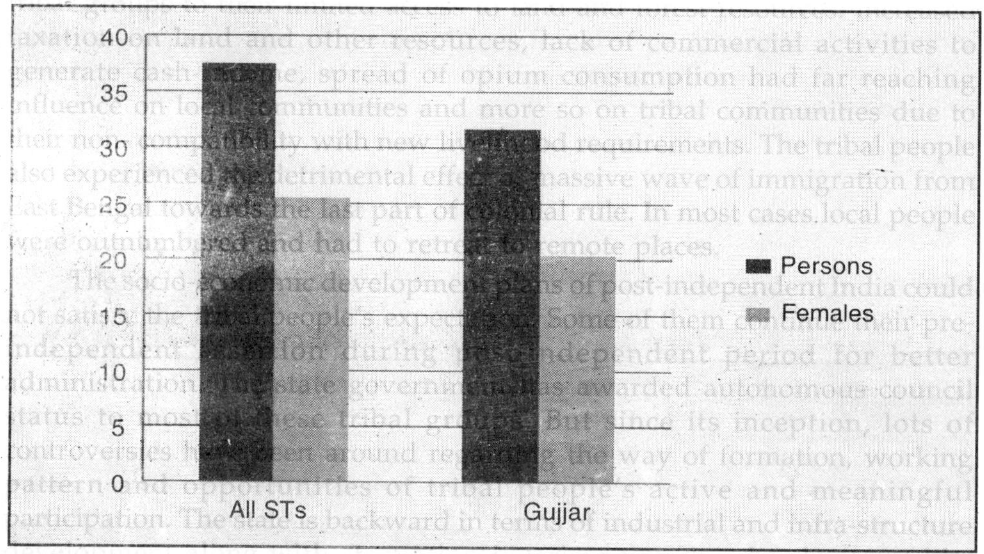

Fig. 4.5:

Table 4.6: Levels of Education among the Major Scheduled Tribes

Various Levels of Education:	All STs	Gujjars
I. Educational levels (Informal Education)		
• Literate without educational level	8.4	9.9
• Below primary	26.5	28.6
II. Educational levels Attained (Formal Education)		
• Primary	26.2	27.6
• Middle	22.1	22.1
• Matric/Sec./Higher Sec/Intermediate etc.	14.7	10.3
• Technical and Non-technical diploma etc.	0.1	–
• Graduate and above	2.0	1.5

Source: Census of India, 2001.

Among the ST literates, 34.9 per cent of tribal literates are either without any educational level or have attained education below primary level. The primary level literates constitute 26.2 per cent followed by literates up to middle level (22.1%). The persons educated up to matric/secondary/higher secondary constitute 14.7 per cent whereas 2 per cent only are graduates and above. Non-technical and technical diploma holders form negligible percentage (0.1) which cannot even be depicted in the figure 4.6 given below.

The figure 4.6 shows that the Gujjars are above the all STs Population in the state till primary level which means given the opportunity, the Gujjars in the state go to schools and get education. Till the level of middle school they are in proportion with all STs Population of the state.

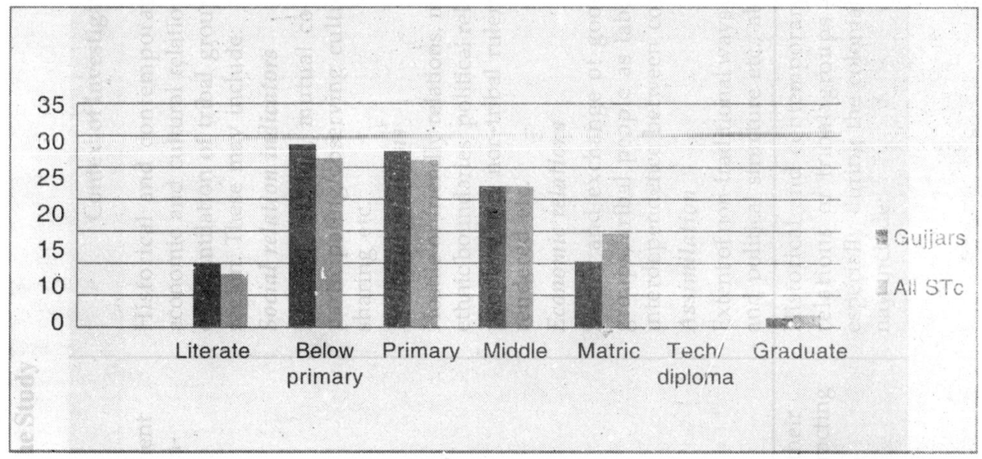

Fig. 4.6: Education Exculsion of Gujjars

However the proportion of literates after middle school drops down approximately half in the High school/secondary level of education and declines sharply after matric. This shows that in the absence of Secondary schools/colleges in the mountains where the Gujjars actually live, the gujjar children either do not have access to schools and colleges or discontinue their education due to their nomadic life making them further excluded educationally.

Economic Exclusion of Gujjars

Agriculture is the main occupation of the tribal population of Jammu and Kashmir as 58.5 per cent of total workers are 'Cultivators' which is significantly higher than the national average of 44.7 per cent. 'Other Workers' constitute 32.7 per cent and this proportion is also twice that of the national average (16.3%). 'Agricultural Labourers' constitute only 6.4 per cent which is significantly lower than that of all STs at the national level (36.9%) and workers in 'Household Industry' account for 2.4 per cent which is at par with the national average of 2.1 per cent. According to Census 2001, the

Work Participation Rate (WPR) of the ST population is 43.9 per cent which is lower than that of the total Schedule Tribes at the national level (49.1%). Both male (50.9%) and female work participation rate (36.1%) among the tribes are lower than the corresponding figures (53.2 per cent male WPR and 44.8 per cent female WPR) recorded by total Schedule Tribes at the country level. Among the total workers, 57.4 per cent are main workers and this proportion is considerably lower than the national average (68.9%).

Table 4.7: Percentage Distribution of Workers

Economic Category	All STs	Gujjar
Cultivators	58.5	61.5
Agricultural Labourers	6.4	7.7
HHI Workers	2.4	2.7
Other Workers	32.7	28

Source: Census of India, 2001.

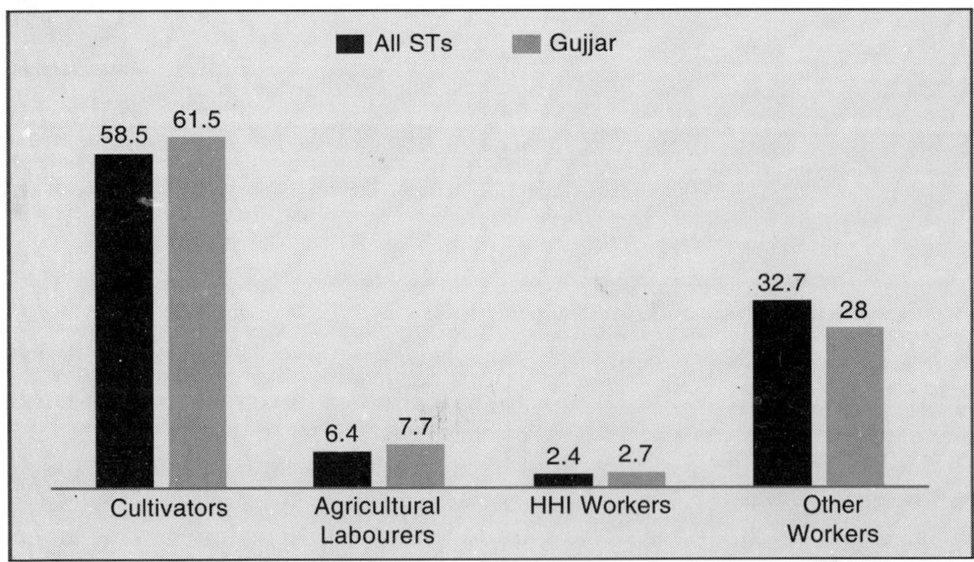

Fig. 4.7:

Linguistic Exclusion

Gujari (or Gojri), has traditionally been the primary language of the Gujjars living in the Jammu and Kashmir. The widely spoken *gojri* language of Gujjars is not given due recognition and has not been included in the schedules of the constitution of India. One of the major reasons for the neglect of Gojri perhaps is the lack of emancipation among this particular linguistic group. Several representations at the groups and individuals levels are submitted by the community to the political leadership for inclusion of Gojri into the eighth schedule of the constitution of India. *Gojri* one of the oldest and significant languages of the South Asian Sub Continent is a strong case for inclusion into eighth schedule of the constitution of India based on its significance, merit and vivacity.

It is the first language of 20 million people in South Asia and nearly eight million people in India, majority of them live in the state of Jammu and Kashmir. Gojri is a language which is easily understood and spoken by the people belonging to the other linguistic groups also. The Government of Jammu and Kashmir has already recognised Gojri by including it in the sixth schedule of the constitution.

Exclusion of the Gujjar Women

Of the twelve different tribal communities of Jammu and Kashmir, the nomadic Gujjar women are most marginalised. Apart from doing all house hold chores, the women from this nomadic tribe sell milk, help their men at farming and cattle feeding and also walk long distances with their children and house hold luggage on their back during migration.

A survey conducted by Tribal Research and Cultural Foundation[3] reveals that Gujjar women in Jammu and Kashmir are among the most backward and discriminated strata of the society not only in the Jammu and Kashmir but also in the country. Compared to women of other communities, Gujjar women face utter gender discriminations in Jammu and Kashmir. The survey claimed that early marriage system, illiteracy, extreme poverty and nomadic way of life are causing marginalization of Gujjar women. The 14 per cent of total female population of Jammu and Kashmir, gujjar women face utter gender discriminations as compared to women of other communities in the state. Since Gujjars live in the most backward and remote hilly areas of the state, most of the men are illiterates. The situation of women's education under such circumstances obviously is expected to be deplorable. This is evident from the fact that there is only one Government Girls Hostel for the gujjar women of the state. Only 100 girls could manage to get the seat in this hostel which is situated at Jammu. In such a situation only a few girls go to the Colleges or the Universities for higher education.

Since Independence, they have been excluded from all major institutions in the state as their presence is almost negligible there. The survey revealed that the presence of gujjar women in political and government organizations is almost zero although the state government has declared 10 per cent reservation to Gujjars since 1991 under Scheduled Tribe category. Due to illiteracy they are not aware of the government schemes. Following data reveals various dimensions of the exclusion of gujjar women in the state of Jammu and Kashmir:

- No Gujjar woman has either been elected or nominated as member of state Legislative Assembly or Legislative Council or Parliament since 1947.

- No women from Gujjar tribe has ever served as under Secretary or above rank in Jammu and Kashmir Civil Secretariat since its establishment, and none of them have become Sub Divisional Magistrate or above in state administration.
- Jammu and Kashmir police department has completely excluded gujjar women. Among 390 DSPs, 163 SPs/SSPs, 21 DIGs and 19 IGs/ADGs/DGs there has never been a single woman from the community so far.
- In the state judiciary there are 85 Munsifs, 56 Sub Judges 67 District and Sessions Judges and 14 High Court Judges while only one woman from Gujjar community has served as Sessions Judge till now.
- In Jammu and Kashmir Bank, there are 3352 officer ranking staff members from Probationary Officers/Managers to the Chairman of the Bank. No woman from Gujjar tribe has yet become as Probationary Officer above in this institution since its establishment.
- There are 303 teachers in the University of Jammu and 364 in Kashmir University. No single Gujjar woman has ever been appointed as faculty by either of the universities since their establishment.
- No Gujjar woman from Chairman to the lowest rank has ever been on the board in Civil Secretariat at State Advisory Board for the Development of Gujjars.

Since Independence, the professional status of nomadic gujjar Muslim women is shown in Table 4.8 given below:

Table 4.8: Exclusion of Gujjar Women in Employment

S. No.	Professions	Number of Gujjar Women
1.	K.A.S and allied Services	2
2.	Lawyers	6
3.	Judicial Services	1
4.	Ph.D	3

Source: Tribal Research and Cultural Foundation

The data demonstrates that the women from Gujjar community are most marginalized in Jammu and Kashmir as they are most illiterate and have no representation in employment neither in banking and Police nor in Schools and Universities. They are also not visible even in planning boards and politics. The cumulative effect of their exclusion from the development process has further aggravated the problem of socio-economic exclusion of gujjar women in the state of Jammu and Kashmir.

Conclusion and Recommendations

Providing tribal Gujjars legal, constitutional and economic safeguards both by the Central and State governments are very necessary for their socio-economic inclusion as they face multi-dimensional exclusion at various levels in the state. Recognising their nomadic culture and living conditions, special inclusionary strategies are needed to be designed by the policy-makers and the planners of the country.

Of all the inclusionary policies and strategies education should be given top priority. Special Education Model to suit the nomadic life styles of gujjars needs to be developed. Education through both, formal and informal modes should be provided to them even when they are on the move. This could be possible if the state provides education and skill development programmes, also through *mobile schools and training centres* that travel along with them. The teachers and trainers should also be from the nomadic background so that the mobile schools and training centres do not get disturbed at the time of migration. Inclusionary programmes must be taken to gujjars in such a way that they along with their children are not required to abandon their daily duties such as: collecting woods, selling milk and herding and feeding the animals. Rather good incentives should be provided by the State to gujjars and their children who continue their education and training programme through mobile set-ups during migration.

The inclusionary programmes should also focus on the integration of nomadic gujjars with their own household economy, their own cultural forms, modes of subsistence and advantages of their specific environments so that they feel more inclined towards poverty alleviation measures meant for their inclusion. India's development agenda of *'inclusive'* growth will certainly be more justified if the most marginalized and most excluded Muslim gujjars are made part of the planning and implementation of the inclusionary programmes in Jammu and Kashmir. This will in real sense promote 'inclusion' of excluded and help them getting out of the trap of vicious circle of age-old chronic poverty in the state of Jammu and Kashmir.

NOTES

1. "These People used to Enjoy a Title of 'Gorjan' (Leader of masses). In Sanskrit the Word Gurjar was used and Now-a-days Gujjar is used in Place of Gurjar which Predicts the Qualities of a Warrior Community". Office of the Registrar General (1961). Census of India, Volume 20, Part 6, Issue 27.
2. Jeremy Page (30 May 2008). "India's Gujjar Caste Fight for a Downgrade". The Times. (www.timesonline.co.uk)
3. Tribal Research and Cultural Foundation is a National Organization which is Working on Indian Tribes with Special Focus on Gujjars.

REFERENCES

A. O. A. C. (1990), Official Methods of Analysis. Association of Official Analytical Chemists, 15th Edition, Arlington, Virginia.

Bhandarkar, Ramakrishna (1989), Some Aspects of Ancient Indian Culture. Asian Educational Services. p. 64.

Census of India (1961), Government of India, Ministry of Home Affairs, Office of the Registrar General, India.

Census of India (2001), Government of India, Ministry of Home Affairs, Office of the Registrar General, India.

Curtis, Glenn E. (2004), Georgia a Country Study. Kessinger Publishing. p. 89.

Govind D, (1977), The History and Culture of the Indian People: The Classical Age. Bharatiya Vidya Bhavan. India, p. 153.

Jeremy page (2008), India's Gujjar Cast Fight for a Downgrade. The Times (http://www.timesonline.co.uk)

Kapoor, Raha, Basu and Kapoor (1994), Ecology and Man in the Himalayas. M. D. Publications. India, pp. 43-44.

Khatana R P (2007), "Gujari Language and Identity in Jammu and Kashmir". Kashmir News Network: Language Section (koshur.org).

Koul, Minoti Chakravarty (1998), Transhumance and Customary Pastoral Rights in Himachal Pradesh: Claiming the High Pastures for Gaddis. Mountain Research and Development, India, Vol. 18, No. 1:5-17.

Lal, Permanand (1974), The Tribal Man in India: A Study In the Ecology of Primitive Communities. pp. 281-329. In: M. S. Mani (ed.) Ecology and Biogeography. W. Junk Publishers, The Hague.

Miller, D. J and Craig, S. R. (1996), Rangeland and Pastoral Development in Hindu-Kush Himalayas. Proc. of a Rangeland Expert Meeting. (November 5-7, 1996), Kathmandu, Nepal.

Shankar, Vinod and Singh J. P (1996), Grazing Ecology. Tropical Ecology. 37 (1): 67-78.

Singh, P (1986), Status of Himalayan Rangelands in India and their Sustainable Management. In Proc. Rangeland and Pastoral Development in Hindu Kush-Hiamalayas (1996), Kathmandu, Nepal. (Ed. By Daniel J. Miller and Sienna R. Craig). pp. 13-22.

Smith, V. A. (1999), The Early History of India; From 600 B.C. to the Muhammadan Conquest Including the Invasion of Alexander The Great. Atlantic Publishers and Distributors. India, pp. 166-174.

Stephen M. Lyon (2007), Gujars and Gujarism: Simple Quaum *vs* Network Activism. University of Kent, Canterbury, (http://sapir.ukc.ac.uk/SLyon/Reports/gujarism.html).

Parvez D. (2004), Jammu, Kashmir, and Ladakh. Manas Publications. India, p. 361.

Tyagi, R. K and Shankar Vinod (1988), Pastoralism and Grazing Systems in the Central Himalayan. 3rd International Rangeland Congress. Abstract Vol. II. Range Management Society of India. Indian Grassland and Fodder Research Institute, Jhansi, India.

Tyagi, R. K. And Singh, P. (1988), Grazing Resources and Grazing Systems in India, pp. 17-34. In P. Singh (ed.), Pasture and Forage Crops Research: A State of Knowledge Report. Range Management Society of India, Indian Grassland and Fodder Research Institute, Jhansi, India.

Verma, V. (1996), Gaddis of Dhauladhar. A Transhuman Tribe of the Himalayas. Indus Publishing Company, New Delhi. India, pp. 149.

Warikoo, Som S. (2000), Gujjars of Jammu and Kashmir, Indira Gandhi Rashtriya Manav Sangrahalaya. Bhopal, Madhya Pradesh, India.

Warikoo K. (2000), Tribal Gujjars of Jammu and Kashmir, Himalayan and Central Asian Studies Vol. 4 No. 1, Jan. India.

5

Indigenous Population and Strategies for Inclusion

With Special Reference to Souria Paharia Tribe of Sahibganj, Jharkhand

*J. Nelson

ABSTRACT

Next to Africa, India has the largest tribal population in the world. There are 580 different tribes in India. With a population of about 90 million people, this constitutes about 9.5 per cent of our country's total population. Some are still primitives and others are developing and a few are distinctive culture, language and life style. To be inclusive is a core value of democratic governance, in terms of equal participation, equal treatment and equal rights before the law. This implies that all people – including the poor, women, ethnic and religious minorities, indigenous peoples and other disadvantaged groups – have the right to participate meaningfully in governance processes and influence decisions that affect them. It also means that governance institutions and policies are accessible, accountable and responsive to disadvantaged groups. This study is based on the works done by Evangelical Fellowship of India Commission on Relief (EFICOR) which is a National Christian Relief and Development Organization.

The following are the objectives of the paper:

*Working in EFICOR, Rajmahal Food Security Project, Sahibganj - 816 109.

- To explore the reason for exclusion of indigenes population.
- To record the indigenous population and strategies.
- To know the real condition of the Souria Pahadia tribes of Jharkhand.

The study was conducted in six villages of Souria Paharia community having habitat in Taljari Block of Sahibganj District of Jharkhand State. The Paharias, as the name indicates, are a hill tribe settled in the hilly ranges of the Rajmahal Hills. The paper ends with certain suggestions for the welfare and upliftment of the tribal people under study.

Keywords: Tribal Development, Millennium Development Goals, EFICOR, Souria Paharia.

Introduction

Next to Africa, India has the largest tribal population in the world. There are 580 different tribes in India. With a population of about 90 million people, this constitutes about 9.5 per cent of our country's total population. Some are still primitives and others are developing and a few are having distinctive culture, language and life style. Each of them has their own problems due to their socio-economic situation and their own religious and cultural experience. The scheduled tribe is undisputedly considered as the weakest section of the society in view of common socio-economic and socio-demographic factors like: poverty, illiteracy, lack of developmental facilities, lack of adequate primary health facilities etc. In this situation government spending more than one crore for one tribal community but result is not satisfactory. With hard work they are implementing more activities for uplifting the condition of Indigenous population. Millennium Development Goal is one of the strategies for inclusive growth at world level, national level and state level.

Various Definitions of a Tribe

- A Tribe is a collection of families bearing a common name, speaking a common dialect, occupying or professing to occupy as common territory and is not usually endogamous, though originally it might have been so – Imperial Gazetteer of India.
- A Tribe is a group of people in a primitive or barbarous stage of development acknowledging the authority of a chief and usually having a common ancestor – Oxford Dictionary.
- A Tribe is an independent political division of a population with a common culture – Lucy Mair.
- A Tribe is a group united by a common name in which the members take a pride by a common language, by a common territory, and by a felling that all who do not share this name are outsiders, enemies' infect – G.W.B. Huntingford.

- A tribe is a social group with territorial affiliation, endogamous, with no specialisation of functions, ruled by tribal officers, hereditary or otherwise, united in language or dialect, recognising social distance with other tribes or castes, without any social obloquy attaching to them as it does in the caste structure, following tribal traditions, beliefs and customs, illiberal of naturalisation of ideas from alien sources above all conscious of homogeneity of ethnic and territorial integration – D. N. Majumdar.

Major Problems of Tribals

1. *Indebtedness:* Has been and still is probably the most difficult problem facing almost the entire tribal population of India. Consequently one of the worst forms of exploitation which the tribal people are exposed is through traditional money lending.
2. *Sifting Cultivation:* Is an age old institution among the Indian Tribes. This in principle means cultivating a plot of land for a temporary period and then leaving it fallow. It consists of clearing the forest slopes ash covered soil.
3. *Poverty and Exploitation:* Are now synonymous with the majority of tribal population. Chronic and mass poverty had been embedded in India's colonial history. The effort to solve our economic problems and achieve all round development began with our plans which have transformed the country in numerous ways to substantial industrialisation. Green revolution is leading to surplus food production, improvement in the average life span and a fast increasing middle class opulence. For the 493 million people below the poverty line development has been a distant phenomenon watched from the way side (UNDP, 1993).
4. *Health:* The normal health of the tribal people cannot be said to be very bad but their condition often chronic after repeated infections. The tribals suffer from many chronic diseases but the most prevalent taking heavy toll of them are water borne. This is mainly due to the very poor drinking water supply.
5. *Alcoholism:* The tribal communities has been widely prevalent. The sentimental attachment of the tribals with one kind of liquor or the other is evident form the fact that mahua tree is treated as sacred by many of the tribals and is worshipped.
6. *Housing:* The problem of housing for the tribal has to be viewed from the aspects of – Shelter and sanitation.
7. *Drinking:* Water is a major problem in tribals. Most of the tribals are taking the water from well and stream.
8. *Education:* The whole formal education has made very little impact on tribal groups. In the light of the past efforts it is not shocking because

prior to 1950 the government of India had no direct programme for the education of the tribals.

9. *Land Alienation:* According to latest statistics nearly 88 per cent of the scheduled tribes are engaged in agriculture. The tribals have great emotional attachment with their lands. Agriculture is the only source of livelihood which most of them have known for centuries.
10. *Communication:* Tribals have been living in isolation for centuries past. The main reason for this isolation is lack of communication.

INDIGENOUS POPULATION

The tribes in India broadly belong to five stocks namely: *(i)* the Negritos, *(ii)* the Austro-Asiatics, *(iii)* the Mongoloids, the *(vi)* Mediterranean and the *(v)* Aryans. The Negritos are believed to be the earliest inhabitations of the Indian Peninsula. They have almost disappeared. However, some traces of Negritos are still found among the tribals of Andaman and Nicobar Islands, Known as the Onges, the Great Andamanese, the Sentinels and the Jarwas and also in Kerala among the Kadars, the Irulars and the Paniyans. The Austro-Asiatics are represented by the Kols or Mundas, Khasis and the Santhals. The Mongoloids race is represented by the tribal people of the sub Himalayan region. They may be divided into two categories, namely: *(i)* the Palaeo Mongoloids and *(ii)* the Tibeto Mongoloids. The Dravidians – the Malars, the Oraons and the Gonds who speak dialects of the Dravidian family while the Aryans are supposed to be the last to come to India.

Inclusive Governance for Societal Upliftment

To be inclusive is a core value of democratic governance, in terms of equal participation, equal treatment and equal rights before the law. This implies that all people – including the poor, women, ethnic and religious minorities, indigenous peoples and other disadvantaged groups – have the right to participate meaningfully in governance processes and influence decisions that affect them. It also means that governance institutions and policies are accessible, accountable and responsive to disadvantaged groups, protecting their interests and providing diverse populations with equal opportunities for public services such as justice, health and education.

MILLENNIUM DEVELOPMENT GOALS (MDGs)

The Millennium Development Goals (MDGs) are eight international development goals that all 192 United Nations member states and at least 23 international organizations have agreed to achieve by the year 2015. They include eradicating extreme poverty, reducing child mortality rates, fighting disease epidemics such as AIDS and developing a global partnership for development.

What is MDG?

The Millennium Development Goals (MDGs) were developed out of the eight chapters of the United Nations Millennium Declaration signed in September 2000. There are eight goals with 21 targets and a series of measurable indicators for each target.

Goal 1: Eradicate Extreme Poverty and Hunger

- ***Target 1A: Halve the proportion of people living on less than $1 a day***
  - Proportion of population below $1 per day (PPP values).
  - Poverty gap ratio (incidence x depth of poverty).
  - Share of poorest quintile in national consumption.
- ***Target 1B: Achieve decent employment for women, men, and young people***
  - GDP Growth per Employed Person.
  - Employment Rate.
  - Proportion of employed population below $1 per day (PPP values).
  - Proportion of family-based workers in employed population.
- ***Target 1C: Halve the proportion of people who suffer from hunger***
  - Prevalence of underweight children under five years of age.
  - Proportion of population below minimum level of dietary energy consumption.

Goal 3: Promote Gender Equality and Empower Women

- ***Target 3A: Eliminate gender disparity in primary and secondary education preferably by 2005, and at all levels by 2015***
  - Ratios of girls to boys in primary, secondary and tertiary education.
  - Share of women in wage employment in the non-agricultural sector.
  - Proportion of seats held by women in national parliament.

Goal 4: Reduce Child Mortality Rate

- ***Target 4A: Reduce by two-thirds, between 1990 and 2015, the under-five mortality rate***
  - Under-five mortality rate.
  - Infant (under 1) mortality rate.
  - Proportion of 1 year-old children immunized against measles.

Goal 5: Improve Maternal Health

- ***Target 5A: Reduce by three quarters, between 1990 and 2015, the maternal mortality ratio.***
- Maternal mortality ratio.
- Proportion of births attended by skilled health personnel.

- ***Target 5B: Achieve, by 2015, universal access to reproductive health***
  - Contraceptive prevalence rate.
  - Adolescent birth rate.
  - Antenatal care coverage.
  - Unmet need for family planning.

Goal 6: Combat HIV/AIDS, Malaria, and Other Diseases

- ***Target 6A: Have halted by 2015 and begun to reverse the spread of HIV/AIDS***
  - HIV prevalence among population aged 15-24 years.
  - Condom use at last high-risk sex.
  - Proportion of population aged 15-24 years with comprehensive correct knowledge of HIV/AIDS.
- ***Target 6B: Achieve, by 2010, universal access to treatment for HIV/AIDS for all those who need it***
  - Proportion of population with advanced HIV infection with access to antiretroviral drugs.
- ***Target 6C: Have halted by 2015 and begun to reverse the incidence of malaria and other major diseases***
  - Prevalence and death rates associated with malaria.
  - Proportion of children under 5 sleeping under insecticide-treated bed nets.
  - Proportion of children under 5 with fever who are treated with appropriate anti-malarial drugs.
  - Prevalence and death rates associated with tuberculosis.
  - Proportion of tuberculosis cases detected and cured under DOTS (Directly Observed Treatment Short Course).

Goal 7: Ensure Environmental Sustainability

- ***Target 7A: Integrate the principles of sustainable development into country policies and programmes; reverse loss of environmental resources***
- ***Target 7B: Reduce bio-diversity loss, achieving, by 2010, a significant reduction in the rate of loss***
  - Proportion of land area covered by forest.
  - CO_2 emissions, total, per capita and per $1 GDP (PPP).
  - Consumption of ozone-depleting substances.
  - Proportion of fish stocks within safe biological limits.
  - Proportion of total water resources used.
  - Proportion of terrestrial and marine areas protected.
  - Proportion of species threatened with extinction.

- ***Target 7C: Halve, by 2015, the proportion of the population without sustainable access to safe drinking water and basic sanitation (for more information see the entry on water supply)***
  - Proportion of population with sustainable access to an improved water source, urban and rural.
  - Proportion of urban population with access to improved sanitation.
- ***Target 7D: By 2020, to have achieved a significant improvement in the lives of at least 100 million slum-dwellers***
  - Proportion of urban population living in slums.

Goal 8: Develop a Global Partnership for Development

- ***Target 8A: Develop further an open, rule-based, predictable, non-discriminatory trading and financial system***
  - Includes a commitment to good governance, development, and poverty reduction – both nationally and internationally.
- ***Target 8B: Address the Special Needs of the Least Developed Countries (LDC)***
  - Includes: tariff and quota free access for LDC exports; enhanced programme of debt relief for HIPC and cancellation of official bilateral debt; and more generous ODA (Overseas Development Assistance) for countries committed to poverty reduction.
- ***Target 8C: Address the special needs of landlocked developing countries and small island developing States***
  - Through the Programme of Action for the Sustainable Development of small Island developing States and the outcome of the twenty-second special session of the General Assembly.
- ***Target 8D: Deal comprehensively with the debt problems of developing countries through national and international measures in order to make debt sustainable in the long-term***
  - Some of the indicators listed below are monitored separately for the least developed countries (LDCs), Africa, landlocked developing countries and small island developing States.
  - Official development assistance (ODA):
    - Net ODA, total and to LDCs, as percentage of OECD/DAC donors' GNI.
    - Proportion of total sector-allocable ODA of OECD/DAC donors to basic social services (basic education, primary health care, nutrition, safe water and sanitation).
    - Proportion of bilateral ODA of OECD/DAC donors that is untied.

- ❖ ODA received in landlocked countries as proportion of their GNIs.
- ❖ ODA received in small island developing States as proportion of their GNIs.

➢ Market access:

- ❖ Proportion of total developed country imports (by value and excluding arms) from developing countries and from LDCs, admitted free of duty.
- ❖ Average tariffs imposed by developed countries on agricultural products and textiles and clothing from developing countries.
- ❖ Agricultural support estimate for OECD countries as percentage of their GDP.
- ❖ Proportion of ODA provided to help build trade capacity.

➢ Debt sustainability:

- ❖ Total number of countries that have reached their HIPC decision points and number that have reached their HIPC completion points (cumulative).
- ❖ Debt relief committed under HIPC initiative, US $.
- ❖ Debt service as a percentage of exports of goods and services.

- ***Target 8E: In co-operation with pharmaceutical companies, provide access to affordable, essential drugs in developing countries***
  - ➢ Proportion of population with access to affordable essential drugs on a sustainable basis.
- ***Target 8F: In co-operation with the private sector, make available the benefits of new technologies, especially information and communications***
  - ➢ Telephone lines and cellular subscribers per 100 population.
  - ➢ Personal computers in use per 100 population.
  - ➢ Internet users per 100 Population.

India's Progress

Development has always occupied centre-stage in the Indian Policy. Achievements since independence include improvements on several fronts like the food security status, literacy rate, life expectancy, health care improvements among many others. India Ranks 127 in a total of 177 countries. (Table 5.1)

Promoted to Achieve MDGs through EFICOR

Evangelical Fellowship Of India Commission On Relief (EFICOR) is a National Christian Relief and Development Organization, formed in 1967, as a relief and development arm of Evangelical Fellowship of India (EFI) to provide relief to the drought hit state of Bihar. EFICOR serves the poor and

Table 5.1: India's Ranking out of 177 Countries

Country	Rank
Japan	11
Singapore	25
Argentina	34
Mexico	53
Brazil	63
Thailand	73
The Philippines	84
China	85
Srilanka	93
India	127

Table 5.2: India's Progress 1991-2001 Selected Economic Indicators

Indicator	1990	2003
GDP Growth Rate	3.9	6.9
Per Capita Income (US $)	380	480
GNI (US $billion)	330.6	571.3
Trade (%of GDP)	15.7	30.5
External Debt. (% of GNI)	26.7	19.0

Table 5.3: India's Track Record

Country	People Living Below Poverty Line (% of Total Population)	Undernourished (% of Total Population)	Undernourished Children (% of Total Population)
India	26.1	52	47
China	4.6	11	10
Thailand	13.1	20	19
Sri lanka	22	22	29
Pakistan	32.6	20	38
Malaysia	15.5	2	12
Mexico	10.1	5	8

the marginalized in the country irrespective of caste, creed or religion in situations of poverty, injustice and disaster. EFICOR is accorded consultative status with ECOSOC-UN and is a member of Core group of NGOs with the National Disaster Management Authority (NDMA). EFICOR is part of many national and international movements and networks, for *e.g.*, Sphere India Management, Disaster Co-ordination Committee, Micah Network, a global network of over 331 Christian Relief, development and justice organizations from over 81 countries, WANGO (World Association of NGOs), VANI (Voluntary Action Network, India), FAN (Freshwater Action Network), Reuters Alert Net and South Asia Climate Action Network. EFICOR works with poor communities in the states of Andhra Pradesh, Assam, Bihar, Chhattisgarh, Delhi, Gujarat, Jharkhand, Maharashtra, Mizoram, Orissa, Rajasthan, Tamil Nadu, Uttar Pradesh and Uttarakhand. EFICOR today is involved in a wide range of integrated development programmes for Tribal, BPL, and Dalit Communities in Sahibganj district Jharkhand. Last fifteen years EFICOR working with Souria Paharia community in Jharkhand. Through EFICOR Souria Paharia community learned the literacy, advocacy, Self-Help Group activities, plantation and watershed structures (Stone bending, Cully plaguing, Terrace making, counter trench). Now EFICOR is focusing on Stainable Livelihood programme for this community. Through this programme EFICOR providing Social forestry and agro forestry saplings, Seeds, Piglets, Goats, Agriculture trainings, Forest management trainings, well construction, Exposure visit on Forest management, Exposure visit on Agriculture, SHG leader ship trainings, Livestock management trainings, SALT (Slob agriculture land technology), awareness training on forest management and Income generation training like Leaf plate making trainings, Bamboo training, Candle training, Food processing trainings.

Objectives of the Study

- To explore the reason for exclusion of indigenes population.
- To record the indigenous population and strategies for development.
- To know socio-economic condition of Souria Paharia community of Sahibganj district of Jharkhand state.

Reason for Choosing the Topic

To understand social exclusion process of Indigenous population and to suggest development strategies for Souria Paharia community of Taljari Block, Sahibganj District of Jharkhand state.

Area of Study

Jharkhand Tribes

The ancient tribes of the state of Jharkhand include Birhor, Asur, Birajia and Mal Paharia. Some other ancient tribes of Jharkhand are Sauriya Paharia, Hill Kharia or Sabar, Parahiya and Korba.

Sahibganj District at a Glance

Set within the lush green region, the district of Sahibganj with a predominantly tribal population is a part of Santhal Pargana division and forms the eastern most tip of the division. The Rajmahal and Pakur subdivisions of old Santhal Pargana district were carved out on 17th May, 1983 to form Sahibganj district. Subsequently Pakur sub-division of Sahibganj district was carved out on 28th January, 1994 to constitute Pakur District.

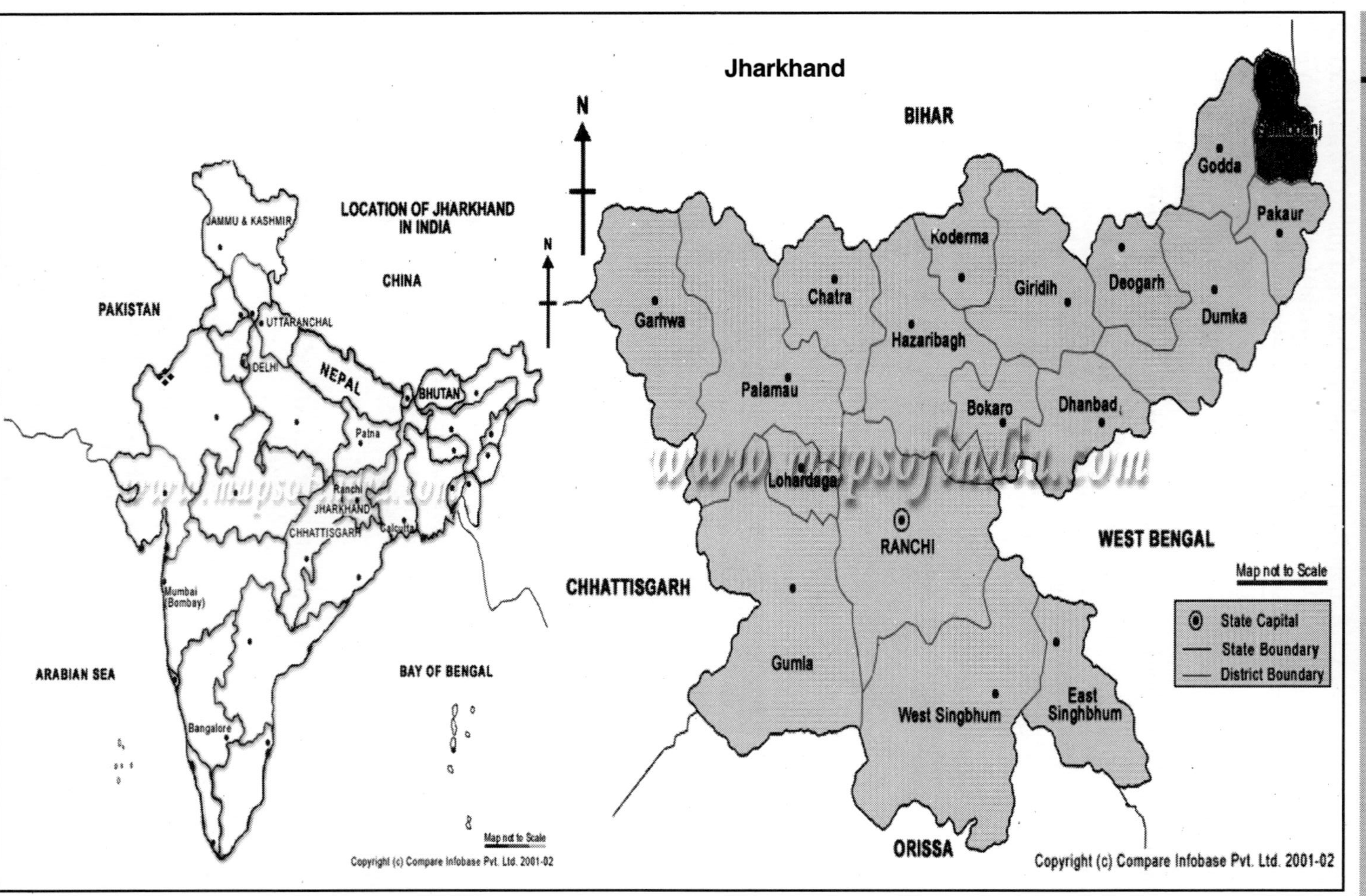
LOCATION OF JHARKHAND IN INDIA
CHINA
PAKISTAN
JAMMU & KASHMIR
UTTARANCHAL
DELHI
NEPAL
BHUTAN
Patna
Ranchi
JHARKHAND
CHHATTISGARH
Calcutta
Mumbai (Bombay)
Bangalore
ARABIAN SEA
BAY OF BENGAL
N
Map not to Scale
Copyright (c) Compare Infobase Pvt. Ltd. 2001-02
Jharkhand
N
BIHAR
Godda
Pakaur
Koderma
Chatra
Garhwa
Giridih
Deogarh
Dumka
Hazaribagh
Palamau
Bokaro
Dhanbad
Lohardaga
RANCHI
WEST BENGAL
CHHATTISGARH
Gumla
West Singhbhum
East Singhbhum
ORISSA
Map not to Scale
State Capital
State Boundary
District Boundary
Copyright (c) Compare Infobase Pvt. Ltd. 2001-02

Table 5.4: Sahibganj District Details as per Census 2011

Population	1150038
Males	590359
Females	559648
O – 6 Population	216402
Males	110704
Females	105696
Literates	501630

Source: Census 2011.

Table 5.5: Sahibganj District details

Longitude (Approximate)	87°25′ East to 87°54′ East
Latitude (Approximate)	24°42′ North to 25°21′ North
Height from sea level	37.185 m.
Total Area	1599.00 Sq. Kms.
ST Population	270423
No of Block	9
Sex Ratio (Females Per 1000 males)	942
Total Literacy Rate	37.61%
Male Literacy Rate	47.93%
Female Literacy Rate	26.56%

Source: http://sahibganj.nic.in/glance.htm

Table 5.6: EFICOR Target Village in Taljari Block

S. No.	Village Name	H/H	M	F	Population	Panchayat	Blocks
1.	Bekchuri	15	29	34	63	Batbanga Santhali	Taljhari
2.	Batbanga	27	61	69	130	Batbanga Santhali	Taljhari
3.	Balko	12	37	28	65	Batbanga Santhali	Taljhari
4.	Kaldibitta	23	57	59	116	Karanpura	Taljhari
5.	Sarsha	17	39	36	75	Karanpura	Taljhari
6.	Chamdibedo	15	40	33	73	Karanpura	Taljhari

Source: EFICOR Annual Report.

Taljari Block, Sahibganj District, Jharkhand State

Primitive Tribes

The Shilu Ao Committee constituted by the planning commission in 1969 for reviewing the tribal situation had observed that a large number of tribal communities continued to be extremely backward and some of them were still in the primitive food gathering stage. It was emphasised that these communities needed special attention. As a part of Tribal sub plan strategy, 75 tribal groups with a total population of about 13 lakhs have been identified as the primitive tribes/groups in 28 states and 7 Union Territory. The main criteria adopted for identification of such tribes are:

(i) Pre-agricultural level of technology.

(ii) Very low level of literacy.

(iii) Stagnant of declining population.

Sauria Paharia Adivasi

The Paharias, as the name indicates, are a hill tribe settled in the hilly ranges of the Rajmahal Hills and the neighboring region in the Santhal Parganas, The Saurias are concentrated mainly in the *Damin-i-koh* region called the Rajmahal hills. The land of the Malar consists of a succession of hills, plateaus, valleys and ravines, the general elevation of which varies from 500 to 800 feet about the sea level though some hills have an altitude of 1500 feet and a few are said to rise to the height of 2000ft. (O.malley 1938:3). The Paharia villages are ten to thirty houses are made. This community not interested in hard work. Leaving the land to be cultivated by the sandals and taking part of the produce. Although, the British government warned these people that the ownership would be given to those who actually ploughs but they carelessly fail to heed.

Table 5.7: Details of Souria Paharia Community

S. No.	Name of the Block	No. of Village	Name of the Paharia Group	Total Families	Total Population	Male	Female
1.	Taljari	86	Souria Mal	2073	8432	4294	4138
2.	Berhait	106	Souria Mal	2163	9727	4722	5005
3.	Patna	66	Souria	1331	5838	2899	2939
4.	Borio	53	Souria	1181	4965	2528	2437
5.	Barharwa	3	Souria	52	214	128	86
6.	Sahibganj	1	Souria	8	53	25	28
7.	Rajmahal	5	Souria	49	232	106	126
8.	Mandro	81	Souria	1384	5668	2891	2777
	Total	**401**		**8229**	**35129**	**17593**	**17536**

Source: Census 2011.

Details of Souria Paharia

Language

The *Sauria Paharia* (Devnagri) language is spoken in Bihar and West Bengal states of India and some pockets of Bangladesh. Most of the speakers are in India with around 1,10,000. There are about 7,000 speakers in Bangladesh. It is a member of the Northern branch of the Dravidian language family.

Settlements

The Sauria Paharia erect houses with bamboo, Wood, bushes mud, leaves, grasses, and tiles.

Family

Family and marriage form the core of any society. The family life of Sauria Paharia of Rajmahal Hills shows intense grouping and intimate relationship. The eldest male member is the head of the family. There is no restriction on widow remarriage. Clearing and leveling of fields are done by the all 10 years above people. Feeding, nursing, cooking, fetching water are the jobs attributed to the women.

Marriage

Marriage among the tribal is not religious sacrament but a jovial contact for the purpose of enjoyment of sex, procreation and companionship. During the marriage time the groom will give the pig and money to the bride. Monogamy is the usual form of marriage because of the hard rules for bride price (known as 'PON', ranges for Rs. 2000/ Rs. 8000) and poverty to maintain two wives. A child marriage is not preferred. The young men ready for marriage at the age of 20-21, must be ready to look after his family. Divorce is weighed more in favour of husband as he may charge his wife for bad temperament, bareness and laziness. Nuclear family is the most common type of family which prevails among them.

Birth

Birth is regarded as very joyous occasion in the society of the Sauria Paharia. The birth of a female child makes family exalt but in the case of boy they feel proud to be parents.

Death

The Sauria Paharia is aware of death reality. They have a conviction that death is caused by anger of God and Deities. The corps is buried along with clothes, utensils, even bow and arrows. Even some fish and rice is kept for the soul of the body. Souria Paharia is now because of awareness they believe death caused by any diseases. Now-a-day there are not keeping the food items.

Economy

Main economic activities of Sauria Paharia have been classified under the shifting cultivation type of tribal economic categorisation. An extensive area under Khallu cultivation and relatively speaking fairly large section of this tribe today depends for their livelihood on this cultivation. As it would be evident from the following description, the study and understanding of the cycle of Khallu cultivation provide us a comprehensive understanding of the total Maler culture generally. Khallu cultivation is marked with the series of processes of selection and cutting of forest; burning and removing of wood; sowing; weeding; watching and harvesting. Presently their economy rests upon resources like Khallu cultivation, selling the firewood, selling the mango, cotton, jackfruit, tamarind, custard apple, paddy cultivation and livestock.

Size of the Land Holding

Each Souria Paharia is having the land for their cultivation. Minimum land holding size is 5 bigga and maximum land holding size is 200 bigga. The tribes in this settlement do not possess the title deeds for their land but have possession certificates.

Cropping Pattern

The main crops cultivated by the tribal groups are cowpea, maize, paddy, wheat, grams, mustard, kesari, millet, rahard and sutra etc.

Forest Dependency

The Souria Paharia used to depend a lot on the forest products like: maquva, Manga, Kendu, Amla, Bear, Jackfruit, Bamboo, Sal leaf, tendu leaf and Chandu gad etc.

Political Organization

The Sauria Paharia's political authorities mark the boundary of a village in these hilly areas. The traditional system of this community had following political posts in hierarchy: Manjhi, Nayak, Sardar, Paraganait, Chakladar and Chaukidar. Following authorities are taking care of boundary of a village council: Manjhi (Administrator), Koddth (Informer), Chaukidar for four to five villages in charge from Police department.

Religion

They are having a strong belief in super-natural powers. Traditionally they are animists. They worship the spirits out of fear by offering sacrifices. They believe their lives are controlled by gossanyis, the ancestral spirits, the spirits and witchcraft. But in recent days most of Souria Paharias believe in Christianity. In every village there are two Kerija, munisi and church committee people who are in charge for the all religious activities.

Food Habits

The Souria Paharia people eats vegetarian and non vegetarian. These people not using the milk. Their foods are rice, cowpea, and various kind of cereals, hill green leaves like Kondro, Adro, Sarso, Achoadro, Mutton, Chicken, Wild pork, pork, fish, potato, Brinjal, Tomato, Poruval, Ladies finger, Kaksha and kundri etc.

Dress

The common dress of elderly male consists of a cloth locally known as Dhothi, and Kanchi. The women wear a half saree in top cloth tokkuvaro and second cloth shirts cover their back and chest.

Some Accomplishments: Buds of Hope

1. Asra Mahila Vikas Samitte (SHG) is from Chamdhi village, Taljari Block Sahibganj district of Jharkhand state. From this village fifteen women gathered and started the Self Help Group through EFICOR, all from the Souria Paharia tribal background. SHG president is Mrs. Thile Paharin (widow) 45 years old, Vice president Mrs. Chimri Paharin (widow) 43 years old, Treasurer Mrs. Thuve Paharin. This group met weekly once and collects money from each member. This group received the government loan amount Rs. 250000.
2. In this village one well was constructed through EFICOR. The well is used for agriculture purpose and for their daily necessities. For this well construction, EFICOR brought nontribal people to dig the well. Through the discussion with the community we find the place and amount of digging charges. After the discussion few days after SHG Group came and asked the well digging work. EFICOR fulfilled community desire to dig the well. Through that request from the community EFICOR made the agreement with SHG. The agreement conditions are that: *(i)* The labourers should be from the Chamdhi village. *(ii)* Payment should be made through the Asra Mahila Vikas Samittee. *(iii)* Working days should be counted on a weekly basis before market day and payment deposited in the SHG account.

After the agreement, the community people started the work. In between that the EFICOR faced a lot of struggle due to local marriage, some people busy with their own work. Because of this delayed work the seasonal rain started and faced the materials transportation problem. During that time all village tribal people came and help to take the sand, cement from down. EFICOR lost their hope but with the villager's confidence and co-operation we completed the work of digging the well. Through that they earned money, experience and skill. Now they are cultivating the vegetables like: potato, tomato, brinjal in the hills. Thus, EFICOR is providing a chance to improve the quality of life of Sauria Paharia community.

Conclusion

Sauria Paharia Tribals are very talented when we are respecting them as a human being. They are having the fundamental knowledge of development. Recalling the famous words of Pandit Jawaharlal Nehru the First Prime minister of India. "The tribals may be allowed to develop on their own genius and should not impose any thing on them". There is need for working with the tribals rather than working for the tribals.

REFERENCES

L. P. Vidyarthi, The Malar: A Study in Nature – Man-spirit Complex on A Hill Tribe of Bihar – Book Land Private Limited Calcutta.

Evangelical Fellowship of India Commission on Relief – Monthly Planner 2012.

www.eficor.org (2012).

V. Richard, Tribal Development Strategy Shanti Nivas Dumka, Jharkhand 2008.

www.Micah network.com (2012).

Jharkhand Government Website: www.Jharkhand.org (2012).

R.C. Verma, Indian Tribes through the Ages, The Director Publications Division, Government of India, New Delhi (1990) (pp. 43 and 44, 167 to 209).

Sahibganj Details http://sahibganj.nic.in/glance.htm

S. D Ponraj, Tribal Challenge Mission Educational Books Bihar India (1996).

District Census Office (2011), Censes of Sahibganj District, Jharkhand.

Nadeem Hasnain, Tribal India, Palaka Prakashan 3930/18 Kanhiya Nagar, Tri Nagar Delhi 110035.

Sr. Francina A. Karippadathu (Eds), (1997), Development and Cultural Dynamism of Two Tribes in Idukki District.

J. Nelson., Dr. L. Raja (2011), Sustaining Life-long Learning for Achieving MDG's with Special Reference to EFICOR RSLP Sahibganj, Jharkhand.

6

Indigenous Population of Irulas and Social Exclusion At Vasantham Nagar, Thiruppachur Village Thiruvalluvar District

A Case Study

*Prof. S. Antonysamy
**Prof. A. Baskar Jayabalan

ABSTRACT

Irulas are one of the tribal communities in Tamil Nadu. They are socially, economically, and culturally excluded than others. Around 35 families are temporally live in huts at Thirupachur village in Thiruvalluvar district. They have less facility like water and street light. They live in isolated place and waste lands and there is no electricity for them. The land is not also belonging to them. The policy of inclusive growth has to cover welfare. The Panchayat officials are also pin pointing at others and present exclusive policies of the government for not anything good had happened to the Irulas community. These people used to go for catching snakes and sell it for taking poison for medicinal purpose. Now-a-days, some of them changed their occupation to construction sector. The issue comes from inadequate of policy and less value ascribed by other communities. These people stay away from main Thiruppachur village. They have to walk 2 km., to buy commodities. Basically the Irullas' culture is different from others. They do not want to live in any village. They would like to prefer

* Lecturer, Department of Outreach, Loyola College, Chennai - 34.

** Lecturer, Department of Outreach, Loyola College, Chennai - 34.

a separate place and to preserve originality of their culture. The Irulas suffer from a set of social disabilities, social discrimination and stigma that cuts down their dignity. Social exclusion has been happening in the world. It has existed in almost all the societies of the world in different forms. Social exclusion occurs when people suffer from a combination of problems such as underemployment, poor skills, high crime, bad health and family breakdown, low social status, marital and relationship barriers. Both the state and central government has not only bringing the welfare scheme but also sensitize other communities to read them with fellow human beings. The government has to reframe the policy to reach every one of the excluded communities.

Introduction

The Irulas tribes of Tamil Nadu occupy the lower slopes and forests at the base of the Nilgiri Hills. They constitute the second largest group of tribes after the Badagas and are similar to the Kurumbas in many ways. This tribe produces honey, fruits, herbs, roots, gum, dyes etc., and trades them with the people in the plains. The Irulas are scattered in various parts of India, but are centralised in Thiruvallur. In the recent times the Irulas help in catching snakes and collect the snake venom. The Irulas inhabit the northern districts of Tamil Nadu, a state in southeastern India. Located not far from the city of Madras, they live in a tropical area subject to monsoon rains. Their language, Irula, is related to Tamil and Telugu, which are southern Dravidian languages. In the Tamil language, the name *Irula* means 'people of darkness'. This could refer to their dark-coloured skin or to the fact that all important events traditionally took place in the darkness of night. The Irula were greatly affected by the spread of plantation agriculture during the time of British colonization. The Kancheepuram and Thiruvalluvar districts are located very near to Chennai City. While the Irula in general merit additional fieldwork, it is only the Nilgiri Irula who are considered here. Tamil Nadu is the south easternmost state of India. It is thus a region within the tropics that is subject to westerly monsoonal rainfall. During the monsoon season Irulas have to struggle with water. It is same thing is happening at Vasantham Nagar, Thiruppasur, Thiruvallur district of Tamil Nadu. This indigenous population is migrated here. In this place they do not have any facility to reside here. The government schemes are not enough to address these people. The panchyat president was mentioning that this place is a water bond area. So the government scheme is social exclude from the development. The local people make use of them as cheap lobour for agricultural work. Though India has brought many schemes for addressing the indigenous people for development, but in reality they are social excluded from the development.

Population in India

The Irulas are a scheduled tribe of India. Irulas are present in various parts of India, but are mainly located in the Thiruvallur district of Tamil Nadu. Their population in this region is estimated from 1000 to 2000. The Irulas are a tribal community living in different parts of India. One of their habitats is in the Thiruvallur district of Tamil Nadu. Their population in this region is estimated to be at least 25,000. They are a recognised Scheduled Tribe (ST) by the Government of India.

Background of the Irulas

The origin of the word 'Irula' is not clear. One surmise is that it could have been derived from Tamil word, Irul either implying the dark complexion of the Irulas or their being constantly spotted by villagers in the ancient past as distant silhouettes in the forests. Anthropological literature says that Irulas belong to the Negrito (or Negroid) race, which is one of the six main ethnic groups that add to the racial mosaic of India. Negroids from Africa were the oldest people to have come to India. These people are now found in patches among the hill tribes of south India (Irulas, Kodars, Paniyans and Kurumbas) on the mainland. Unlike the survivors in the Andaman Islands who have retained their language, Irulas in Thiruvallur have adopted the local regional languages, namely Tamil and Telugu. The Irulas lived in the forests and until about three to four decades ago maintained a system of mild interdependence with the neighboring villages. They used to sell honey, honey wax, fire wood, etc., and in return get village products for their use. Their food was obtained mainly within the forests – the vegetation and wild animals. As per the Forest Protection Bill of 1976, the traditional homes, livelihood and lifestyle of the Irulas had become illegal. The Irulas started moving to the neighboring villages in hope of rebuilding their lives.

The Present Situation of Irulas

Irulas as a tribe are traditional snake and rat catchers. This is no longer their means of living, and over these years of existence they have been unable to find a sustainable occupation for themselves. They are unskilled in doing any kind of job. They earn their living by doing 'coolie' work. This could be either by working as labourers in the fields of the landlords during the sowing and harvesting seasons or by working in the rice mills. Fishing is also an occupation in some of the Irulas' villages. Some of them also collect firewood from the forest to sell. The problem of these people is that, only some get money while the remaining just get some rice or other things in kind as a payment for their labour. Their economic hardships are also due to the fact that the society at large has been neglecting them over the years. The landlords under whom they work treat them as bonded labourers in many of these villages. The rice mill labourers live in appalling conditions. They stay, work, eat and sleep in the rice mills, as they have no other place to live in. Moreover the fear of the outer world, forces them to continue their livelihood within the four walls of the mills. This is also due to the fact that they have no money or savings with which they could start a living. Lastly for those who are able to live outside, the owners have been acting as obstacles, as they would be losing extremely cheap labour. Non-rice mill workers are equally worse. They don't have a fixed means of livelihood. The living conditions in the villages are not favorable. Many of them don't even have a land certificate for the place they stay in. Due to this they are unable to draw any benefits that may be forthcoming to them from the government. As a result they don't have basic amenities like electricity and roads connecting their villages. Another problem being commonly faced by the Irulas is the apathy of the authorities towards their concerns. They are not even given the Schedule Tribe certificate that may help them in getting some benefits extended to them by the government. Some children who manage to study and go through the exams don't get the certificates. These circumstances have resulted in a situation where the Irulas are virtually cut off from the mainstream of the society. They are totally ignorant about the happenings in the external world to the extent that they don't even know the benefits that they are eligible to receive as a Schedule Tribe. This state of affair is the result of their illiteracy. Taking advantage of this, the local village people cheat them in terms of employment and security. The facts stated is only a tip of the iceberg of the kind of life that the Irulas lead. It would suffice to say that this community needs a lot more attention from the government and the society at large. They had nothing. The education and health conditions of the people were very bad. They had no community certificates.

Occupation of Irulas

Their main occupations are snake and rat catching. They also work as labourers (coolies) in the fields of the landlords during the sowing and harvesting seasons or in the rice mills. Fishing is also a major occupation. Rats destroy a quarter of the grain grown on Tamil Nadu – area farms annually. To combat this pest, Irula men use a traditional earthen pot fumigation method. Smoke is blown through their mouths, which leads to severe respiratory and heart problems. Irulas have no formal methods of locating or catching snakes. Skilled at their art, Irulas can track a snake by following snitch signs on the ground, following tracks to burrows where the snakes may be hiding. Using nothing more than crowbar to dig the soil and bare hands, these tribal easily catch highly poisonous snakes like cobras, vipers and kraits. Each Irula hunts the area radiating from his village or campsite as far as the distance he can easily walk with his family in one day. Usually, the area is within a 10 km radius of their villages. They usually get one to three large snakes in a good day's hunt, which they sell to their society.

Economic Situation

The Irula economy was based on collecting food from the jungle and hunting small game. Today, however, most of the Irula are small-scale farmers. Irula houses are built together in small settlements or villages called *mottas*. The mottas are usually situated on the edges of steep hills and are surrounded by a few dry fields, gardens, and forests or plantations. The typical house consists of only one room with an earthen floor, thatched roof, and a front porch. Less traditional houses have tile roofs and stone walls. The people sleep on mats, which they roll up and store in a corner during the day. In some villages different tribes and castes live alongside the Irula, but in other villages the Irula live alone. When compared to the Hindu plains-peoples that surround them, the Irula have preserved a relatively simple, democratic social structure. Marriage partners are selected from within the tribe, but outside the clan. Social control is exercised by a tribal council of men representing the different clans. Today, typical Irula dress is rarely worn, but tattooing is still frequently seen, especially on the forehead. The women enjoy wearing jewelry, and the men take pleasure in making their own drums and flutes.

Religion

Although 95 per cent Irulas are Hindus, elements of their traditional ethnic religion are still part of their lives. Many of them have retained their own tribal beliefs that revolve around the spirit world. 'House deities' are very important. They are the inherited clan-gods that are passed down through the male descendants. *Bujaris*, or priests, are used to contact the supernatural world of deities and spirits.

Education

The Irulas do not own the land on which they build their small fragile huts, they are often expelled and face constant displacement. This is one reason why their children are often cut off from the education system. In other cases, the children are not allowed to go to school. The Indian society has been neglecting the Irulas as other tribal communities over the years. They belong to one of the most marginalised fractions of the rigidly stratified Indian society. Their poverty and resulting disempowerment make them particularly vulnerable to all types of discrimination and injustices.

Culture

The Irulas are sub-divided into the following groups; Poongkaru, Kudagar Kalkatti, Vellaka, Devala and Koppillingam. Marriage ties are rather loose. The Irula marriage and funeral ceremonies are simple. The Marriages are followed by feast and dance.

The Irulas are said to worship Vishnu in their own temple. Irula temples aren't imposing, consisting as they do of circles of rough stones, each enclosing an upright one with iron tridents fixed in the ground. There are many traditions concerning their power over wild beasts. They are accredited with being able to tame tigers, and the fable goes that the women when in the woods leave their children in the care of tiger.

Identification

Most Irulas inhabit the state of Tamil Nadu, India. Although they form a Scheduled Tribe, the Irula are in many ways similar to their nearby Hindu caste neighbors. They have pantheistic and animistic tendencies of their own, but prolonged contact with more orthodox Hinduism has also had its indelible impact.

Social Exclusion of Tribals

Social exclusion is fundamentally about inequality; thereby it directly addresses the question of social justice. Any system of social or economics organization that gives rise to categories of individuals of groups that are included would fail the elementary test of justice of fairness. On the other hand, if there is a historical legacy of long years of exploitation or oppression perpetuated against some individual or groups then one may legitimately justify a pattern of development that improves the condition of the oppressed to the exclusion of other better-off groups. In other words, exclusion may be justified only if the pattern of development were to help only those who are already socially and economically excluded. The notion of exclusion may also be extended to incorporate the notion of rights. Eradication of caste based exclusion is however, a much slower and yet more daunting task. We look at a dimension of social exclusion that is of central importance in India. This has to do with exclusion on the basis of caste. This is in some sense the most potent form of exclusion because this sociological characteristic is fixed at birth and is hence completely inflexible. A number of other forms of exclusion from certain basic rights deserve careful consideration. One may identify several other important dimensions of exclusion like exclusion from education, exclusion from housing, exclusion from property ownership, exclusion from democratic participation, exclusion from access to health services, exclusion from public goods, to name a few. In addition to these, one may think in terms of gender based exclusion of the old and infirm, exclusion of widows, and exclusion of the physically handicapped etc. We have recognised the problem of exclusion but we have not made our party politics, the executive namely: the state, decision-making bodies, administration and above all our polices sufficiently inclusive so as to address the problem of poverty and deprivation and of participation and representation of excluded groups like Scheduled Castes, Scheduled Tribes and religious minorities that are linked with the societal process of exclusion in multiple spheres. It has to be recognised that the problem of Dalilts, Adivasis and religious minorities is one of exclusion and oppression in multiple spheres.

It is essential that political and government mechanisms, the system of governance and development of the state, therefore, very much depends upon the indication of the change that happens in these communities. The Scheduled Tribes seem to suffer from isolation and greater disadvantage in rural non-farm labour market. They also suffer from what Sen would call 'constructive relevance". This type of exclusion of the group to relate to others and to take part in the life of the community directly impoverishes a person's life, apart from reducing economic opportunity that comes from the social contract. Adivasis being isolated and not being able to relate with others face exclusion in more general ways from the network of opportunities. This possibly explains as to why poverty is highest among the tribes in rural areas despite better access to agriculture land. General access to market and information that is needed in the production economy is thus lacking.

Social Exclusion of Irulas at Vasantham Nagar, Thirupasur, Thiruvallur District – Case Study

Around 35 families are residing at Vasantham Nagar. These people had migrated from some other villages. Vasamtham Nagar is just 3 km., away from Thirupasur village. These people are living in waste land of water lagging area. They have one street light and one water tap for thirty five families. Their houses are huts with 3 feets wall. They are residing more than five years in the same area. During the monsoon season, their condition is very pathetic and their house's floor is also wet. The entire place will get filled with water. Irulas mainly go for hunting snakes and sell it. They do not have adequate income to look after their families. Many of them are working as coolie. A few of them are going to high school at Thiruvallur. Irulas just have one connection of water tap and only one street light. They have to manage with hurricane light. They are staying in waste land which is not permanent to them. The local government has not provided basic facilities to these people. The panchayat president had been blaming that this place is not permanent to them. So the local government could do anything to them. The local people have not recognised the Irulas as human beings and use them for agricultural work. They pay lower wages to them compared to others. The children also do not have enough dress to wear. The people expressed regret on lack of infrastructure for their living and water logging at rainy days. Hence, the government has to reaffirm the polices to available Irulas (tribal) and implement them.

Conclusion

The need of Irulas, today, is an acceptance and empathy of all people, make them understand us and thus create a bond of affection and understanding. After the achievement of independence, the basic problem of India is still to address the problems of Irulas. Political integration is now complete but that is not enough. We must bring about changes much more basic and initiate a social transformation than mere political integration. All we can do is to nurture it and create conditions where it finds pleasant soil. So, the greatest problem of India today is not so much political as psychological integration and consolidation. India must build up for herself a unity which will do away with provincialism, communalism, and address the various other infrastructure facilities.

REFERENCES

Book on the tribal people of India, publications Division, Ministry of Information and Broadcasting.

Article on Social Exclusion and Inclusiveness of a Tribal Community in Tamil Nadu: Reality and Challenges. By S. Rajangam and Dr. S.Gurusamy – Social Action Vol. 61. January – March 2011.

http://www.everyculture.com/South-Asia/Irula-Orientation.html#ixzz1gsMMbAON

http:// www.en.wikipedia.org/wik/Irulas

http://www.ashanet.org/proects/tamilnadu/irulas/Irulas.html

http:// www.rediff.com.com/us/2000/aug/08us.htm

http://www.indianetzone.com/22/tribes_tamil_nadu_india.htm

SECTION – II

Indigenous Population

Poverty, Health and Crisis to Survival

7

Issues of Poverty among Indigenous Communities

*Dr. P. Anandharajakumar

ABSTRACT

What do we mean by – Indigenous? There is no widely accepted definition of indigenous peoples. But we have developed a modern understanding of this term-based on: self-identification as indigenous peoples at the individual level and accepted by the community as their member; historical continuity with pre-colonial and/or pre-settler societies; strong link to territories and surrounding natural resources; distinct social, economic or political systems; distinct language, culture and beliefs; form non-dominant groups of society; and resolve to maintain and reproduce their ancestral environments and systems as distinctive peoples and communities (UNFPII).

Rough estimates suggest that there are more than 5,000 different groups living in more than 70 countries (IFAD). It has been further estimated that there are approximately 250-350 million indigenous peoples worldwide, representing 5 per cent of the world's population (IWGIA 2008). The United

* Head and Associate Professor, Department of Rural Development, GRI, Deemed University, Gandhigram, TN.

Nations Permanent Forum on Indigenous Issues (2006) estimates the indigenous population to be over 350 million. It is also estimated that up to 15 per cent of the world's poor, and up to one-third of the rural poor, are indigenous (UNPFII).

Poverty among indigenous communities has been increasingly recognised in the development literature. The relationship between being indigenous and experiencing economic inequality in developing countries has come to the fore in recent years. Still, very little investigation has been made into the different economic experiences of the indigenous population within a society. It is important to consider indigenous peoples in discussions about economic development – but not often done.

This paper attempts to explain issues such as whether poverty among indigenous peoples higher and more severe than poverty among the general population in the countries in which they live? Do poverty trends differ between the indigenous and non-indigenous population? More specifically, do indigenous poverty rates remain stagnant when national poverty rates change? What is the extent of access to basic infrastructure services (water, sanitation) and major social programmes available to indigenous communities?

Keywords: Indigenous Communities, Poverty, Health, MDG.

Introduction

Indigenous peoples are ethnic groups that are defined as 'indigenous' according to one of the various definitions of the term, though there is no universally accepted definition. Most uses of the phrase refer to being the 'original inhabitants' of a territory. In the late twentieth century, the term began to be used to refer to ethnic groups that have historical ties to groups that existed in a territory prior to colonization or formation of a nation state, and which normally preserve a degree of cultural and political separation from the mainstream culture and political system of the nation state within the border of which the indigenous group is located. The political sense of the term defines these groups as particularly vulnerable to exploitation and oppression by nation states. As a result, a special set of political rights in accordance with international law have been set forth by international organizations such as the United Nations, the International Labour Organization and the World Bank. The United Nations have issued a Declaration on the Rights of Indigenous Peoples to protect the collective rights of indigenous peoples to their culture, identity, language, employment, health, education and natural resources. There are more than 370 million self-identified indigenous peoples in some 70 countries around the world. In Latin America alone there are more than 400 groups, each with a distinct language and culture. But the biggest concentration of indigenous peoples is in Asia and the Pacific – an estimated 70 per cent.

Origins of the Phrase

During the late twentieth century the term *Indigenous peoples* evolved into a legal category that refers to culturally distinct groups that in various ways had been affected by the processes of colonization. These are usually collectives that have preserved some degree of cultural and political separation from the mainstream culture and political system that has grown to surround or dominate them economically, politically, culturally, or geographically. "'Indigenous peoples'... is a term that internationalises the experiences, the issues and the struggles of some of the world's colonized peoples". "The final 's' in 'indigenous peoples' ... [is] a way of recognising that there are real differences between different indigenous peoples". Used politically, the term defines these groups as particularly vulnerable to exploitation and oppression by nation states, and as a result a special set of political rights in accordance with international law have been set forth by international organizations such as the United Nations, the International Labour Organization and the World Bank. The United Nations issued a Declaration on the Rights of Indigenous Peoples, with the intent to protect the collective rights of indigenous peoples to their culture, identity, language, employment, health, education and natural resources. However, the phrase is not applied consistently in all cultures. The notion of an indigenous group depends on context and other issues. The World Bank's policy for indigenous people states: Because of the varied and changing contexts in which Indigenous Peoples live and because there is no universally accepted definition of 'Indigenous Peoples', this policy does not define the term. Indigenous Peoples may be referred to in different countries by such terms as 'indigenous ethnic minorities', 'aboriginals', 'hill tribes', 'minority nationalities', 'scheduled tribes', or 'tribal groups'. Different states designate the groups within their boundaries that are recognised as indigenous peoples according to international legislation by different terms. These include, for example 'Native Americans' and 'Pacific Islander' in the United States; 'Aboriginals (Inuit', 'Métis' and 'First Nations)' in Canada; Aborigines in Australia; Hill tribes in Southeast Asia; indigenous ethnic minorities, scheduled tribes or Adivasi in India; tribal groups, or autochthonous groups.

Understanding the Phrase 'Indigenousness'

Ethnic group or community may be described as being *indigenous* in reference to some particular region or location. Key to a contemporary understanding of 'indigenousness' is the political role a cultural group plays, for all other criteria usually taken to denote indigenous groups (territory, race, history, subsistence lifestyle, etc.,) can, to a greater or lesser extent, also be applied to majority cultures. Therefore, the distinction applied to indigenous groups can be formulated as "a politically underprivileged group, who share a similar... identity different to the nation in power", and who share territorial rights to a particular area governed by a colonial power. However, the specific term *indigenous peoples* has a more restrictive interpretation when it used in the more formalized, legalistic, and academic sense, associated with the collective rights of human populations. In these contexts, the term is used to denote particular peoples and groups around the world who, as well as being native to or associated with some given territory, meet certain other criteria (such as having reached a social and technological plateau thousands of years ago.

Who are Identified as Indigenous Communities?

There is no widely accepted definition of indigenous peoples. Indigenous Peoples may be referred to in different countries by such terms as 'indigenous ethnic minorities,' 'aboriginals,' 'hill tribes,' 'minority nationalities,' 'scheduled tribes,' or 'tribal groups'. This term based on a variety of characteristics – self-identification at the individual level and accepted by the community as their member; historical continuity with pre-colonial or pre-settler societies; a strong link to territories and surrounding natural resources; a distinct social, economic, or political system; a distinct language, culture, and beliefs; individuals that form non-dominant groups of society; and those that resolve to maintain and reproduce their ancestral environments and systems as distinctive peoples and communities.

Criteria for Indigenous

A contemporary working definition of 'indigenous people' for certain purposes has criteria which would seek to include cultural groups (and their continuity or association with a given region, or parts of a region, and who formerly or currently inhabit the region) either before or its subsequent colonisation or annexation; or alongside other cultural groups during the formation or reign of a colony or nation-state; or independently or largely isolated from the influence of the claimed governance by a nation-state, and who furthermore have maintained at least in part their distinct cultural, social/organizational, or linguistic characteristics, and in doing so remain differentiated in some degree from the surrounding populations and dominant culture of the nation-state. To the above, a criterion is usually added to also include peoples who are self-identified as indigenous, or those recognised as such by other groups. Even if all the above criteria are fulfilled, some people may either not considers themselves as indigenous or may not be considered as indigenous by governments, organizations or scholars. The discourse of indigenous/non-indigenous may also be viewed within the context of postcolonialism and the evolution of post-colonial societies.

Common Characteristics

Characteristics common across many Indigenous groups include present or historical reliance upon subsistence-based production (based on pastoral, horticultural and/or hunting and gathering techniques), and a predominantly non-urbanised society. Not all indigenous groups share these characteristics. Indigenous societies may be either settled in a given locale/region or exhibit a nomadic lifestyle across a large territory, but are generally historically associated with a specific territory on which they are dependent. Indigenous societies are found in every inhabited climate zone and continent of the world.

Key Facts about Indigenous Communities

- There are more than 370 million self-identified indigenous people in the world, living in at least 70 countries.
- Most of the worlds' indigenous peoples live in Asia.
- Indigenous peoples form about 5,000 distinct groups and occupy about 20 per cent of the earth's territory.
- Although indigenous peoples make up less than 6 per cent of the global population, they speak more than 4,000 of the world's 7,000 languages.
- One of the root causes of the poverty and marginalization of indigenous peoples is loss of control over their traditional lands, territories and natural resources.
- Indigenous peoples have a concept of poverty and development that reflects their own values, needs and priorities; they do not see poverty solely as the lack of income.
- A growing number of indigenous peoples live in urban areas, as a result of the degradation of land, dispossession, forced evictions and lack of employment opportunities.

Population and Distribution

Indigenous commiunties range from those who have been significantly exposed to the colonizing or expansionary activities of other societies through to those who as yet remain in comparative isolation from any external influence Precise estimates for the total population of the world's Indigenous peoples are very difficult to compile, given the difficulties in identification and the variances and inadequacies of available census data. Recent source estimates range from 300 million to 350 million as of the start of the 21st century. This would equate to just fewer than 6 per cent of the total world population. This includes at least 5000 distinct peoples in over 72 countries. Contemporary distinct indigenous groups survive in populations ranging from only a few dozen to hundreds of thousands and more. Many indigenous populations have undergone a dramatic decline and even extinction, and remain threatened in many parts of the world. Some have also been assimilated by other populations or have undergone many other changes. In other cases, indigenous populations are undergoing a recovery or expansion in numbers. Certain indigenous societies survive even though they may no longer inhabit their 'traditional' lands, owing to migration, relocation, forced resettlement or having been supplanted by other cultural groups. In many other respects, the transformation of culture of indigenous groups is ongoing, and includes permanent loss of language, loss of lands, encroachment on traditional territories, and disruption in traditional lifeways due to contamination and pollution of waters and lands.

Rights, Issues and Concerns: The Question of Poverty

Indigenous peoples confront a diverse range of concerns associated with their status and interaction with other cultural groups, as well as changes in their inhabited environment. Some challenges are specific to particular groups; however, other challenges are commonly experienced These issues include cultural and linguistic preservation, land rights, ownership and exploitation of natural resources, political determination and autonomy, environmental degradation and incursion, poverty, health, and discrimination. The interaction between indigenous and non-indigenous societies throughout history has been complex, ranging from outright conflict and subjugation to some degree of mutual benefit and cultural transfer. The situation can be further confused when there is a complicated or contested history of migration and population of a given region, which can give rise to disputes about primacy and ownership of the land and resources. Wherever indigenous cultural identity is asserted, some particular set of societal issues and concerns may be voiced which either arise from (at least in part), or have a particular dimension associated with, their indigenous status. These concerns will often be commonly held or affect other societies also, and are not necessarily experienced uniquely by indigenous groups. Despite the diversity of Indigenous peoples, it may be noted that they share common problems and issues in dealing with the prevailing, or invading, society. They are generally concerned that the cultures of Indigenous peoples are being lost and that indigenous peoples suffer both discrimination and pressure to assimilate into their surrounding societies. It is also sometimes argued that it is important for the human species as a whole to preserve a wide range of cultural diversity as possible, and that the protection of indigenous cultures is vital. The moot point of view is that indigenous peoples are increasingly faced with threats to their sovereignty, environment, and access to natural resources and thus poverty.

Poverty among Indigenous Communities

As the global community looks for ways to meet the Millennium Development Goal (MDG) of halving the share of people in poverty by 2015 from its 1990 level, it cannot afford to ignore the plight of indigenous peoples. Although they make up roughly 4.5 per cent of the global population, they account for about 10 per cent of the poor – with nearly 80 per cent of them in Asia. Indigenous peoples continue to be over-represented among the poor, the illiterate, and the unemployed. Indigenous peoples number about 370 million. While they constitute approximately 5 per cent of the world's population, indigenous peoples make up 15 per cent of the world's poor. They also make up about one-third of the world's 900 million extremely poor rural people. In China, the national and indigenous poverty rates are strikingly low. Elsewhere, indigenous poverty rates approach or exceed 50 per cent. While the majority of indigenous peoples come from China and India, the proportion of the indigenous poor is more spread out across regions, given lower poverty rates in these two countries, particularly China. In other countries, indigenous peoples have disproportionately high poverty rates – meaning that they deviate from the non-indigenous poverty rate by a great margin However, there is evidence of rapidly declining poverty rates, even among indigenous peoples, in emerging Asia (notably, China, India, and Vietnam). But research from Latin America – and to some degree Australia, Canada, New Zealand, and the United States – shows a sticky persistence of poverty rates for indigenous peoples over time. Indigenous people suffer from the consequences of historic injustice, including colonization, dispossession of their lands, territories and resources, oppression and discrimination as well as lack of control over their own ways of life. Their right to development has been largely denied by colonial and modern states in the pursuit of economic growth. As a consequence, indigenous peoples often lose out to more powerful actors, becoming among the most impoverished groups in their respective countries.

Indigenous peoples also face huge disparities in terms of access to and quality of education and health. Indigenous peoples also suffer from discrimination in terms of employment and income. In different parts of the world, differential progress is being made by indigenous peoples in their social and economic development, reflecting specific national legal and policy frameworks with regard to recognising, respecting and promoting their rights. Historical and ongoing globalisation has trapped many of them in conditions of deepening impoverishment, even as others have made important advances in asserting recognition of their distinct identities as indigenous peoples and promoting models of development with cultural identity and integrity, applying a human rights-based approach. It is clear that the advancement of indigenous peoples' social and economic development is predicated on international and national recognition of their human rights and on pursuing development strategies based on their own definitions and indicators of poverty and well-being. The poverty gap, or shortfall of the poor below the poverty line, provides a measure of the resources required to eliminate poverty. It is expressed as the total amount of money which would be needed to raise the poor from their present incomes to the poverty line, as a proportion of the poverty line, and averaged over the total population. This measures the depth of poverty. In all cases the poverty gap measure is higher for indigenous/minority groups. Research by the Institute of Human Development, India, has shown how official statistics could shed light on the discrimination experienced by indigenous peoples. Analysis of official data on Scheduled Tribes and Scheduled Castes from the UNDP Human Development Index (HDI) and the Planning Commission of the Government of India showed that while the caste system discriminates against the poorest caste – the *Dalits* – the level of poverty among Scheduled Tribes is deeper, despite the constitutional rights that apply uniquely to them. It is found that while poverty among the general population had declined between 1993-94 and 1999-2000, there had been little change in poverty levels among indigenous peoples. The Scheduled Castes have fared better than Scheduled Tribes in terms of poverty reduction. The poverty gap between Scheduled Castes and other groups in India has decreased while that between the Scheduled Tribes and other groups has widened.

Similar results were found using the Human Poverty Index (HPI). Whilst India is considered a middle-ranked country in the UNDP HPI ranking of countries, the indigenous communities as a group are comparable to Sub-Saharan countries, which are ranked in the bottom 25. By taking into account the poverty of indigenous peoples, the MDG goal of halving poverty by 2015 may not be achieved in India. Scheduled Tribes also score lower in education, health and other social and economic aspects measured by the HDI. Indigenous communities in India are typically rural, and poverty among rural communities is higher than that in urban areas. There are few people without land among the Scheduled Tribes, but their lands have low productivity. The more productive lands, especially in low-lying areas, have been taken over by other communities. There is also less job diversification among Scheduled Tribes. Deprived of formal education and with little access to capital, they fail to find work, either self-employed or within regular jobs, ending up in casual employment or in agriculture.

Health Issues

Despite generally improving conditions in many countries, health deficits among indigenous populations are severe. In December 1993, the United Nations General Assembly proclaimed the International Decade of the World's Indigenous People, and requested UN specialised agencies to consider with governments and indigenous people how they can contribute to the success of the Decade of Indigenous People, commencing in December 1994. The WHO notes, that "Statistical data on the health status of indigenous peoples is scarce. This is especially notable for indigenous peoples in Africa, Asia and eastern Europe", but snapshots from various countries, where such statistics are available, show that indigenous people are in worse health than the general population, in advanced and developing countries alike: higher incidence of diabetes in some regions of Australia; higher prevalence of poor sanitation and lack of safe water among the households in Rwanda; a greater prevalence of childbirths without prenatal care among ethnic minorities in Vietman; suicide rates among Inuit youth in Canada are eleven times higher than the national average; infant mortality rates are higher for indigenous peoples everywhere. Indigenous groups are more likely to suffer from health issues and they are less likely to seek or receive medical attention, even the most basic preventive care. For example, in India, where poverty reduction achievements have been sizeable, indigenous peoples are less likely to be not covered by health programmes nor receive vital vaccinations.

Potentials of Indigenous Communities

Indigenous peoples have in-depth, varied and locally rooted knowledge of the natural world. And because traditional indigenous lands and territories contain some 80 per cent of the planet's bio-diversity, indigenous peoples can play a crucial role in managing natural resources. Indigenous peoples and their knowledge systems have a special role to play in the conservation and sustainable management of natural resources. Unfortunately, indigenous peoples too often pay a price for being different and far too frequently face discrimination. Over the centuries, they have been dispossessed of their lands, territories and resources and, as a consequence, have often lost control over their own way of life. Worldwide, they account for 5 per cent of the population, but represent 15 per cent of those living in poverty. One of the most effective ways to enable indigenous peoples to overcome poverty is to support their efforts to shape and direct their own destinies, and to ensure that they are the co-creators and co-managers of development initiatives.

Conclusion

Indigenous peoples have rich ancient cultures and view their social, economic, environmental and spiritual systems as interdependent. They make valuable contributions to the world's heritage thanks to their traditional knowledge and their understanding of eco-system management. But indigenous peoples are also among the world's most vulnerable, marginalized and disadvantaged groups. We must ensure that their voices are heard, their rights respected, and their well-being improved.

REFERENCES

Joji Carino, (2005), State of the World's Indigenous Peoples, UNICEF.

World Bank (2007), Economic Opportunities for Indigenous Peoples in Latin America, Washington D.C.: The World Bank.

UNPFII. 2006, UN Economic and Social Council, Permanent Forum on Indigenous Issues, Fifth Session. Action Programme for Second Indigenous Decade Launched. 15 May 2006.

Sanders, Douglas (1999), Indigenous Peoples: Issues of Definition, *International Journal of Cultural Property*.

WGIP (2001). *Indigenous Peoples and the United Nations System*. Office of the High Commissioner for Human Rights, United Nations Office at Geneva.

8

Historical Locks and Economic Deprivation of Indigenous Population

Evidence From Kerala

*M. P. Saji

ABSTRACT

Social exclusion, a term that has recently claimed its territory in development parlances, is meant to accommodate a wider dimensions socio-economic deprivation of a section of the society. The current discussions on social exclusion, in-variably, recognised the socio-economic marginality experienced by the indigenous tribal population across India. Despite of high economic development of the country and the eventual claim of trickle down effects of economic development by the neo-liberal advocates, this section of the Indian population is still the least to gain. In fact, it is the indigenous population living in remote areas of the nation, who bear the brunt of the economic development. Though there are several targeted initiatives to bring the tribal population to be part of the changing socio-economic milieu, the development in this regard is not as desired. There are several reasons for that. One major issue is that, they are encircled by a set of historical locks – a situation created by the historically attributed factors. On the one hand it takes longer period for them to come of a

* Research Scholar, Department of Extension Education, GRI, Gandhigram, Dindigul, Tamil Nadu.

completely different circumstances and cultural values created over several millennia. On the other hand, the current phase of changes in socio-economic and political milieu is too fast for them to catch up with. The factors contributing to the social and economic exclusion of the indigenous communities can, then, be understood only if we look into their deprivation on a relative context.

The present paper is an attempt to look into the economic deprivation of the tribal people in Kerala state by analysing the historical locks in the economic empowerment of over three lakh indigenous tribal population in the State. The paper, mainly focusing on three major contributories of the economic deprivation of the tribal people in the state, *i.e.,* the poor land ownership, skill orientation of the working population and the relative backwardness in the formal education. All these issues have historical backgrounds that continue to lock the tribal people the access to the current economic environment. In the present era of economic globalisation, these locks seem to be getting more complex and in such situation, the social and economic exclusion of the tribal people is going to be widened.

Keywords: Social Exclusion; Indigenous Population; Economic Development; Land Alienation; Educational Backwardness.

Introduction

Social exclusion, a term that has recently claimed its territory in development parlances, is meant to accommodate a wider dimensions socio-economic deprivation of a section of the society. Social exclusion is the process through which individuals and groups are wholly or partially excluded from full participation in the society in which they live (Atkinson and Divoudi, 2000). The current discussions on social exclusion, in-variably, recognised the socio-economic marginality experienced by the indigenous tribal population across India. Despite of high economic development of the country and the eventual claim of trickle down effects of economic development by the neo-liberal advocates, this section of the Indian population is still the least to gain. In fact, it is the indigenous population living in remote areas of the nation, who bear the brunt of the economic development. The indigenous people are disadvantaged from several dimensions that lead to social exclusion. Sonowal (2008), mentions two broader forms of disadvantages of the indigenous population – the identity based forms of disadvantages and the special disadvantages. While the former reflects the cultural devaluation of the groups in a society and the later lies in the remoteness and isolation of a location that makes it difficult for its inhabitants to participate in broader socio-economic processes. Both from economic and market perspective, the exclusion of indigenous people cater relevance in present situation. They are more likely to have lower income, access to labour market, land and capital market. All of which leads to economic exclusion of a social class from the modern life. Just as their counterparts in rest of modern India, the indigenous people living in Kerala are also facing the problem of social exclusion and the economic deprivation. There are several reasons for that. One major issue is that, they are encircled by a set of historical locks – a situation created by the historically attributed factors. On the one hand it takes longer period for them to come of a completely different circumstances and cultural values created over several millennia. On the other hand, the current phase of changes in socio-economic and political milieu is too fast for them to catch up with. The factors contributing to the social and economic exclusion of the indigenous communities can, then, be understood only if we look into their deprivation on a relative context.

Tribals in Kerala

The Western Ghats and its peripheries form the main abode of the tribal people in Kerala. The scheduled tribe population of the state is 364,189 which is 1.14 per cent of its general population (GoK, 2005). There are 36 different tribal communities in the state, of which five are primitive tribes. Highest concentration of scheduled tribes is seen in Wayanad district (37.4%), followed by Idukki and Palakkad districts. A total of 72.8 per cent of tribal population is concentrated in six districts: Wayanad, Idukki, Palakkad, Kasaragod, Thiruvananthapuram and Kannur (Table 8.1).

Table 8.1: Regional Distribution of Tribal Population in Kerala, 2001

State/Districts	% of ST to Kerala Population	District-wise % Total ST Population
Kerala	1.14	100.00
Kasaragod	2.52	8.33
Kannur	0.83	5.48
Wayanad	17.43	37.36
Kozhikode	0.21	1.63
Malappuram	0.34	3.37
Palakkad	1.52	10.89
Thrissur	0.16	1.33
Ernakulam	0.32	2.76
Idukki	4.51	14.00
Kottayam	0.94	5.04
Alappuzha	0.15	0.86
Pathanamthitta	0.53	1.80
Kollam	0.20	1.43
Thiruvananthapuram	0.65	5.72

The tribal communities of Kerala not only differ from the non tribals but also from one another. But they have some uniform~ characteristics. The tribal people in Kerala, like their counter [arts as elsewhere in India, live in the midst of poverty, sufferings and exploitation in everywhere of their life. Being the most backward and excluded community, their economy is characterised by dependency ion mainstream society, land alienation, indebtedness, bonded labour system. (Mathur, 1977; Kunhaman, 1989; Mohandas M, 1992).

Economic Development of Kerala and Tribals

For almost three decades between the late 1950s and the late 1980s, Kerala's economic performance was rather dismal despite its high human development, reflecting a 'human development lopsided' pattern of development. In recent years, a series of studies observe a turnaround in the development experience of Kerala. Subramanian and Azeez (2000), Pushpangadan (2003) have come out with the observation that economic growth has not completely eluded Kerala. From 1994-95 onwards per capita income and its growth rate in Kerala is greater than all India average. A striking feature of the Kerala economy in the turnaround growth scenario is the drastic change in the pattern of sectoral composition of output, increasingly inclining towards the tertiary sector. It is quite natural that averages explain a phenomenon. However, as in all distributions, Kerala has certain sections of its population for whom the general tendency or the pattern of the development cannot be applied, indigenous people are one such segment.. Getting insights into such populations is important since the credit of Kerala's success is driven by enlightened state policy based on equity and public action rather than market led-individual initiatives.

When we look at the structure of employment among the tribal population in comparison with that of the non-tribal, we find that the growing sector of Kerala's economy has not absorbed the tribal population. The major chunk of the tribal population is still engages in agriculture and allied activities whereas for the state as a whole the structure of the employment is showing a transformation from the primary to the tertiary sector. It is also observed that the change in the social and economic status of the tribal community has been marginal than that of the average population of Kerala. The decline in these sectors was compensated by a corresponding increase in the service sectors, especially trade and commerce. But with respect to the tribal population a positive change in the employment was observed in the III category, *i.e.*, Livestock, Fishing, Hunting and Plantations, Orchards and Allied Activities. This indicates that as the economy progressed and the employment pattern was shifting towards the service sector activities for the general population, the Tribal communities were still caught up in the traditional economic activities. The preceding analysis reveals that 88 per

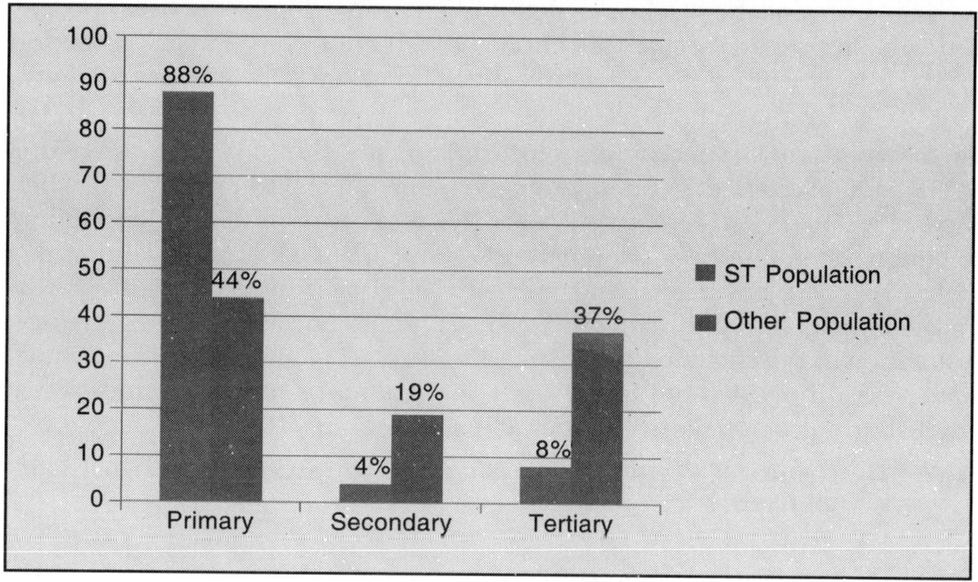

Fig. 8.1: Sectoral Composition of Working Population – Tribal *vs.* Non-Tribal

cent of the tribal population is still working in the primary sector of the economy, while only 44 per cent of the general population works in this sector. Only 8 per cent of the working population among tribals is into the tertiary sector as against 37 per cent of the general population. This clearly shows that the structural transformation in the economy since the 1980s could not accommodate the tribal population at all. They remain still in the periphery of the development process as outliners to the distribution of the fruits of development.

Land Alienation

As seen in the previous section, the ST population in the state is very much depending on farming and other primary sector for their livelihood. However the basic resource of living, the land of their own, still remains a dream for most section of the ST population. While they have been living in the vast forest areas of the state for generations, they never be aware of the concept of private ownership of land. And the history witnessed a systematic alienation of tribal people of owning land.

It is considered that over half of the tribal families in the state do not possess any land of their own. They come around 45000 families. For most of the tribal families who were given forest land under various tribal development plans, did not have Pattas (possession certificate). They reason the government says is to avoid transfer of tribal land to non tribal people. Though this claim is valid, one of the negative outcomes of this act was that, the agriculture development become stagnant in this land, as the tribal lands become non-bankable. Consider that a large proportion of the tribal people depends on primary sector, this implies that there is very limited scope for capital investment for farm diversification and improvement in productivity.

Those families who do not have land, working as daily labourers under land owners in the nearby agriculture land are the only way to ensure livelihood. A section of them also depends sonly on collection of Non-Timber Forest Produce. The Government, over the decades promises of distribution of land to these families. Even there are about 1.39 lakh acres of land in the State identified as surplus land. But only hold of it is distributed to poor households in the state. Though Debar Commission in 1950s suggested of restoration of the alienated tribal land, the successive governments in Kerala state took different route to sidelines the real spirit of the Commission's order to protect the interest of the land grabbers than the tribal people.

Table 8.2: Historical Perspective on the Government Stand on Tribal land Restoration

1950s	The Debar Commission suggests restoration of alienated Tribal lands back to Tribals with effect from January 26, 1950.
1975	The Kerala Assembly passed the Tribal Land Act to restore all the lands lost by Kerala tribals from January 26, 1960.
1986	Rules were formulated to implement the Act with retrospective effect from January 1, 1982.
1996	Kerala Assembly passes the Kerala Scheduled Tribes (Restriction on Transfer of Land and Restoration of Alienated Lands) Amendment Bill, 1996 (it held legal and valid all transactions of tribal land between 1960 to January 24, 1986).

Education Backwardness

In the changing economic conditions, education is a key factor that determines the participation of the people in the new economic system. In the present Knowledge economy, and inclusive education scenario determines the employment, income and movement of people of various social strata (George, 2011). While Kerala has succeeded in attaining universal literacy and better positioning their population in the educational attainment, the segregated data for ST population in the state shows that this achievement is actually excluded a large percentage of them. (Table 8.2). While over 90 per cent of its population is literate, the ST population in the State has just 64.4 per cent having the ability to read and write. Thus the targeted literacy programmes of the 1990's have not very much made inroads into the Tribal colonies of the state.

Thus education still remains a luxury for majority of the Tribal people. The main reasons for the very low spread of education are the peculiar nature of their habitation that in most case lies far from the educational institutions.

Table 8.3: Literacy Rate General Population *vs.* ST Population in Kerala

Year	1961	1971	1981	1991	2001
Total population	–	60.42	70.42	89.81	90.9
ST population	17.26	25.72	31.79	37.22	64.4

Source: Census data, from 1961 to 2001.

Further, the socio-economic condition preailining in the tribal settlements are not conducive for studies. This is evident from the fact that the drop out rate among the ST students as high as 42.3 per cent in primary level and at elementary level and at Secondary level the drop out rate is even worse with 65.9 per cent and 79 per cent respectively. Besides, the disparities increase at higher and higher levels of education, particularly in technical and professional education which provide better access to more remunerative jobs. In a way, it is these disparities within the state that matter more in view of the high unemployment rate in the state and consequently the highly competitive nature of the labour market.

Towards an Explanation

As it has been mentioned earlier, there have been two distinct phases in Kerala's development experience; first, before the mid-1980s, characterised by a high social sector development and low economic growth; and second, turnaround phase since the mid-1980s with high social sector as well as economic development. A pertinent question that arises here is: why have the tribal communities in Kerala remained deprived both in terms of social and economic development unlike the average Keralite. Our macro explanation is that those very factors, 21 which stand in favour of the celebrated development experience of Kerala, themselves constitute the reasons for the relative deprivation of the tribal communities in the state. Various factors have been identified by scholars, within as well as outside the country, for the social sector development of Kerala sans economic progress (Franke and Chasin, 1991). Most important among them are:

(a) Politically motivated institutional intervention, *viz.*, the land reforms which gave entitlement to the tenants.

(b) The social reform movements which paved way for the lower castes attaining a social space like: entry into temples, access to education, healthcare.

(c) The influence of the Christian missionaries in spreading English education and literacy, etc.

However, evidence suggests that these three factors have not been imparted any influence on the tribal communities of the State. There is a long-standing view that the tribal population of the State has not at all been the beneficiaries of the programme of land reforms (Ravi Raman, 2005). Again their cry for land and the agitation resulted in *Muthanga* firing is an eye opener in this regard. Again, there is hardly any evidence to suggest that the social reform movements of the State spread over the tribal belts unlike among the other communities, especially the Ezhava and the Scheduled Castes.

The role of Christian missionaries in spreading education and literacy has been marginal among the tribal communities until recently. Thus, we may argue that the various factors that contribute to the sector development of the State rarely imparted any influence on the tribal folk and that the kind of social development enjoyed by an average Keralite during the initial phase was therefore not inclusive of the Tribal communities. Similarly, during the second phase, of the turnaround growth too, the tribal communities remained as unaffected by the very factors that led to the turnaround. Studies point out that factors such as economic reforms, remittances and human capital were the main source of the turnaround since the mid-1980s. In fact, these three factors are mutually reinforcing. To Chakravarthy (2005), the outstanding levels of basic education provided to the people of the State during earlier periods gave opportunities to them to find employment outside the country. The overseas migration resulted in large increase of private income (huge amounts of remittances). The outcome of economic reforms, according to Kannan (2005) was the discontinuation of the fixed-exchange rate system, in favour of a market-determined one, which contributed to the strengthening of the role of remittances. Here education has been highlighted to be a precursor of the remittances and the subsequent turnaround in economic growth of the state. Since the tribal population could not achieve a significant improvement in educational standards, one may argue that their human capital became of little competitiveness in coping up with the development process of the State. Notwithstanding the poor performance in education, the sheer chance of the Tribals to emigrate was also rare. Available data on emigration give a clear picture that the percentage of Tribals who migrated outside the country has been too small and that no comparison is possible of their performance in this respect with that of any other single community of the State. With a meager proportion of tribal NRKs, we cannot expect much by way of remittances, to become of influence for the development of the ST communities. Thus, we may argue that both in the lopsided and in the turnaround phases of Kerala's development experience, thanks to certain factors, the average population could perform well but the same reasons ironically kept the ST population depressed and forced to remain as outliers.

Conclusion

The Kerala model of development experience has been widely discussed all over the world. Its high social sector attainments attained with near stagnant economic growth rates were hotly debated topic in the 1980s and the 1990s. But after the later 1980s the economy showed 23 a turnaround in the growth performance of the state when it translated its human development into growth, basically in the service sector, thus making it a sound model of development. In the period of lopsided development itself, it was found that there were outliers to this central tendency. The foregoing analysis verifies this hypothesis, with reference to tribal communities of the state. It was found that deprivation was higher and the lack of educational attainment much greater for the tribal people in Kerala than general population in the State. The structural transformation of the State – increasing dependence on the tertiary sector and the decreasing dependence on the primary sector – has not been applicable to this outlier community. The whole development of the State happened in a context of its exclusion; could not accommodate tribal communities in the distribution of the fruits of development. Since the factors such as land reforms, educational attainments and foreign remittances have contributed to the particular development pattern of the State economy and since these factors impart little influence on the tribal population, the study raises a case for a second generation land reforms which should reach the really deprived – the outliers – of society. Active government intervention is also necessary to ensure quality education to the tribal and other marginalized communities of the state in order to empower them with high human capital.

REFERENCES

Atkinson Rob, Divoudi Simin 2000. The Concept of Social Exclusion in the European Union: Context, Development and Possibilities. *Journal of Common Market Studies*, 38(3): 427-448.

Chackraborhy, Achin (2005), "Kerala's Changing Development Narratives", *Economic and Political Weekly*, Feb, 5.

Franke, Richard and Chasin, Barbara (1991), 'Kerala: Development Through Radical Reform', *Monthly Review*, New York, January.

George KK (1993), Higher Education in Kerala: How inclusive is it to Scheduled Caste and Schedule Tribes, Education Exclusion and Economic Growth, Working paper series, Vol. 1 (1), CSSEIP, CUSAT, Cochin.

GoK (2005), "Kerala Human development Report 2005." Planning Board of Kerala, Thiruvananthapuram.

Kannan K. P. (2005), "Kerala's Turnaround in Growth: Role of Social Development, Remittance and Reform, *Economic and Political Weekly*, Feb, 5.

Kunhaman, M. (1989), Development of Tribal Economy, Classical Publishing Company, New Delhi.

Mathur P.R.G (1977), Tribal Situation in Kerala, Kerala Historical Society, Thiruvanthapuram.

Mohandas, M. (1992), Impact of New Settlers in the Western Ghat Region on the Socio-economic Conditions of the Tribal Population. The Case of Wayanad

District in Kerala. Research Report, Ministry of Environment and Forest Government of India.

Pushpangadan, K (2003), "Remittances, Consumption and Economic Growth in Kerala: 1980-2000", Working Paper No. 343, Centre for Development Studies, Thiruvananthapuram.

Ravi Raman (2005), "Belonging and Deprivation: The Political Economy of Adivasi Resource Conflict in Kerala", Paper prepared for the Planning Commission Unit of the CDS, Thiruvananthapuram.

Sonowel (2008), Indian Tribes and Issues of Social Inclusion and Exclusion, Stud. Tribes Tribals, Vol. 6 (1), pp 123-134.

Subramanian, KK and Azeez (2000), "Industrial Growth in Kerala: Trends and Explanations, Working Paper No. 310, Centre for Development Studies, Thiruvananthapuram.

9

Determinants of Marriage and Natal Care among Tribal Communities in India

*Dr. A. K. Ravishankar

ABSTRACT

Tribals are considered to be the autochthonous people of the land. About half of the world's autochthonous population *i.e.* 84,326,240 peoples (8.2% of total population) are living in India. Indian tribals are known for their unique ways of living, distinct culture, traditions, beliefs and practices which provide them a distinct identity on the national scene. High level of poverty, inadequate health resources, ignorance and high-risk beliefs and practices among the tribal communities has contributed to the vulnerability of this population. Under this backdrop an attempt was made to explore the marriage practices and incidence of early pregnancies in the tribal community; to understand their delivery management practices among the tribals and to study the influence of SED characteristics on early marriage and pregnancy among the tribal community in India.

The data were collected from National Family Health Survey-III, a large-scale sample survey conducted in India during 2005-06. Information collected from a nationally representative sample of 10,815 tribal women

* Assistant Professor, Department of Population Studies, Annamalai University, Annamalainagar Tamil Nadu.

aged 15-49, from various States and Union Territories of India. Relatively a significant proportion of tribal women in India are still likely to marry and begin childbearing in their middle teenage years. A significant association between age at marriage and attainment of education was observed that the mean age at marriage for illiterate tribal women was 16.78 years, whereas for the women who completed higher education was 23.44 years. The logistic regression analysis results indicate that the early marriage was much consistently improving with the improving socio-economic conditions of tribal women (except place of residence and WI). Seven out of 10 babies were born at home itself among the India tribal communities, it indicates that the tribal women perceive delivery as a natural phenomenon and no advance preparations are made. More than two-third of the tribal women who had deliver their latest birth at home believed that institutional care is not necessary (69.0%). In the light of the above discussion it can be inferred that female literacy should be enhanced so that it can act in a multidimensional way to boost the mean age at marriage and utilisation of natal care services.

Keywords: Tribals, Marriage, Natal Care, Child delivery practices.

Introduction

Tribals are considered to be the autochthonous people of the land. Article 366 (25) of the Constitution of India refers to Scheduled Tribes as those communities, who are scheduled in accordance with Article 342 of the Constitution. This Article further says that only those communities who have been declared as such by the President through an initial public notification or through a subsequent amending Act of Parliament will be considered to be Scheduled Tribes (Ravishankar, Ramachandran, and Subbiah, 2008). About half of the world's autochthonous population *i.e.* 84,326,240 peoples (8.2% of total population) are living in India. India has these tribal communities across its length and breadth. Nevertheless, more than half of the Indian tribal population is concentrated in the States of Madhya Pradesh, Chhatisgarh, Maharastra, Orissa, Jharkhand and Gujarat, whereas in Haryana, Punjab, Delhi, Pondicherry and Chandigrah no community has been notified as a specific tribal group (Nayak, and Babu, 2001). They form the lowest rung of the social and economic ladder and most of the Scheduled Tribes had been leading primitive lives, cut off from the mainstream for centuries *i.e.,* are living in isolation in natural and unpolluted surroundings far away from civilization with their traditional values, customs, beliefs and myth intact.

Indian tribals are known for their unique ways of living, distinct culture, traditions, beliefs and practices which provide them a distinct identity on the national scene. Most of the tribals are relative seclusion from the main stream of population, dwelling in remote inaccessible hilly terrains and unaffected by the developmental process undergoing in the country, in addition they are lacking in adequate access to basic amenities, education, employment opportunities and affordable health care services. There is a consensus that these scheduled tribes are the descendants of aboriginal population in India (Bhasin and Walter, 2001). High level of poverty, inadequate health resources, ignorance and high-risk beliefs and practices among the tribal communities has contributed to the vulnerability of this population. Under this backdrop an attempt was made to:

- Study the practice of early marriage and incidence of pregnancies among Indian tribals.
- Understand their delivery management practices among the tribals.
- Study the influence of SED characteristics on early marriage and pregnancy among the tribal community in India

Method and Materials

The data were drawn from NFHS-III (National Family Health Survey-III), a large-scale sample survey conducted in India during 2005-06. The NFHS-III sample covers 99 per cent of India's population living in all the States/ UTs. Information collected from a nationally representative sample of 109,041 households, 124,385 women age 15-49. Out of this, 10815 currently married tribal women aged 15-49, were selected from various States and Union Territories of India for this study to examine the practice of marriage, pregnancy, and its determinants.

Background Characteristic of Tribals in India

Percentage distribution of tribal women by background characteristics in India shows that about forty-four per cent of the currently married tribal women were adolescents (6.2% in 15-19) and young (37.9% in 20-29). About thirty per cent of the women fall in the 30-39 year age groups. The remaining one-fifth falls in the above 40 age group. It can be inferred that the age structure of the tribal women reflects the younger population.

Table 9.1 also reveals that majority of them were residing in rural areas (75.3%) and Hindus and Christians were the prominent religious groups among the tribal communities (48.4 and 39.9% respectively). Further, it is evident that tribals were having a preference to live in nuclear families (57.4%). As per 2001 Census, the overall literacy rate for Scheduled Tribes was 47.1 per cent, in particular 34.8 per cent of the ST female were literate. In their study Roy, Saha, and Abbad (2010) found only about 16 per cent of the tribes in Madhya Pradesh were literates. However, in this study it is found little above half of the respondents were literates (51.7%), although only 3.6 per cent had completed higher level of education. In this study, the gap between male and female literacy seems to be quite wide (68.4% for male and 51.7% for female) as seen by Manoj and Sameera (2005).

Table 9.1: Percentage Distribution of Tribal Women by Background Characteristics in India

Background Characteristics	Tribal Women	
	Number	Percentage
1	2	3
Age of the Women		
15-19	669	6.2
20-24	1858	17.2
25-29	2235	20.7
30-34	2045	18.9
35-39	1743	16.1
40-44	1320	12.2
45-49	945	8.7
Place of Residence		
Urban	2672	24.7
Rural	8143	75.3
Religion		
Hindu	5223	48.4
Muslim	193	1.8
Christian	4313	39.9
Other	1072	9.9
Respondent's Educational Level		
No education	5228	48.3
Primary	1723	15.9
Secondary	3478	32.2
Higher	386	3.6
Respondent's Occupation		
Not working	4224	39.1
Agricultural employee	4463	41.3
Non-Agricultural employee	2128	19.7
Household structure		
Nuclear	6033	57.4
Joint	4470	42.6

Contd...

1	2	3
Wealth Index		
Poorest	2969	27.5
Poorer	2225	20.6
Middle	2015	18.6
Richer	2001	18.5
Richest	1605	14.8
Total	**10815**	**100.0**

In the surveyed population about two-fifth of the respondents (41.3%) were agricultural employee and 39 per cent were fall in the not working category. Around one-fifth of them were employed in the non-agricultural sectors. As far as the wealth index was concerned the data reveals that little less than half of the women were both poorest and poorer categories (48.1%), and only one-third fall in the richest (14.8%) and richer group (18.5%). The present study result found similarities with the study on the demographic characteristics of Abujhmaria tribe in Madhya Pradesh by Pandey and Goel (1999) that majority of population were poor and illiterate. It can be concluded from the above discussion that the married tribal women were living in barbarous conditions.

Marriage and Pregnancy Practices

Age at first marriage remains an important variable in any comprehensive study of the demographic characteristics of population. In India, several national policies have advocated special programmatic attention to helping young women delay marriage/prevent early marriage and to enforcing existing laws against child marriage (Prohibition of Child Marriage Act, 2006). Despite these efforts, substantial proportions of young women continue to marry during adolescence (Santhya, Usha, Acharya, Shireen, Jejeebhoy, Ram, and Abhishek, 2010). The NFHS-III findings also finds that marriages occurs relatively early in India even today (IIPS and Macro International, 2007), despite legislation enforcing minimum ages of consent to 21 and 18 for males and females respectively.

In the tribal communities, ignorance and high-risk beliefs and practices, high level of poverty, inadequate and non-accessibility of health resources has contributed to the early marriage that nearly 61 per cent respondents were married below the age of 18 and 17.6 per cent of the pregnant mothers were 12 to 15 years old at the time of marriage (Gaur, 2008). A study conducted by Roy *et al.* (2010) found that the mean age of marriage for females was 14-23 years and a significant number of women became pregnant at younger ages (<20 years). Another study by Ravishankar *et al.* (2008) reveals that almost half of tribal women aged 20-24 were married by age 16 in India.

Table 9.2: Percentage Distributions of Tribal Women by Incidence of Early Marriages and Early Pregnancies

Incidence of Early Marriage and Pregnancy	Tribal Women	
	Number	Percentage
Age at First Marriage*		
Less than 15 years	1783	16.5
15-17 years	3746	34.6
Below legal age at marriage	5529	**51.1**
Above legal age at marriage	5286	48.9
Total	**10815**	**100.0**
Mean age at marriage (20-49)	**18.22 years**	
Age at First Birth	Number	Percentage
11-14	497	5.1
15-17	2580	26.3
Early Pregnancy	3077	31.4
18-19	2352	23.9
20-22	2423	24.7
23-24	872	8.9
Above 25	1099	11.1
Pregnancy after 18 years	6746	68.6
Total	**9823**	**100.0**
Mean age at marriage (20-49)	**19.79 years**	

*Marriage refers to cohabitation with a spouse.
It excludes women who are married but have not yet had *gauna* performed.

The present study result was also coexist with the above studies that 51 per cent of the tribal women were got married before they reached the legal age at marriage (18 years), particularly seventeen per cent of the tribes are get into the marital life before they reached the age of 15. The mean age at first marriage among tribal women age 20-49 was 18.22 years, over time there was a slight increase in the mean age at marriage among the tribal communities.

The age at which women starts childbearing is influences a variety of demographic and non-demographic phenomena. Age at marriage also has a profound impact on childbearing because women who marry early have on average a longer period of exposure to pregnancy and a greater number of lifetime births. The marriage of girls at young ages in India leads to teenage pregnancy and motherhood (IIPS and Macro International, 2007).

Of the 9823 total tribal women who reported their age at first birth, 497 women (5.1%) had given their first birth before they reach the age of 15 years and more than one-fourth (26.3%) had given their first child between age of 15-17 years. In total about thirty-one per cent of the tribal women had given their first birth under the age of 18. In other words, more than half of the tribes (55.3%) had given their first births when they were in teenagers. It is evident from the analysis that the incidence of early and teenage pregnancy was quite common in the tribal community. On contrary, Singh Uday Narayan (2001) observed that no girl could marry before she was 20 years of age and no boys before 25 years of age among the Santals of Bihar. Similar findings are reported by Raj, Praveen, and Pawan (2008) that majority of the Gaddis (95%), Kinnauras (79.23%) and Bhots (72.86%) tribals in Himachal Pradesh has been reported 19-21 years as girl's marriage age. However, few studies corroborated with the present findings. Further, data on childbearing by an adolescent's 18th birthday-before she is legally old enough even to marry-show that 22 per cent of all Indian young women have already given birth by that age (Ann, Susheela, Usha, Lisa and Suzette, 2009). This percentage for the young tribal women was 37.2 per cent that shows relatively a higher proportion of tribal women given birth before they reach the legal age at marriage. In India, the transition from wife to mother usually occurs about two years after marriage, as young couples are expected to have their first child soon after starting their life together (Ann *et al.* 2009). A similar result found among the tribal women that the mean age at first birth was 19.79 years. It can be inferred from the above analysis that relatively a significant proportion of tribal women in India are still likely to marry and begin childbearing in their middle teenage years.

Determinates of Age at Marriage

The mean age at marriage of currently married tribal women by background conditions have been presented in Table 9.3. The mean age at marriage was lowest among rural tribal mothers (17.6 years), young tribes (17.10 years), Hindus (16.66 years), poorest wealth index group (16.45 years), higher birth order mothers (16.75 years), mother who had longer marital duration (16.61 years) and women who not at all had exposure to TV (17.02 years) than their counterpart. Table 9.3 further reveals that the Christians had the highest mean age at marriage (19.65 years) than the rest of religious groups which is coincide with findings of Premi (2005). A significant association between age at marriage and attainment of education was observed from Table 9.3 that the mean age at marriage for illiterate tribal women was 16.78 years, whereas for the women who completed higher education was 23.44 years. A similar inverse relationship between education and early marriage was found by Ann *et al.* (2009). Further, the Table 9.3 discloses that the poorest tribal women had the lowest mean age at marriage

(16.45 years) when compare to the richest tribal women (20.40 years). The mean age at marriage was remained mostly unchanged between nuclear and joint family systems of tribal communities.

In India, the persistence of early marriage reinforces women's low status and social isolation, and such marriages almost always force girls to prematurely end their education to assume household responsibilities. Consequently, early marriage reduces women's employment prospects as well (Baru and Kurz, 2008). Under this backdrop the Table 9.3 explains the determinants of early marriage among the tribal community. Raj *et al.* (2008) found that nearly half of the Indian women aged 20-24 marry before their 18th birthday, in clear violation of the nation's official legal age at marriage for women of 18. The present study results also confirmed that a relatively a higher proportion of tribal women in all age groups break the official legal age of marriage. With data on marriages of tribal women below the legal age of marriage by residence shows that more than half of the rural tribal women (56.1%) performed marriages before reaching the legal age of 18 years, whereas this proportion for urban tribal women was 36.0 per cent. It is observed from Table 9.3 that there was a wide difference between religious groups in marriages performed before age of 18 years (66.9% of Hindus, 32.4% for Christians). This is corroborated by the findings of Premi (2005) among the general population.

Table 9.3: Percentage Distribution of Incidence of Early Marriage among Tribal Community by Background Characteristics

Background Characteristics	Age at First Marriage				Mean Age at Marriage
1	2				3
	Before 18 Years			After 18	
	< 15	15-17	under 18	> 18	
Age of Women 396.328**					
20-24	16.5	39.6	56.1	43.9	17.10
25-29	15.4	33.0	48.4	51.6	18.02
30-34	16.9	31.2	48.1	51.9	18.51
35-39	15.4	32.3	47.7	52.3	18.53
40-44	16.1	32.2	48.3	51.7	18.51
45-49	12.4	28.5	40.9	59.1	19.27
Place of Residence 328.410**					
Urban	10.3	25.7	36.0	64.0	19.40
Rural	18.5	37.6	56.1	43.9	17.61

Contd...

1	2				3
Religion 1164.69**					
Hindu	23.1	43.8	66.9	33.1	16.66
Muslim	18.1	34.7	52.8	47.2	17.88
Christian	8.7	23.7	32.4	67.6	19.65
Others	15.3	33.3	48.6	51.4	18.42
Household Structure NS					
Nuclear	16.7	34.0	50.7	49.3	18.08
Non-nuclear	16.3	35.5	51.8	48.2	18.00
Respondent's Educational Level 1423.66**					
No education	24.3	42.3	66.6	33.4	16.78
Primary	15.7	37.7	53.4	46.5	17.70
Secondary	6.8	24.8	31.6	68.4	19.54
Higher	1.6	4.9	6.5	93.5	23.44
Respondent's Occupation 261.232**					
Not working	13.0	31.0	44.0	56.0	18.51
Agric-employee	20.3	39.9	60.2	39.8	17.24
Non-Agric-employee	15.4	30.9	46.3	53.7	18.86
Wealth Index 1024.711**					
Poorest	24.3	46.2	70.5	29.5	16.45
Poorer	19.0	38.8	57.8	42.2	17.45
Middle	15.3	32.3	47.6	52.4	18.13
Richer	10.8	27.2	38.0	62.0	19.14
Richest	7.2	19.7	26.9	73.1	20.40
CEB 373.488**					
0	8.0	30.1	38.1	61.9	19.42
1	11.7	30.4	42.1	57.9	19.15
2	13.3	31.1	44.4	55.6	18.64
3	16.0	36.9	52.9	47.1	17.84
4	19.7	37.0	56.7	43.3	17.42
5	21.3	39.0	60.2	39.8	17.19
6+	25.5	38.5	63.9	36.1	16.75
Marital Duration 507.36**					
0-4 Years	5.9	29.1	35.0	65.1	19.74

Contd...

1	2				3
5-9	13.2	33.2	46.4	53.6	8.57
10-14	15.5	36.4	51.9	48.1	8.08
15-19	20.3	35.0	55.3	44.7	17.57
Above 20 years	25.7	38.6	64.3	35.7	16.61
Exposure to TV 544.2**					
Not at all	21.6	42.0	63.6	36.4	17.02
Less than once in a week	15.0	32.1	47.1	52.8	18.30
At least once in a week	13.1	30.6	43.7	56.3	18.69
Almost every day	11.3	26.9	38.2	61.8	19.15
Total	**1783**	**3746**	**5529**	**5286**	**18.22**

*** Refers to significant at 0.1 per cent level (chi-square results – Age at marriage and SED characteristics).

As expected, the proportion of women married below 18 years age was higher among illiterate tribals than the women who completed higher education. The table reveals that the proportion of women married below 18 years age was ten times higher for illiterate women than the higher educated women (66.6% and 6.5% respectively). The percentage of women married below legal age at marriage was quite higher among the agricultural labourers (60.2%) than the non-agricultural labourers (46.3%) and not working category tribal women (44.0%). About seventy per cent of the poorest tribal women performed marriages before attaining the legal age of marriage, whereas this number for richest wealth index women was only around 3. Mass media are effective in information dissemination which increases awareness and could facilitate behavioural changes allowing for the adoption of new behaviours. The proportion of tribals who married before 18 years was comparatively higher for the women who had expose TV than women who not at all exposed to TV (61.8% and 36.4% respectively).

The marital duration and mean age at marriage also show a strong negative association. The mean age at marriage for the women who had longer marital duration (above 20 years) was 16.61 years and for shorter marital duration women (0-4 years), was 18.57 years. It may be concluded from the above investigation that relatively a significant proportion of tribal women violating the nation's official legal age at marriage. Logistic regression technique has been employed to assess the effect of the each background variables on the probability of early marriage, controlling for other variables. For this analysis, the dependent variable was 'early marriage', which has been coded as 0 (marriage performed under the age of 18 years). The multivariate analysis indicated that most of the predicator variables selected was significantly related to the dependent variable – below legal age at marriage rate.

Table 9.4: Odds Ratios from Logistic Regression Examining the Effect of Selected Background Variables on the Age at Marriage

Background Variables	B	S.E.	Sig.	Exp. (B)	95.0 C.I. for Exp. (B)	
					Lower	Upper
Age of Mother**						
20-24 (ref)			.000	1.000		
25-29	.308	.070	.000	1.361	1.187	1.560
30-34	.295	.072	.000	1.343	1.165	1.547
35-39	.409	.076	.000	1.506	1.298	1.746
40-44	.425	.082	.000	1.530	1.304	1.796
45-49	.844	.091	.000	2.325	1.946	2.777
Place of Residence NS						
Urban				1.000		
Rural	.025	.064	.694	1.026	.904	1.163
Religion **						
Hindu			.000			
Muslim	.614	.159	.000	1.847	1.352	2.524
Christian	.933	.052	.000	2.542	2.295	2.815
Other	.609	.075	.000	1.838	1.587	2.129
Respondent's Educational Level**						
No education			.000	1.000		
Primary	.301	.065	.000	1.352	1.189	1.536
Secondary	1.113	.065	.000	3.043	2.682	3.454
Higher	2.921	.225	.000	18.556	11.948	28.820
Respondent's Occupation **						
Not working			.090	1.000		
Agri employee	-.203	.055	.000	.816	.733	.909
Non-Agri employee	-.252	.063	.000	.777	.687	.880
Wealth Index*						
Poorest			.064	1.000		
Poorer	.147	.065	.025	1.158	1.018	1.317
Middle	.179	.072	.012	1.197	1.040	1.377
Richer	.144	.082	.079	1.155	.983	1.358
Richest	.235	.101	.020	1.265	1.038	1.541
Constant	-1.230	.093	.000	.292		
-2 Log likelihood	12095.436 (a)					

***, ** and * denotes significant at .1 per cent, 1 per cent and 5 per cent probability level respectively. NS- Not Significant.

The old age group was more likely report above legal age at marriage than the young mothers, the odds ratio for 45-49 age group was 147349.6 ($p = 0.000$). The religion shows the well established link between the variables, Christians was 2.4 times more probability of got married after the legal age of 18 years than the Hindus. As expected, the literacy status of tribal women was found to be important predictors. As compared with illiterate women, the probability of getting marriage after the legal age of 18 years among higher educated women was 5.7 times higher. The marital duration shows a strong negative association between the variables. The women who had longer marital duration had a significantly higher probability of being early married. Birth order also again shows the negative association with early marriage. The higher birth order women (above 6: OR = 0.435) had significantly lower probability of being early marriage than the lower birth order women. The place of residence, wealth index and exposure to mass media (TV) was not significant as far as legal age at marriage was concerned. The logistic regression analysis results indicate that the early marriage was much consistently improving with the improving socio-economic conditions of tribal women (except place of residence and WI).

Child Delivery Practices among Tribal Communities

Women were asked whether their babies born during the last one year were born at home or at any health institution (public hospitals, private hospitals or other healthcare institutions). Seven out of 10 babies were born at home itself among the India tribal communities, it indicates that the tribal women perceive delivery as a natural phenomenon and no advance preparations are made. The results of place of delivery by background characteristics are presented in Table 9.5.

Among the tribal communities only about 28 per cent of the deliveries are managed at institute and the remaining 72 per cent of the deliveries are undertaken at the home. It again proved that the tribal women usually do not utilise the public health services. This finding is supported by Salil Basu (2000) that more than 90 per cent of deliveries are conducted at home attended by elderly ladies of the household and no specific precautions are observed at the time of conducting deliveries. A similar result was found by Padam and Yadav (2009) that the proportion of institutional deliveries managed by hospitals and health centres was 41 per cent and the remaining births was at respondents' home. Roumi (2008) findings also coexist with the above results that tribal women who gave birth to a child, 45 per cent delivered in their in-laws house more particularly the Mawkynrew block in East Khasi Hills (Meghalaya) had maximum deliveries in their in-laws home, followed by Pynursla, Mawsynram and Mawryngkneng blocks.

The study on Traditional and modern maternal child health services in tribal areas: a case study of Dhar district by Gaur (2008) validate the home delivery practice that most of the respondents believed in their traditional health culture because they neither felt any necessity of the modern facility, nor they had any awareness about it. The villagers have more faith in these medical measures than the modern medical care simply because they have been depending upon the local medicine, the man and his traditional system of treatment over the ages.

Table 9.5: Percentage Distributions of Tribal Women by Place of Delivery with their Background Characteristics

Background Characteristics	Place of Delivery		
1	2		
	Home	Institution	No. of Mothers
Age of the Women 23.371*			
15-19	70.9	29.1	330
20-24	70.9	29.1	1483
25-29	71.5	28.5	1627
30-34	70.3	29.7	1111
35-39	75.0	25.0	595
40-44	83.0	17.0	230
45-49	81.9	18.1	83
Place of Residence 848.24**			
Urban	39.2	60.8	1224
Rural	81.6	18.4	4235
Religion 59.527**			
Hindu	77.2	22.8	2382
Muslim	75.7	24.3	115
Christian	67.4	32.6	2404
Other	69.8	30.2	550
Respondent's Educational Level 922.91**			
No education	88.4	11.6	2515
Primary	75.7	24.3	885
Secondary	54.0	46.0	1861
Higher	18.7	81.3	198
Respondent's Occupation 454.124**			
Not working	61.9	38.1	2394
Agricultural employee	88.0	12.0	2174
Non Agricultural employee	60.7	39.3	891
Household structure 49.157**			

Contd...

1	2		
Nuclear	76.3	23.7	2934
Joint	67.6	32.4	2339
Wealth Index 1480.131**			
Poorest	93.2	6.8	1625
Poorer	85.5	14.5	1189
Middle	73.5	26.5	1078
Richer	50.5	49.5	958
Richest	21.0	79.0	609
Age at 1st Birth 212.184 **			
> 18 years	83.4	16.6	1551
18-20 years	73.9	26.1	1900
Above 21 years	61.6	38.4	2008
Birth Order 400.718**			
1	54.3	45.7	1220
2	66.2	33.8	1251
3	76.2	23.8	964
4	78.3	21.7	756
5	85.8	14.2	501
6+	89.7	10.3	767
Marital Duration 273.103**			
0-4 years	56.1	43.9	1323
5-9 years	72.5	27.5	1928
10-14 years	78.8	21.2	1154
15-19 years	83.0	17.0	658
Above 20 years	86.4	13.6	396
Exposure to Mass Media (TV) 958.700**			
Not at all	88.1	11.9	2457
Less than once a week	80.5	19.5	838
At least once a week	65.0	35.0	763
Almost every day	42.8	57.2	1399
Full ANC Coverage 120.844**			
No Full ANC coverage	65.2	34.8	2178
Full ANC coverage	36.7	63.3	425
Total	**72.1**	**27.9**	**5459**

*** and, * refers to significant at 0.1 per cent and 1 per cent level (chi-square results – Age at marriage and SED characteristics). NS- Not significant

Further, Saha, Singh, Chatterjee, and Roy (2007) found among tribes of central India that inaccessibility of health posts in remote areas, dissatisfaction with government health providers, availability of traditional medicine men and a shortage of trained medical practitioners all contribute the low utilisation of government health services. Significant difference was observed among the tribals who were young and old in case of institutional deliveries. The proportion of institutional deliveries was quite higher among young tribals (29.1%) than the old age tribal women (18.1%). Lowest level of institutional deliveries was observed among the rural (18.4%), while the urban had the highest (81.6%) level of institutional deliveries. Nearly one-third of the Christian tribal women preferred to deliver their baby at institution this proportion for the remaining religious groups was lesser.

There is a consistent increase in proportion of institutional deliveries from 11.6 per cent among illiterate women to 24.3 per cent among primary completed women then to 81.3 per cent among women who had completed their higher education. When compare to women who working in agricultural sector, the women engage in non-agricultural sector preferred the institutional delivery. It is also found that there is a steady increase in proportion of institutional deliveries from 6.8 per cent in poorest quintiles to 79 in richest quintile. The institutional deliveries are much higher among the women who given their first child at the age of above 20 years (38.4%) than the women who given their first child at the early age (16.6% at less than 18 years). The birth order of the child and the proportion of institutional delivery show a strong negative association. Among the higher birth order the institutional deliveries are quite low (10.3% in 6+order), while the percentage of institutional deliveries are significantly higher among the first birth order (45,7%).

Marital duration data also shows a similar association. A substantial difference was noticed between the institutional delivery and marital duration. It ranges from 13.6 per cent among shorter marital duration (0-4 years) to 43.9 per cent among the longer marital duration (above 20 years). As expected, the exposure to mass media (TV) influences the institutional deliveries. It reveals from the table that relatively a higher proportion of institutional deliveries are evidenced among the women who had almost watched the TV every day (57.2%) than the counterpart. Evidence suggests that delivering in a medical institution is influenced by use of antenatal care services in India (Sugathan, Mishra, and Retherford, 2001). It is corroborated with the present study results that the proportion of institutional deliveries was high among women who availed full ANC package than the counterpart.

Assistance During Delivery

Assistance during delivery is an important component in the reproductive healthcare services: it can reduce the risk of obstructed labour during delivery. Information was collected about who assisted during delivery: health personnel (doctor, Auxiliary Nurse Midwife (ANM), nurse or midwife, trained traditional birth attendant) or non-health personnel (untrained traditional birth attendant, friends or relatives).

Table 9.6: Percentage Distributions of Tribal Women by Delivery Assistance

Deliveries Assistance by	Home	Public	Private	Total No. of Deliveries
Doctor	9.9	61.2	28.8	1307
ANM/nurse/midwife/LHV	26.7	56.7	16.6	1131
Other health personnel	79.2	10.4	10.4	77
DAI/TBA	98.7	0.9	–	1975
Relative, friend	74.4	18.5	7.1	637
No one	100.0	–	–	89
Total	**72.1**	**20.1**	**7.8**	**5457**

Roumi (2008) was found that traditional delivery plays a substantial role in East Khasi Hills, 22.5 per cent went to the traditional birth attendants and trained birth attendants attended 19 per cent. The nurse assisted 15.3 per cent of the women in their last delivery whereas, 33.6 per cent women took assistance from doctor (MBBS and above). The reasons for more home deliveries were the absence of delivery facilities in the nearest CHCs and PHCs (FGD). Other tribal maternal care studies (Pandey and Lakra, 2000) found that the deliveries are usually assisted by elderly ladies (mother-in-law, sister-in-law and other neighboring ladies) and untrained traditional birth attendants, usually called 'DAI'. The present study results also coexists the above result that around half of home deliveries were attended by TBA/DAI in the tribal communities and quite significant proportion were attended by relative/friends.

Table 9.7: Percentage Distributions of Tribal Women by Reason did not Delivery at Health Facility

Reason didn't Deliver at Health Facility (Multiple Response)	Tribal Women	
	Number	Percentage
Not necessary	2713	69.0
Too far/no transport	798	20.3
Cost too much	746	19.0
Facility not open	197	5.0
Not customary	169	4.3
Husband/family members not allowed	127	3.2
Do not trust health facility	72	1.8
No female provider	40	1.0
Total	**3930**	**100.0**

Gaur (2008) in his study entitled, Traditional and modern maternal child health services in tribal areas: a case study of Dhar district found that villagers try to attend to child delivery cases themselves or call Traditional Birth Attendant (TBA) who is more trustworthy than Auxiliary Nurse Midwife (ANM) because TBA belongs to their own culture and lives amidst them. They believe that TBA or an experienced aged woman can easily perform the duty in case of delivery and she can take care at the time of any crisis.

Table 9.7 shows the responses regarding the reasons for not going to health facility. More than two-third of the tribal women who had deliver their latest birth at home believed that institutional care is not necessary (69.0%). Another one-fifth replied the care centre was too far away from their habitat or there was no transport facility to reach the care centre. A similar proportion of tribal women replied that too much of cost was the main reason for not deliver at health facility. Gaur (2008) found that normally the villagers are reluctant to use modern health service unless there is an emergency. They try to help themselves at the time of delivery or call TBA, who is more trustworthy than an ANM. They believe that TBA or an experienced aged woman can easily perform the duty in respect of delivery and she can also take care at the time of any crisis and they have to spend little money to access the local medicine and care provider.

Conclusion

Marriage, pregnancy and natal care practices and its determinants of tribals studied in this paper revealed that getting in to marital life and becoming pregnant are relatively better among tribal communities however, their delivery care seeking behaviour is wretched.

Not only the wide spread poverty, illiteracy, poor maternal and child health services, ineffective coverage of national health and nutritional services, etc., have been found, as possible contributing factors of dismal utilising natal care condition prevailing amongst the tribal communities of the country, but there is no motivating force to help them to use institution for delivery. In the light of the above discussion it can be inferred that female literacy should be enhanced so that it can act in a multidimensional way to boost the utilisation of health care services. In addition, government should implement specific tribal natal care programmes which should consider the cultural practices of the tribal communities. Further, the small and inaccessible tribal villages should be focused and targeted in the national RCH programme.

REFERENCES

Ann M. Moore., Susheela Singh., Usha Ram., Lisa Remez., and Suzette Audam. (2009). *Adolescent Marriage and Childbearing in India: Current Situation and Recent Trends*, New York: Guttmacher Institute.

Barua, A., and Kurz, K. (2008), Reproductive Health-seeking by Married Adolescent Girls in Maharashtra, in: Koenig MA *et al.*, eds., *Reproductive Health in India: New Evidence*, Jaipur, India: Rawat Publications, 32-46.

Bhasin, MK., and Walter, H. (2001), *Genetics of Castes and Tribes of India*. Delhi: Kamla-Raj Enterprises, 26-78.

Gaur, Paul. (2008), Traditional and Modern Maternal Child Health Services in Tribal Areas: A Case Study of Dhar District, Madhya Pradesh. *Journal of Social Sciences*, July.

International Institute for Population Sciences (IIPS) and Macro International. (2007), *National Family Health Survey* (NFHS-3), 2005-06: India: Volume I. Mumbai: IIPS.

Manoj, K.A., and Sameera, M. (2005), A Study of Demographic Structure and Fertility among the Bhotia Tribe of Uttaranchal. *Demography India*, Vol. 34 (1): 85-102.

Nayak, A.N., and Babu, B.V. (2001), Utilisation of Services Related to Safe Motherhood among the Schedule Caste and Schedule Tribe Population of Orrissa: An Overview. *South Asian Anthropologists*, 20 (2): 85-88.

Padam Singh., and Yadav, R.J. (2009), Antenatal Care of Pregnant Women in India. *Indian Journal of Community Medicine*, Vol. 25, No. 3.

Pandey, G. D., and Goel, A. K. (1999), Socio-Demographic Characteristics of Abujhmaria Madhaya Pradesh. *South Asian Anthropologists*, 20 (2):85-88.

Pandey, G. D., and Lakra, V. R. (2000), Maternal and Child Healthcare among Bihors of Madhya Pradesh. *Tribal Health Bulletin*, 8 (1): 21-23.

Premi, M. K. (2005), Marital Status and Religion in India, *Demography India*, Vol. 34 (2):197-215.

Raj Pathania. Praveen, Kaur. and Pawan Pathania. (2008), Marital and Family Practices among Tribals of Himachal Pradesh, *Stud Tribes Tribals*, 6(2): 73-78.

Ravishankar, A. K., Ramachandran, S., and Subbiah, A. (2008), Trends and Issues in Tribal Studies. In: Safe Motherhood Practices among Indian Tribal Communities: Facts from NFSH-II. Soubhagya Ranjan Padhi and Biswajita Padhy (Eds). Abhijeet Publications, New Delhi.

Roumi, Deb. (2008), Utilisation of Services Related to Safe Motherhood among the Tribal Population of East Khasi Hills (Meghalaya): An Overview. *Ethno-Med.*, 2(2): 137-141.

Roy, J., Saha, K. B., and Alpana Abbad. (2010), Some Aspects of Maternal and Child Healthcare among Khairwars of Madhya Pradesh. *Ethno Med*, 4(2): 107-109.

Saha, K.B., Singh, N., Chatterjee, U.S., and Roy, J. (2007), Male Involvement in Reproductive Health among Scheduled Tribe: Experience from Khairwars of Central India. Rural and Remote Health, 7, 605 (on line). Retrieved from http://www.rrh.org.au/publishedarticles/article-print-605.pdf.

Salil Basu. (2000), Dimensions of Tribal Health in India. *Health and Population - Perspectives and Issues* 23(2): 61-70.

Santhya, K. G., Usha Ram, Rajib Acharya, Shireen, J., Jejeebhoy, Faujdar Ram., and Abhishek Singh. (2010). Associations between Early Marriage and Young Women's Marital and Reproductive Health Outcomes: Evidence from India.

International Perspectives on Sexual and Reproductive Health, 36(3):132-139.

Singh Uday Narayan. (2001), Changing Profile of Santals in Bihar. *Man and Dev*, 23(1): 12-19.

Sugathan, K. S., Mishra, V., and Retherford, R. D. (2001), Promoting Institutional Deliveries in India: Role of Antenatal-Care services. National Family Health Survey Subject report No. 20. Mumbai: IIPS and East West Centre, Honolulu.

10

Right to Health and Tribal Communities in India

From a Social Exclusion Perspective

*Jobi Babu
**Dr. Hilaria M Soundari

"The swaraj I dreamt is a swaraj of poor people. Swaraj cannot be complete till the poorest have a guarantee of being provided with the basic necessities of life".

— **Mahatma Gandhi**

ABSTRACT

The 'tribal' or 'indigenous people' constitute around 8.2 per cent of the total Indian population (Census, 2011). Around 636 schedule tribe categories live in geographically scattered areas and in areas which are not easily accessible (Salil Basu, 2000). Even though they have a rich culture they are socio-economically disadvantaged and marginalized. They often suffer social-economic-health problems due to their disadvantages and marginalisation by the non tribal people. The development of a nation depends on the better health status of its citizen. Health is a basic necessity of life. WHO (1946), the apex organization in health programmes, define "health is a state of complete physical, social and mental well-being and not merely the absence of disease or infirmity". Good health confers on a

* Research Scholar, Department of Applied Research, GRI, Gandhigram.

** Assistant Prof. Department of Applied Research, GRI, Gandhigram.

person or groups' freedom from illness – and the ability to realise one's potential. Health is therefore best understood as the indispensable basis for defining a person's sense of well being. Health is a function, not only of medical care, but also of the overall integrated development of society – cultural, economic, educational, social and political. There are multi dimensional components associated with the health. The lack of any one component will adversely affect the total health condition of a person and thereby it will affect the socio-economic well-being and the quality of life of an individual. The government of India adopted several health policies and programmes in the health sector but the sad fact is that the indigenous people are marginalized.

The paper tries to throw light on the diverse health problems among the different target groups of tribal community in India and the exclusion of these underprivileged groups from the realm of better health facilities, their miseries due to the lack of accessibility, affordability and availability of health services etc., are emphasised. The paper also gives certain suggestions to improve the health conditions of the tribal people and there by improve the quality of life of the tribal populace in India.

> *"It is my aspiration that health will finally be seen not as a blessing to be wished for, but as a human right to be fought".*
>
> **— Kofi Annan, (Former UN Secretary General)**

Keywords: Health; Social Exclusion; Tribal; '4A' Concept.

Introduction

The development of a nation depends on the better health status of its citizen. Health is a basic necessity of human life. WHO (1946), the apex organization in health progammes, defined "health is a state of complete physical, social and mental well-being and not merely the absence of disease or infirmity". Within the context of health promotion, health has been considered less as an abstract state and more as a means to an end which can be expressed in functional terms as a resource which permits people to lead an individually, socially and economically productive life. Health is a resource for everyday life, not the object of living. It is a positive concept emphasising social and personal resources as well as physical capabilities. In keeping with the concept of health as a fundamental human right, the Ottawa Charter, (1986) emphasises certain pre-requisites for health which include peace, adequate economic resources, food and shelter, and a stable eco-system and sustainable resource use. Recognition of these pre-requisites highlights the inextricable links between social and economic conditions, the physical environment, individual lifestyles and health. Good health confers on a person's or groups' freedom from illness – and the ability to realise one's potential. Health is therefore best understood as the indispensable basis for defining a person's sense of well-being.

Tribal Communities in India

The 'tribal' or 'indigenous people' constitute around 8.2 per cent of the total Indian population, (Census, 2011) and of the total tribal population around 80 per cent is found in central India and a large part of the rest in the north-eastern states. Almost all tribal communities have their affinity and relationship with traditional ways of life and the forest. Around 636 schedule tribe categories live in geographically scattered areas and in areas which are not easily accessible (Salil Basu, 2000). Even though they have a rich culture they are socio-economically disadvantaged and marginalized. They often suffer social-economic-health problems due to their disadvantages and marginalisation by the non-tribal people.

Health and Tribal Communities

As we discussed earlier, health is a function, not only of medical care, but also of the overall integrated development of society – cultural, economic, educational, social and political. The health status of a society is intimately related to its value system, philosophical and cultural traditions, and social, economic and political organization. Each of these aspects has a deep influence on health, which in turn influences all these aspects. Hence, it is not possible to raise the health status and quality of life of people unless such efforts are integrated with the wider effort to bring about overall transformation of a society. The following Fig. 10.1 shows the dimensions to the concept of health.

Dimensions of Health

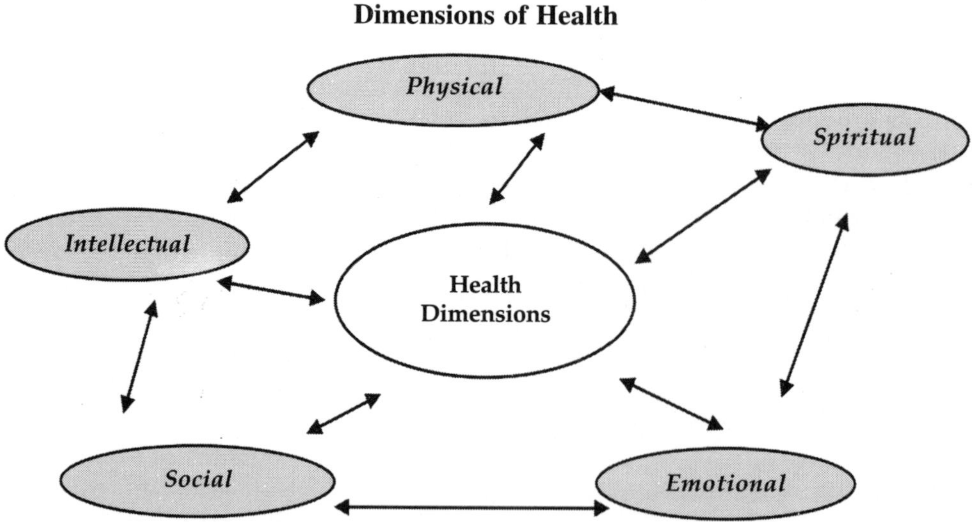

Fig. 10.1:

From the Fig. 10.1 it is clear that health has a multi dimensional face. This includes, physical, intellectual, social, emotional and spiritual. The lack of one aspect will adversely affect the total health condition of a person and thereby it will affect the socio-economic well-being and the quality of life of an individual.

According to World Health Organization (2000), India holds 112th ranks out of the 192 member countries in the arena of health. The difference between rural and urban indicators of health status and the wide interstate disparity in health status are well known. When it comes to the health status of the tribal community, the gap widens. In addition to widespread poverty, illiteracy, under nutrition, absence of safe drinking water and sanitary living conditions, poor maternal and child health services and ineffective coverage of national health and developmental services have been identified by several studies, are possible contributing factors to the dismal health conditions prevailing among the tribal population in India.

Health is associated with the social, economic development of the nation as well the tribal community. "A level of better health that will permit people to lead a socially and economically productive life" (Leo Pantitch, 2011). Lack of betterment in health will affect the social-economic-cultural life of any community. Tribal communities in general and primitive tribal groups in particular are highly disease prone. Also they do not have required access to basic health facilities. They are most exploited, neglected, and highly vulnerable to diseases with high degree of malnutrition, morbidity and mortality (Balgir, 2004). Their misery is compounded by poverty, illiteracy, ignorance of causes of diseases, hostile environment, poor sanitation, lack of safe drinking water and blind beliefs, etc.

Health Issues of the Tribal Community

According to Balgir (2001), "there is a heavy burden of communicable, non-communicable and silent killer genetic diseases prevalent in tribal communities. Many of the infectious and parasitic diseases can be prevented with timely intervention, health awareness, and information, education and communication skilled activities. In spite of the tremendous advancement in the field of preventive and curative medicine, the healthcare delivery services in tribal communities are still poor and need amelioration and strengthening with sustenance on the guidelines suggested to achieve the targeted goals of health for all in India". The Indigenous World 2006, International Working Group on Indigenous Affairs report says that, "Indigenous peoples remain on the margins of society: they are poorer, less educated, die at a younger age, are much more likely to commit suicide, and are generally in worse health than the rest of the population". (The Indigenous World 2006, International Working Group on Indigenous Affairs (IWGIA), ECOSOC

Consultative Status, p. 10). This shows that there are a number of health related issues are found among the indigenous people all over the world.

According to Buddhadeb Chaudhuri (1992), the various issues related to tribal health are:

1. Health and culture-including the traditional belief in the super nature.
2. Health, food habits and environment-covering the sanitation, water supply, settlement pattern, the total physical environment affecting health and food during socio-religious occasions.
3. Medicine, health and community – the traditional health practitioners, their position in the society, concept and treatment of diseases, nature and use of medicine-traditional and modern.
4. Fertility and mortality-variations and reasons, use of traditional and modern practices of birth control.
5. Interaction of traditional and modern systems of medicine at various levels, reasons for non-adoption of modern practices.
6. Traditional medicine – its use and application with certain modification and change, study of indigenous methods of treatment.

As a developing nation, India is also lacking behind the better health delivery to the tribal people. The women, children, elder population and the other groups of tribal population are equally vulnerable to the communicable as well as non-communicable diseases.

- ***Children***

Children are considered to be the assets of the nation. A country's future rests upon the upcoming generation. So the overall development of the children is an essential one. Because of this reason the notion of child health is given much importance in both the developed and developing countries of the world.

As we discussed earlier the health issues of tribal people affect their overall development. The child health is also deprived. The following graph shows the IMR (Infant Mortality Rate) among the tribal community in different nations. As a global phenomenon, the IMR rate is also very high in India.

As per the 2001 census, India's IMR is 47.57, but the IMR in tribal community is 50-55 per 1000 live birth. This gap shows the poor health status of the tribal children. Tribal children suffer from nutritional deficiency diseases like endemic Goitre, Anemia, Pellagra and Beriberi. Other manifestations are small body sizes, underweight adolescents and short life spans etc. Another set of nutritional problems develop from in-sanitary food supplies and water contamination, less calories of food intake, which have much reflection on the health status of tribal children.

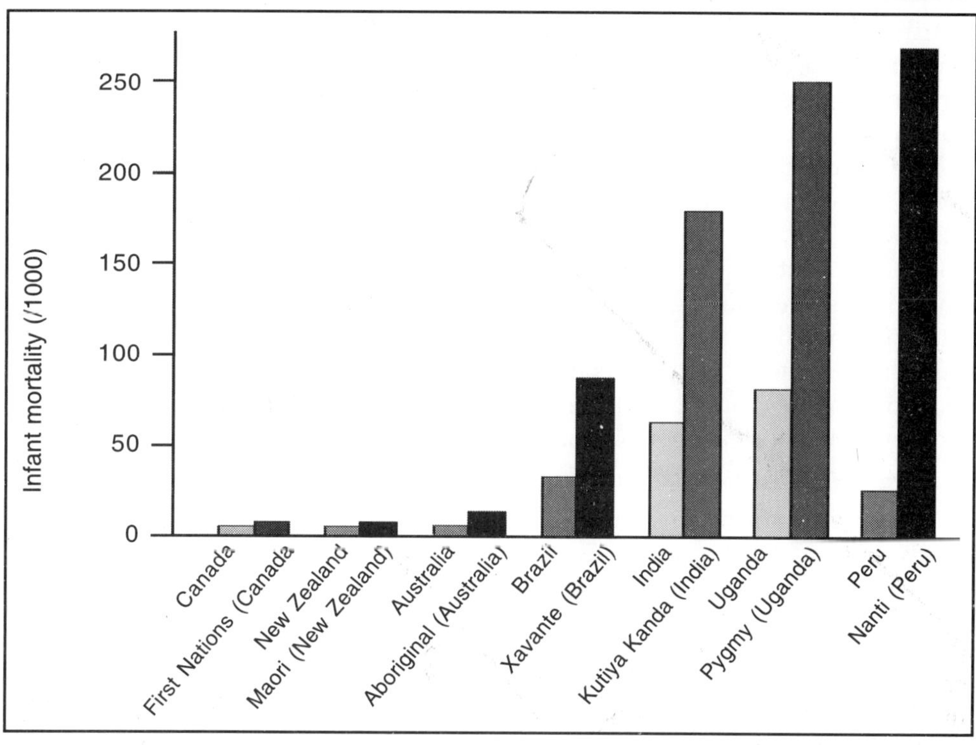

Source: Lancet Series on Indigenous Health, Vol. 367, June 2006, p. 2022.

The hereditary diseases like, Sickle cell Anemia is very high among the tribal communities which badly affect the health condition of the children. The poor health status of the children is a serious issue because it is the matter of the existence of the tribal community in the world. The unhealthy population cannot carry over the rich culture and traditions. So we can say that the children are more vulnerable in the health condition of the tribal community.

- ***Women***

The status of women in a society is a significant reflection of the level of social is a significant reflection of the level of social justice in that society. Women's status is often described in terms of their level of income, employment, education, health and fertility as well as the roles they play within the family, the community and society (Ghosh, 1987). In compare to other community, women occupy a dignitary place in tribal community. Women's health has an important role in determining the health of the family members, especially the health of the children. But due to the inequality, the women are also facing several health problems. Largely they are the victims of the poverty, so automatically they are having the problem of malnutrition. Basu (1993) says that, maternal malnutrition which was quite common among the tribal women was also a serious health problem; especially for those having many pregnancies too closely spaces, and reflected the complex socio-economic factors that affected their overall situation. The nutritional status of pregnant women directly influenced their reproductive performance and the birth is crucial to an infant's chances of survival and to its subsequent growth and development. Nutrition also affected location and breast feeding which were key elements in the health of infants and young children and a contributory factor in birth spacing. The major health problems of the tribal communities are the high incidence of maternal mortality and morbidity. Maternal mortality rate is as high as 619 in rural areas and stands at 358 per 1 lakh live births in Orissa (The Hindu, 2007). Because of the poor health condition of the women, it adversely affect the health of the children and there by the upcoming generation.

- ***General Tribal Population***

The health condition of the adult, male, elderly population of the tribal community is also having a number of health problems. The unhealthy practices such as drinking, chewing, smoking etc., are very prevalent among the tribal people. Suneel R. Qamra *et al* (2006) , says that, many of these practices are attached with their customs. For example, the entire festival, celebration, functions etc., of the Ho community (a tribal group largely found in Orissa) is very much associated with the use of alcohol. The occurrence of Liver cirrhosis due to excessive drinking of country made alcohol, chronic respiratory diseases due to excessive smoking, oral cancer (due to regular betel nut chewing), etc., is the aftereffect of the intake of substance abuse (Balgir 2005). However the tribal people are close to the environment, there are several other environmentally caused health hazards due to poor sanitation, poor disposable facilities for human excreta, animal waste, sewerage and sullage, etc., associated with illiteracy, extreme exploitation by the local elites, etc., are found among the tribal areas. Clean environment is also essential for the well-being of any society. It is noted that tribals do not possess any separate arrangements for waste disposal. Only a low percentage of the households have toilet facilities near their house. This kind of poor sanitation facility also affects the health condition of the tribal community. Colour blindness, cataract (Balgir, 1999a), etc., are encountered among the elder tribal populations. The elder population of tribal community is vulnerable to TB, Malaria, cancer etc. The changing of food habit also affects the health condition of the tribal communities. For instance, Paniya is a tribal group in Kerala. In earlier times their diet was rich enough with the roots, cereals, pulses and fruits; they used more leafy foods and vegetables but nowadays they are depending more on fast foods like *Porotta* maid with fine maida. The over use of these kind of food adversely affect the digestion of the people and also it won't supply any nutrition to the body.

'4A' Concept and Health of Tribal Communities

According to WHO (2011), the health should be available, accessible and affordable to the entire people in the world. When any intervention is initiated in the health sector these three 'As' should be taken into consideration. But when it comes to the tribal community, one more 'A' is added that is the 'acceptability'. Let us have a look on the concepts of availability, accessibility affordability and acceptability of health facilities and the tribal community.

1. Availability

When we speak about the health delivery, availability of health services is an important one. The health services need to be available to the entire population. It largely depends on the health infrastructure and its proper functioning. Infrastructure at sub-centres are lacking in the tribal areas. Medical officers and health officers posted in tribal areas are practically working in non-tribal areas due to lack of basic conveniences in the tribal areas for their stay. In the remote villages, the availability of hospital facility is very poor. The tribals have to walk more than five kilometers to visit a government hospital. A study done by *Samatha*, an organization which is working for the tribal community in Andhra Pradesh says that, the PHCs in scheduled areas are too distant, are inadequately staffed and have few medical supplies. They have very few tribal staff; most staffs are non-resident and are irregular in their work and are not sympathetic to tribal people. The availability of the health facility is lacking in the tribal areas. So it is important that the authorities should open Primary Health Centres (PHCs) or health sub-centres in these remote villages with full medical facilities; otherwise the health needs of the tribal community will remain as unmet.

2. Accessibility

As Gulliford M, (2002) says facilitating access is concerned with helping people to command appropriate health care resources in order to preserve or improve their health. Access is a complex concept and at least four aspects require evaluation. If services are available and there is an adequate supply of services, then the opportunity to obtain health care exists, and a population may 'have access' to services. The extent to which a population 'gains access' also depends on financial, organizational and social or cultural barriers that limit the utilisation of services. Thus access measured in terms of utilisation is dependent on the affordability, physical accessibility and acceptability of services and not merely adequacy of supply. Services available must be relevant and effective if the population is to 'gain access to satisfactory health outcomes'. As a developing country, vast majority of its population lives in the rural areas which are lacking better transportation system, and other facilities. When it comes to the life of the tribal people, as Balgir (2002) pointed

Table 10.1:

Inaccessibility: National Summary								
		Number of Facilities Identified by State			Number of Facilities Identified by NHSRC			
Sl. No.	States	Inaccessible	Most Difficult	Difficult	Inaccessible	Most Difficult	Difficult	Total (Source: Rural Health Statistics, 2009)
1	2	3	4	5	6	7	8	9
	EAG States							
1.	Bihar	1	11	33	44	39	128	1846
2.	Chattisgarh	0	543	35	33	131	215	859
3.	Jharkhand	1	3	5	0	24	64	515
4.	Madhya Pradesh	8	154	509	5	44	237	1488
5.	Orissa	0	227	209	2	60	166	1510
6.	Rajasthan	19	53	112	1	131	217	1870
7.	Uttar Pradesh	2	53	0	1	12	42	4205
8.	Uttarakhand	0	60	67	3	21	82	294
	NE States							
9.	Arunachal Pradesh	19	19	55	15	16	37	160
10	Assam	47	107	72	51	41	51	952
11.	Manipur	0	3	12	9	10	10	88
12.	Meghalaya	1	8	15	4	21	38	133
13.	Mizoram	0	34	25	0	34	17	66

Contd...

1	2	3	4	5	6	7	8	9
14.	Nagaland	0	4	38	3	11	15	144
15.	Sikkim	0	3	6	0	3	3	24
16.	Tripura	0	7	9	0	5	9	87
	Other States							
17.	Andhra Pradesh	55	6	226	5	43	54	1737
18.	Gujarat	0	34	81	0	3	43	1365
19.	Haryana (Mewat)	0	0	0	0	0	0	530
20.	Himachal Pradesh	0	10	29	18	56	124	522
21.	Jammu and Kashmir	0	25	27	27	27	35	460
22.	Karnataka	2	103	217	0	46	156	2517
23.	Maharashtra	0	0	66	3	21	88	2192
24.	Punjab (4 Distt.)	7	1	2	0	1	1	523
25.	Tamil Nadu	0	0	227	0	12	60	1533
26.	West Bengal	90	47	28	49	3	33	1256
	Total	**252**	**1515**	**2105**	**273**	**815**	**1925**	**26876**

Source: NHSRC Report 2009.

out that most of the trial people are lives in the hilly areas which are lacking travelling facilities like: roads, vehicles etc. Transportation is an important variable that determine the health status of the people. The following Table 10.1 given by the NHSRC (2010) which gives the state wise details about the inaccessibility to basic healthcare.

Table 10.1 clearly speaks about the gap between the data given by the state government and the information gained by the NHSRC. So the inaccessibility to the available healthcare facility is another problem which affects the health status of the people like tribals.

3. *Affordability*

The concept of affordability largely depends on the economic affairs of the people. The spending of people on health is another determining factor of their health status. Majority of the tribal people are largely depends on the agriculture related work or unskilled works. The poor earning of the tribal people is not adequate to meet the cost on health. The modern medicines are costlier which is not affordable to the tribal people because they fall in the category of low income group. So the affordability of the health cost is also affect the health status of the tribal community.

4. *Acceptability*

The tribal communities are generally following the traditional health related practices. As Balgir (2003) says they are rooted with several superstitious beliefs. They believe that the prayers and offerings can give relief to their health problems. This kind of beliefs separates them from use of modern treatment and medicine. The study conducted by Jagga Rajamma (1996) says that the lack of optimal utilisation of health services by tribals may be due to a variety of reasons. Some services are inappropriately used, whereas others, such as preventive health programmes, are under-utilised because of the unacceptability of the modern medicine. The study also identified that the change in the food pattern affected the healing power of the traditional medicine. So the tribal people are compelled to follow the modern medicine, however there are tribal groups which are still follows the traditional medicine only. Guite and Acharya (2006) have shown that the acceptance of a particular health care system among the tribal people mostly depends on its availability and accessibility. So the unacceptability of modern health care is due to the unavailability and the acceptability of the health care services.

Efforts for the Betterment of the Health Status of Tribal People

Constitution of India (1950) part IV, article 47, articulated that 'a duty of the State to raise the level of nutrition and the standard of living and to improve public health. The State shall regard the raising of the level of nutrition and the standard of living of its people and the improvement of public health as among its primary duties..." Global level, national level, and state level efforts are taken to address the diverse health problems of the people. United Nation Organization, in the Millennium Development Goals (MDGs) has highlighted the significance of providing better health by setting three out of eight goals of these MDGs, eight of the 16 targets and 18 of the 48 indicators relate directly to health. The fourth goal aims at the reduction of infant mortality and the fifth goal strives to improve the maternal health. The sixth goal moves forward in combating HIV/AIDS, malaria and other diseases. The government of India has implemented several health services and schemes in the realm of community health. For example, the implementation of National Rural Health Mission and its services. The major aim of these kinds of schemes and services is to reach the needy people or the marginalized session in our society. But many a time a large number of people are deprived from these kinds of services. There by the health problems are very prevalent in these kind of people; particularly the rural people. The major aim of these kinds of schemes and services is to reach the needy people or the marginalized session in our society. But many a time a large number of people, especially the so called marginalized community are deprived from these kinds of services. There by the health problems are very prevalent in these kind of people; particularly the tribal community. The National Health Policies dealt with primary healthcare consisting of nutrition for all, immunization, maternal and child healthcare, prevention of food adulteration, water supply and sanitation, environmental protection, school health programmes, occupational health services, prevention and control of epidemic diseases. The role of voluntary organizations and non government organizations (NGOs) are appreciated in the regard of tribal health. Community health is a major intervention area of the NGOs which are working in the tribal areas.

Right to Health and Tribal Communities: ways Ahead

Indian constitution in its A.21 says that every people have a right to live. The concept of right to health has a close association with the right to life. The efforts are on the way to make health as fundamental rights. But as we discussed earlier, the underprivileged section in the society are deprived to get better health. The groups such as tribal community are denied healthcare. So there is a huge gap between the implementation of right to health and the miserable life of the tribal community. Let us have a look on the issues to be addressed or take into consideration before going to implement right to health.

(a) As the Committee on Economic, Social and Cultural Rights (2000) states, the statistical data relate with the health status of the tribal communities are not much available. With improved information on indigenous peoples' health, action can be taken to ensure access to culturally

appropriate healthcare, as well as to safe and potable water, adequate housing and health-related education.

(b) Health is influenced by a number of factors such as adequate food, housing, sanitation, healthy lifestyles, protection against-environmental hazards and communicable diseases. So when we take the effort to improve the health status of the tribal people we need satisfy the factors influencing health; such as quality water supplies, sanitation facility etc.

(c) It is necessary to conduct frequent surveys on the food habits, nutrition, health practices of the tribals. It will help the authorities to take suitable measures to improve the health of the tribals.

(d) In the remote villages, the availability of hospital facility is very poor. The Tribals have to walk more than 5 km to visit a government hospital. Therefore, they make use of private clinic. It is important that the authorities should open Primary Health Centres (PHCs) or Health Sub-centres in these remote villages with full medical facilities. The frequency of free health camps, conducted by the Department of Health, can be increased. The frequency of the health personnel, visiting the villages, may also be increased.

(e) Education, especially the female education, is generally considered a key factor to development. Female education is believed to have a great influence on the maternal and child health as it enhances the knowledge and skills of the mother concerning age at marriage, contraception, nutrition, prevention and treatment of diseases. So by providing education, the health condition of the tribal people can be improved.

(f) The policy-makers should understand that, health and development are interlinked. The nation's development rest on the better health status of all the people as well as the development of the weaker sessions like tribal community.

(g) Instead of a piecemeal approach to the problems of tribal health, a holistic approach would integrate the efforts of the various departments of health. The government need to be considered the spending for the tribal community is for the development of human capital.

(h) Collaborative works of the health department and tribal welfare department is essential to address the health issues of the tribal communities.

(i) Management of health services is another thrust area in health delivery. Proper management in the overall health delivery function can also contribute much to the effective implementation of the health programmes in the rural areas, especially in the tribal areas.

(j) As a matter of the availability of healthcare, quality of health care and quantity of workforce is also essential. The healthcare services that we are provided to the tribal people need to be a quality one and for providing the quality services, the effective employment of the workforce is also essential.

Conclusion

Overt or implicit discrimination violates one of the fundamental principles of human rights and often lies at the root of poor health status. Discrimination against ethnic, religious and linguistic minorities, indigenous peoples and other marginalized groups in society both causes and magnifies poverty and ill-health. The UN World Conference against Racism, Racial Discrimination, Xenophobia and Related Intolerance encouraged States to adopt action-oriented policies and plans, including affirmative action, to ensure equality, particularly in relation to access to social services such as housing, primary education and healthcare.

Health is closely intertwined with economic growth and sustainable development. There is evidence that investing in health brings substantial benefits for the economy. According to the WHO, increasing life expectancy at birth by 10 per cent will increase the economic growth rate by 0.35 per cent a year. On the other hand, ill health is a heavy financial burden. Difference between rich and poor countries is due to ill-health and life expectancy. Health expenditure is, however, too often viewed as a short-term cost, not as a long-term. Investment, and is only now starting to gain recognition as a key driver of economic growth (Goel Rajneesh, 2002). So the policy-makers and its implementators need to give much emphasis to the health of the tribal community. By addressing the health issues we can lead the tribal people into their overall development. As a marginalized group of people we need to address their issue; that means grass root level initiative to be taken to address the health related problems of the nation then only we can achieve the status of a developed country.

"The swaraj I dreamt is a swaraj of poor people. Swaraj cannot be complete till the poorest have a guarantee of being provided with the basic necessities of life".

— **Mahatma Gandhi**

REFERENCES

Arya, S. (1998), *Tribal Activism, Voice of Protest.* Jaipur: Rawat Publication.

Balgir R. S. (2001), Human Genetics, Health and Tribal Development in Orissa. In: P Dash Sharma (Ed.). Environment, Health and Development: An Anthropological Perspective. Ranchi: S. C. Roy Institute of Anthropological Studies. pp. 87-104.

Basu, S. K. (1993), Tribal Health in India (edited). Manak Publishers, New Delhi (in press).

Buddhadeb Chaudhuri (1992), "Health, Religion and Culture: The Tribal Situation", Tribal Transformation in India, Inter-India Publications, New Delhi, pp. 211-215.

et.al., R. V. (Ed.). (2009), *Text Book of Public Health and Community Medicine*. New Delhi: Department of Community Medicine AFMC Pune in Collabration with WHO.

Ghosh, S. (1987), Women's Role in Health and Development. Health for the Millions. Vol. XIII No. 1 and 2 VHAI.

Goel Rajneesh (2002), Community Healthcare, Deep Publications Pvt. Ltd., New Delhi.

Guite and S. Acharya. 2006, "Indigenous Medicinal Substances and Health Care: A Study Among Paite Tribe of Manipur, India", Studies in Tribes and Tribals, 4(2): 99-104, Kamla Raj Enterprises, Delhi.

Gulliford M *et al* (2002), Journal of Health Service and Research Policy. 2002 Jul; 7(3): 186-8. The Royal Society of Medicine Press Ltd N.

Indian Institute of Education. (1981), *Health for All. An Alternative Strategy*. Pune: Indian Institute of Education.

Jagga Rajama, K., D. Vijaya and B. Raw, 1996 "Health Seeking Behaviour, Acceptability of Available Health Facilities and Knowledge about Tuberculosis in a Tribal Area" *Indian Journal of Tuberculosisi*, 43, 195-199, Tuberculosis Association of India, New Delhi.

Leo Pantitch, C. L. (2011), *Health under Capitalism*. New Delhi: Left Word Books.

Naik, J. P. (1977), *An Alternative System of Health Care Service in India*. New Delhi: Allied Publishers Pvt. Ltd.

Park, K. (2004), *Essentials of Community Nursing* (Fourth Edition ed.). Jabalpur: M/s Banarsidas Bhanot Publishers.

Raju, C. B. (2006), *Social Justice and the Constitution of India (With Reference to SC's/ ST's)*. New Delhi: Serials Publications.

Rao, C. N. (2005), *Priniples of Sociology with an introduction to Social Thought*. New Delhi: S Chand and Company Ltd.

http://www.businessdictionary.com/definition/lifestyle.html

http://www.rmrct.org/files_rmrc_web/centre's_publications/NSTH_06/NSTH 06_27.SR.Qamara.pdf

http://www.rmrct.org/files_rmrc_web/centre's_publications/NSTH_06/NSTH 06_27.SR.Qamara.pdf

http://assets.survivalinternational.org/static/files/news/PPM_informe _completo.pdf

http://www.who.int/about/brochure_en.pdf

www.who.int/hpr/NPH/docs/ottawa_charter_hp.pdf

http://www.photius.com/rankings/healthranks.html

http://nhsrcindia.org/hsd_accessibility_health_facilities_data.php

http://www.lrsitbrd.nic.in/IJTB/Year%201996/Oct%201996/OCT-1996%20F.pdf

http://www.samataindia.org/documents/triballandproblems.PDF

11

The Quest for Survival

Nebulous Future of Onge Tribe of Andaman Nicobar Island

*K. Veeramani

ABSTRACT

The dooms day debate may be happening with these Onges population also. They are numbered more than seven hundred during the dawn of the 20th century. But they are numbered now less than a hundred only. They were said to be one of the crudest ethnic stock and flesh of the flesh of this humanity. But they are gradually becoming extinct species threatened by all the maladies of current contexts of globalised world because they cannot be escaped to live in isolation out of this current globalised scenario. Whenever they exposed to the outside world their situation is in dilemma.

One of the oldest Negrito racial stock and hunter-gatherers lives on the southern most edges of Indian sub continent at Dugong Greek Island, a part of Little Andaman. I have done twenty day first hand ethnographic field work study among them along with late Prof. V. Sudersen and other students during 2001. It had given us deep insights into the lives of these kinds of hunter-gatherers. We have enumerated their population on 2001. The depopulation persuaded mainly by the reasons of Man-made activities

* · Guest Faculty, Department of Anthropology, Pondicherry University, Puducherry.

such as: land Alienation; depletion of natural resources (Poaching); cultural contacts; spread of diseases; unbalanced social structure and diminishing of their traditional knowledge systems. It is really of surprise to all of us about their existence even after all kinds of miseries. The administrative policies must be revamped according to the real needs of this egalitarian foraging community. Otherwise they will be fossilised. The inclusive growth can be attained only if the needs of all the communities living in Indian Society will be satisfied.

Keywords: Onge Tribe; Rehabilitation; Demography; Rituals.

Introduction

This study was first hand ethnographic Study among Onge of Little Andaman. This study is an outcome of Late Professor V. Sudarsen's (Department of Anthropology, University of Madras) two decades of association with the Onge, one of the Six Primitive Tribes of Andaman Archipelago. The field work was undertaken in the Dugong Creek settlement of the Onge in Little Andaman during January-February 2001. This was also a part of the Department of Anthropology's academic activity. We the Post-Graduate students (Anthropology) carried out our field work and, in addition, two doctoral students of the department accompanied with us.

Objectives

This paper intended to analyse important glimpses of an ethnographic account of Onge tribal group along with the following core objectives:

1. To identify the forces and agents of social exclusion of the Onges of Little Andaman.
2. To evaluate the changing patterns of land rights and ramifications of forest policies endangering the livelihood of them.
3. To critically assess the phenomenon of 'development deficit' causing social exclusion of this indigenous population.
4. To suggest inclusive measures and mechanism at policy level imperative for the Resilience and sustained livelihood to them.

The Little Andaman and Onge

The origin of the name Little Andaman is curious and obscure. In some maps the names Isle de Andaman and Isle de Maon appeared to indicate great Andaman and little Andaman respectively.

Flora and Fauna

The presence of coral reefs around the island of little Andaman provides evidence of its emergence of from sea bed. The island is almost flat, except at the extreme north where it rises in to a height of about 500 foot. There is no river in little Andaman but a number of perennial streams are located here and there in the forest. The vegetation of little Andaman is very similar to that of the other islands of the Andaman. The tropical Andaman forest distinctly Indo-chinese and Malaysian in character can be broadly divided into the littoral and non littoral types of forests. The littoral coastal forest is characterised by an extensive growth of mangroves, pandanus, nipapalm etc., which acts as shore protector and also have economic value as firewood. The coconut and causirina are the characteristic little flora of little Andaman. The whole coastal forests of the Andamans is very comprises of evergreen trees, climbers and patches of growth deciduous. The stock of timber has been the main source at revenue for these islands. There is no carnivorous animal in Little Andaman or for that matter in any of the islands of the Andaman, mention may be made of the wild pig (sus andamanesis) available in plenty , the wild cat (paradoxurus) and the iguana. Besides many varieties of fish, turtles, crocodiles and dugong (herbivorous sea mammals) constitute the important marine fauna of Little Andaman.

The climate, generally warm and tempered by pleasant sea breezes tends to become warmer with the movement of the sun towards the north. The island is exposed to both the northeast and southwest monsoons which bring comparatively dry and very wet weather respectively. Calm weather prevails from February to April and in October. The average annual rainfall is 127.35 inches for the whole of the Andaman Islands.

Little Andaman is one of the greatest repositories of the tropical rain forest. Little Andaman is an island with 721 sq Km of area; it is once the exclusive habitation of Onge. Onge are one of the four earliest inhabitants of Andaman Islands. Till 1922 Onge were the only inhabitants of Little Andaman, when the British entered the island. The population of the Onge in 1922 was estimated to be about 600, today they are 94 (Based on 2001 enumeration we have done during our field work). Today they are pushed to the northern corner of the island. They are resettled in Dugong Creek in 1976. Dugong Creek is the new settlement of Onge. Andaman administration has constructed house in 1976, when the Onge were first settled in this area.

Onge had three territorial units, two them were settled here and the third one in South Bay. There are several houses, which have been dismantled and reconstructed. The entire life is spent on the platform when they are at home. The thatched roof will be placed over the berai structure – a communal hut.

In addition to the changes in the Onge habitation, several new structures have come up in Dugong Creek. Some of them very gaudy and not in sink with local ecology. The temple to serve the needs of the administration staffs at settlement. There are school buildings and a community hall.

Rehabilitation and Settlement of Onges

Inspite of the resistance of the onge, they were killed during the course of reconciliation attempted by the British. They were left almost in a state of destitution to languish for a considerable time. Subsequent changes in the administrative control of the territory from the British to the Japanese and back again to the British further aggravated the situation. It was only after the formation of the Andaman Adim janjati vikas samiti, a tribal welfare agency, that cetrtian welfare measures taken up among the onge. The samithi was constituted under special assistance from the government of India, Ministry of Home affairs, in March 1976.

When the Andaman administration and samithi approached the onge, they were living in groups at Dugong creek, Jackson creek, and South Bay. As a first step towards the welfare the onge of Dugong creek and Jackson creek were rehabilitated at Dugong creek, and the South Bay group was settled where it was. The settlement of the rehabilitated onge is situated at the north eastwern corner at Dugong creek. One can also reach dugong creek from Hutbay in about two hours by motor boat. The boats of the settlers are frequently engaged by the samithi for the transport of essential goods to the settlement in time.

The onge settlement at Dugong creek stands only a few furlongs away from the seashore. This was set up during 1976-79. Twenty six wooden buildings with raised platforms have been distributed among the heads of the onge families. Apart from onge houses, there are good wooden buildings for the community hall, dispensary, power house, onge multipurpose cooperative society and for the residence of the staff of the samithi. The houses provided to the onge do not have any structural resemblance either with the indigenous temporary hut or the communal hut of the onge. Even when they are provided with houses, most of the onge do not stay in them and rather prefer their own korale built on adjacent land. The samithi provides some food and other essential articles, free of cost to the onge. Rice and wheat though never a part of their traditional diet, have now become their staple food.

Education

Balwadi-cum-adult education with 16 children and a few adults under the non-formal education programme was introduced among the Onge in 1978. The performance has been very poor due to the irregular service of the school. Besides schooling the onge are taught stitching, plastic basketing and other crafts.

Health Services

The permanent medical sub-centre at Dugong creek established in 1978 with a doctor, a nurse and a ward attendant to extend service as full-fledged centre. Prior to resettlement of onge, they were dependant on traditional medicines which are still used by the onge. The health workers were given the task of teaching and improving hygienic conditions of the onge.

Onge Multi-purpose Co-operative Society

The Onge Multipurpose co-operative society was started with the idea of collecting coconuts, honey, resin, cane from the onge to sell them in the market .the profit was kept for the welfare of the onge. But with irregular collection forest produce, except coconut, from the Onge and lack of supervision and management, the co-operative society is not functioning according to expectations. Its main function, at present is distribution of rations and other essential articles among the Onge. The free ration includes: rice, wheat, flour, sugar, milk powder, cooking oil, pulses, spices, onion, salt, tea-leaves, tobacco, matches, candles, washing and bathing soaps and kerosene.

Coconut Plantation

A Coconut plantation was stated by the Samiti has been in and around the settlement under the supervision of a plantation in-charge. The Coconut plantations are giving good yields.

Power House

An electric generator has been stationed at Dugong creek to provide electricity to the onge huts and to the government offices as well as staff quarters.

Population and Demography

In 1901, an attempt was for the first time made by the census department to estimate actual number of the Onge. This remains only an estimate because actual enumeration was not possible due to the hostality and nomadism of the Onge. In 1901, the estimated population of the Onge was 672. The Trend and pace of decadence of the Onge population in recent years is thus evidently not as alarming as it was till 1961. As far as the depopulation of the Onge is concerned, the studies suggest that both the inherent character at the population and the diseases prevalent are responsible.

Source	Population
Census 1901 (Estimated)	672
Census 1911 (Estimated)	631
Census 1921 (Estimated)	346
Census 1931 (Estimated)	250
Census 1951 (Estimated)	150
Census 1961 (Estimated)	129
Census 1971 (Estimated)	112
B. K. Basu 1984 (enumerated)	102
B. K. Basu 1987 (enumerated)	98
Xavier and Veeramani (2001 February 15th) (77+19)	96

Social Organization

The Onges have lived in three bands spread over the whole of the island of the Little Andaman till the early fifties, Members of each band, which comprised of a few *berai*, shared a beehive shaped communal hut. The sleeping places, the raised platforms of cane and wood, had social significance for the Onge because they were associated with all the important events in the life of its members. For example, the placenta was buried under the sleeping platform after a child was born. Initiation ceremonies (tanagiru) and marriages were performed there and the dead body of a member was buried under his or her sleeping platform in the communal hut.

Patrilineal Nature of Berai

Banda and patrilineal, *i.e.,* the members are descended through the male lines only, resulting in a group of agnates. Partilineally or the agnatic position of persons seems to be the recognised criterian of recruitment in to the onge bands.

Exogamous Nature of Berai

A study of all the married couples of Dugong creek shows that in each case husband and wife belongs to different bands. Even in case of remarriage, the exogamous character of the band is maintained. However now 10 *berai* only exist in Dugong creek settlement. These bands distributed over 25 families. The existing bands are: Tokabae; Entije; Chamalae; Toibabu; Titaje; Thangulumae; Beradalu; Konamae; Thorakandadu and Thongalang.

Korale

The *Korale* (family) is the constituent unit of the berai among the Onge. In earlier day, all the families of band lived in a common hut. Now the families stay in individual wooden huts or in *Korale.*

Though a clear division of labour is recognised at the family level, the economic burden of the family as a whole is not expected to be shouldered only by the husband or head of the family. Usually men only go for foraging and women go for collection tubers and roots. It is not expected that the wife alone should do all the household chores. Onges are always kind with their children and never harsh with them.

Neither the adults nor the children were ever found fighting, quarrelling or even exchanging hot words with one another. This does not mean, however, that conflict is completely unknown to them. If and when there is a dispute or conflict within them, the concerned individuals are kept apart until the feelings of anger subside.

Marriage

Monogamy is the only form of marriage among the Onge. Marriage within close relatives and within the same *berai* is strictly avoided, but cross cousin marriage is in vogue. Remarriage of widows and widowers is a common feature among the Onge.

The limited population of ones, the restriction on marrying within the prohibited degrees of relatives, and band exogamy led to scarcity of suitable mates for marriageable boys and girls. In compatible pairing leads to unproductive marriages and stabilise the population.

Kinship System

The Kinship structure appears a bit complex due to the presence of levirate and sororate marriages in addition to the practice of re-marriage. Band exogamy has resulted in a situation where all the members of the bands are found to be related one another directly or indirectly. This is evident from geneology. All the surviving onge are related to one another in varying degrees. It is evident from Genealogy diagram in page no.

The terms *Umari* and *Kairi* for father and mother respectively are normally not used for any other relative. The Kindship terms are as follows:

Kolodi	–	Father's elder brother
Kakodi	–	Father's elder brother's wife
Ecaikwe	–	Step father
Etukete	–	Step mother
Agichebe	–	Husband
Angechibe	–	Wife
Obeletene	–	Father-in-law
Uteesy	–	Mother-in-law
Agegi	–	Elder brother's wife
Agjentezi	–	Husband's elder brother
Ayentenegi	–	Husband's younger brother
Atilanka	–	Younger brother and younger sister
Elketa	–	Elder brother and elder sister
Mairi	–	Children
Dabaigi	–	Son
Debaigi	–	Daughter
Aye	–	Step children

There is no separate term of address for brother and sister as such. However a single term is used to refer to younger brother as well as sister and a separate term to refer to elder brother and sister.

Economy

Till the advent of administrators, onge economy revolved around the hunting, fishing and the collection of edible roots, fruits, and tubers. This is done for immediate consumption. The concept of property does not exist. The large resources provided by the forest and the sea have been the source of food for the subsistence of the Onge.

There is clear division of labour on the basis of sex, with activities like hunting, fishing, collection of honey, preparation of dug-out canoes, implements etc., which require skill and strength entrusted to the men and the women. On the other hand, for collecting edible roots, tubers, fruits and firewood from the forest and also to catch the smaller fish with nets in creeks curing low tide women always go out in group.

The economic activities of the Onge are to some extend followed by the climate conditions of the island. In the rainy season, *i.e.* April to September most of the Onge remain preoccupied with pig hunting and the collection of forest produce. During the south west monsoon the pigs become fat by gorging on the forest vegetation. The onge relish the meat most during rainy season. Turtle and dugong hunting are among the most adventurous and delightful economic pursuits of the Onge men. Dugong is a rare and precious sea mammal. Using dug-out canoes they catch dugong and turtle. Turtles' eggs are a delicacy for the Onge, who roam about on the seashore in search of turtle's eggs, with baskets and sticks in their hands. Besides hunting and fishing, the collection of honey also one of the main economic pursuits of the Onge men. Of late, the Onge were employed by the government as unskilled casual labour on daily wages (at the rate of Rs. 70 per day). They are employed mainly to clean the plantation area, collect and store the coconuts under the guidance of a worker of the plantation in charge.

Distribution

A hunter is relieved of his responsibilities once he brings the kill to the settlement. Immediately two or three men take charge of the game, quickly cut into pieces and put them in the boiling water.

Consumption

Cooking among the Onge is limited to simple roasting or boiling of the items without using spices and salt. The boiled pork, turtle's meat or fish which is left over after consumption is spread over the racks made for the purpose and take it for next couple of days.

Apart from the above activities the social worker maintaining the personnel account against each member. Their labour wages calculated and are added into their account and expenditures is subtracted from the savings.

Onges can also sell the honey to outsiders through plantation incharge and the amount is to be added in the account. Besides these things few of the m among the Onges has an amount of their savings in the state bank, co-operative bank and post office. Sometimes they get reward from the government such as during the birth of child the parents are given amount of Rs. 1000.

Political Organization

Among the onge people, there are no explicit judicial institutions or administrative leaders as chiefs or military machinery and very many and relationships. However the concept of Raja or King used to mark a leader, seems to be an alien induction, for there is no such word in the Onge terminology. It was introduced by the administrators to ensure better administrative control centre the onge through the raja from the continuous projection of the Raja system the onge have now causally started identifying or affiliating themselves with one leader or the other. The Pradesh Council of Andaman and Nicobar Territory appointed member represent in Pradesh council to attending the council meetings at Port Blair.

Rituals and Beliefs

The onge have a few rites and rituals associated with birth, adolescence, marriage and death.

Birth

The Onge believe that none of their women can conceive without the grace of 'Onkoboro', a spirit, which is in sky. The childless couples are considered to the victims of the anger of Onkoboro. During the pregnancy the mother is fed nicely with pork, crab, turtle and fish so that the child in the womb becomes healthy.

Childbirth takes place in one's own karale itself. Experienced elderly women come forward to assist the mother. When we were in the settlement, Babai, the wife of Baragegin gave birth to a male child which we witnessed.

Koye is a kind of leaf which was tied around the waist of the mother. The Koye was spread out on which the mother delivers the kid. Her busband was holding her. The whole body of the mother was applied with white clay to make the delivery easy.

After the child was born, he was decorated with the white clay. White clay was applied to make the baby clean. The placenta, along with the blood stained leaves is buried in the ground at the spot where the birth took place. The husband stays with wife for certain period of time at koraley to help her. As a post – natal restriction, the new mother is not offered pork, turtile's meat, dugong's meat, certain variety of fishes, prawn, crab, honey, certain fruits and tubers. Today the Onges go to hospital either in the settlemtn or at Hutbay in contrast to the traditional systems of childbirth. They think that there would be less risk of deaths in the deliveries.

Adolescence and Adulthood

The transition from adolescence to adulthood in the life of the onges is marked by ceremony called *tanagiru* for boy and for 4 the girl, it is known as *porangabe.*

Tanagiru (Male Initiation Ceremony)

Tanagiru is a ceremony where in the onge boy proves his efficiency as an onge hunter to earn his entry into the world of adults and acquire the status of good hunter. A hunting party is led by the boy to be initiated. If he succeeds in killing toothed male wild boar, he comes back to the settlement with the party. It is to show the boy is powerful and capable of hunting. If the Onges do not celebrate thanagiru function they feel guilty and something is lacking in their life. They strongly believe that they would not get wild boar when they go for hunting.

Porangabe (Puberty)

An Onge girl attains the most important phase of her life through the performance of the rituals of puberty. By doing this the onges believe that 'she attains the status of an adult and sub-sequently a prospective onge wife and the mother.

Marriage

Marriage among the onge is a simple ritual. Marriage partners are fixed when the child is born by both the parents. It is done to avoid conflicts in acquiring spouse later. The parents of the bride and bridegroom fix the date of the marriage. Two beds are prepared in korale .The parents, relatives and the friends of the bride stand on the one side of the bed and the bride is made to sit on the bed. The parents, relatives and the friends of the bridegroom will stand close to other bed. Both the bride and groom are well decorated with white clay to differentiate them from other. Then both are called together and asked to hold their hands. Then both of them go to bedrooms and sleep together.

Death

After the death, the deceased person is buried under his/her own bed, often in a koraley. The corpse is then bent in such a way that the knees touch out the chest, and the palms are made to cover the eyes. The elbows rest against the ribs of the corpse. The corpse is laid on its back in the grave, with the head facing the sea. They believe that if they bury the dead in some other place, some misfortunes will happen in the forest. The spirit of the dead will become evil spirit and get angry with those who are alive. So they bury the dead underneath the koroley or close to it. They are also of the opinion that the deceased is always with them and they are always on watch that the dogs never disturb burial ground.

Belief System Associated with Hunting and Gathering

When dugong is caught, the onge widows use to weep holding dugong thinking of their deceased husbands. They believe that if their husbands been alive they would have been happy to relish the meat of the Dugong. Whenever they go for hunting and gathering they think of the spirit and are convinced they would get wild boar, turtle etc. Dogs have been domesticated not only for hunting but also for watching the whole settlement.

The Andaman Adim Janjati Vikas Samithi

Various developmental activities were under taken by the different departments of the Andaman Nicobar administration. The Andaman Adim Janjati Vikas Samithi is the agency set up to carry out the welfare activities for the tribes. This agency is an autonomous organization fully financed by the Government of India. This organization is headed by Lt. Governor, with the Chief Secretary as Vice Chairman, the Assistant Commissioner of tribal welfare, as the member secreratary, the executive and all the heads of the government departments as executive members. The secretary and the tribal welfare department are also the members of the executive committee. They formulate the welfare schemes and communicate the field level workers living in the settlement for implementation.

Wild Boar Hunting and Poaching

The hunting of wild boar was the main stay of onges livelihood. They also lay the traps – and comeback the next day to see whether any animal has got trapped. But it is becoming difficult to continue their traditional subsistence activities. As there is poaching in both forest and sea. Both the local community and foreign fishing vessels come and poach. Often what happens is that by the time they return the next day the poachers from the other side of the forest come and theft the animal.

Out Trigger Canoe for Fishing

Dug out and out trigger canoes are good enough for Onge sea-going activities and the creeks. Canoe making starts with the identification of a trunk and felling it. Scooping out starts right in the forest, when a major part of scooping out is over it is moved to the habitation for finishing. The technique is very simple and the only instrument used to scoop out is chisel. Fishing in a creek is a major subsistence activity which contributes considerably to their subsistence pattern, they use the out rigger canoe to move in the creek. Today the use of hook and line for fishing is also becoming popular among youngsters. It is more a pastime rather than a major contribution for their subsistence. But real fishing is done in the creek and shallow waters.

Dugong Hunting

Dugong or the sea cow, a mammal once available abundantly in Dugong Creek, today is very scarce. Onge relish dugong meat very much. There is a ban on dugong hunting but Onge are sometime tempted to have dugong meet. There is a convention here that as soon as the hunted dugong is brought to the shore, the widows come to the shore and place their hands on it and weep, is supposed to be a remembrance of their passed husbands.

Onge relish the meat of wild boar, they also use its lard both for ritual purpose and also in their food system. Whatever is hunted and gathered is generally on hand to all the people as long as it lasts. The hunter or who gathered they have a right on certain parts, rest is open for consumption to everybody in the habitation, of course it is a reflection of their hunting and gathering past.

'Thanagiri' Ceremony of Onge and Scarcity Crisis

There are several problems both social and otherwise, which the Onge facing today, the social dilemmas whether they should continue with their original social system, rules and regulation, norms and values or they should deviate. These were some of the questions, which were discussed with this group. 'Thanagiri 'is a very important ceremony of Onge, it is the adulthood ceremony, a transitory ritual from adolescence to adulthood, wherein the boy prove his ability as a hunter by hunting a fixed number of wild boars. But today they are facing a great crisis. For more than 10 years they could not hold thanagiri as the number of wild boars is decreasing in numbers, as the poaching is increasing. It is a group activity. Many of the boys within the age of 12-16 years of age undergo the thanagiri ceremony at a time. But today whether such a ritual is possible or not is a dilemma. Whether the ambit of recent food security act has any scope for making inclusive to their folder also need to be known.

Child Delivery and Fading away of their Traditional Knowledge Systems

In this social crisis within the Onge society, there is the new birth of an Onge boy. All the people practically the entire settlement are around this hut where the delivery is taking place. The children bring lots of leaves. The woman sits in the husband's lap where the leaves are placed beneath. We observed they are in dilemma to go by their traditional medical practices or modern bio medicine of outsider or parallel to both of it.

It is true that mankind may have found a common future. But the Onge still have to find a path to their future. A path which looks to be very rough and path which looks to be very long one. Will these children find a future, as they are wishing to be?

Recommendations for the Inclusive Development

1. Safeguarding their rights over the lands, forests and also Sea limits through suitable protective policies (*e.g.*, through recent forest dwellers act of 2006).
2. Augmentation of their Indigenous knowledge Systems through Community Participation. The National knowledge Commission can be involved.
3. The Stringent restrictions on intrusion of outside element into their world of culture.

4. Intervention of team of experts (especially anthropologists) to identify their unmet needs of livelihood.
5. Educational policy suitable to their livelihood.

Conclusion

The inclusive growth attained only if all the minorities living in Indian society being inclusive to all of the developmental activities. The policies should be revamped according to the real met needs of all those Primitive Tribal Groups. The fate of their livelihood and destiny of forthcoming generations of these indigenous groups altered only by the collective efforts of all of the actors involved in it.

12

Social Exclusion of Populations with Indigenous Knowledge is Crisis to the Nation

*Ashok Das Gupta

ABSTRACT

Community autochthonous to a given territory or living in there from time immemorial is indigenous and also regarded as being traditional. They might be pre-agricultural, agricultural, and post-agricultural affecting their production-trade relationship and property concept. In their long-run; these people too close to nature have innovated so many things intentionally or unintentionally, recorded these knowledge traits in their documents and literature, and while being scriptless just used culture as a text. For systematic application of knowledge traits in order to get so many public services, people in an ecosystem develop social structure, Indigenous Knowledge System and Indigenous World View.

Knowledge in advanced, scripted, civilized, modern, urban-industrial, rational, secular, widely-impacted, fragile, post-structural and individualistic societies are more scientific and proved; whereas in indigenous communities more ethno-scientific, magic-oriented, gender-related, trial and error based, philosophical, religious, believed, more

* Department of Anthropology, University of North Bengal, Darjeeling District, West Bengal, India, 734013, nbu_ashokanthro@rediffmail.com.

conceptualized and less proved. So, there is always a tendency to underestimate the later by the former. But it is also a fact that when the first system fails, the second fills the gap. The advanced section could treat them in an inclusive way, and in turn get so many good services from them making the nation more educated and wiser in this era of globalisation. There is always a confrontation between the two. And the highest oppression has been targeted to the indigenous communities still living with folk lives. The suppressed groups could struggle for their resources, right and justice in local, national and international grounds. The suppressed many know such things that are impossible for the so called advanced.

In this paper, social exclusion of indigenous communities is considered as a crisis to the Indian Nation with support from historical evidences and with three suitable examples, implications of Indigenous Knowledge Systems/Indigenous World View for all the time and all the humanity.

Keywords: Social Exclusion, Indigenous Knowledge, Folk Life, River System.

Introduction

Knowledge, an eminent part of human culture and set of facts and experiences, is of two types: *(i)* Traditional and *(ii)* Modern. Former is still nourished by the autochthons or people still living very close to the soil. These peoples are basically treated as Natives during colonial periods also known as Indigenous.

Traditional knowledge of these peoples is treated as Indigenous Knowledge System. This Indigenous knowledge which is empirical, local and basically oral is scattered unevenly. These people use their traditions or cultures as their holy books with chapters regarding substructure, structure, super-structure; artifacts, mentifacts, psychofacts; nature, human and supernature – in a single word: the folk life.

Intellectual reasoning of common people, intimate understanding, informal experimentations on trial and error are the main attributes of indigenous knowledge and its cognate indigenous knowledge system where the technical and non-rational symbols are quite inseparable. Many of these indigenous knowledge traits are useful in mitigating various challenges caused due to negative side effects of modernity that could not be solved by the latter. Alternative public services are treated as Ethno-Sciences or Peoples' Science – a set of unqualified but quire effective facts very much used in day to day lives and still to be tested in scientific laboratory.

Indigenous Knowledge is also related with social, economic, political and religious systems. Holders of this knowledge should not be excluded rather included. Otherwise, that would produce crises in front of humanity.

In this global era with subsequent booms and recessions, we can learn a lot from these people. Issues like Global Village, Indigenous Peoples and Indigenous Rights are already there. With suitable examples, author is going to prove that the indigenous knowledge holders should be included for benefit of the Nation.

Indigenous Knowledge (IK)

Indigenous knowledge may not be as abstract as scientific knowledge. It is often concrete and always dynamic. It relies strongly on intuition, directly perceivable evidence, and an accumulation of historical experiences. IK encompasses the following issues of factual data, theory, interrelations, concepts, and attributive information of a high degree of accuracy. It is a multidisciplinary subject and incorporates the following dimensions: physical sciences and related technologies, social sciences and humanities (Atte in Agarwal, 1989). Indigenous knowledge (IK) is the local knowledge – knowledge that is unique to a given culture or society. IK contrasts with the international knowledge system generated by universities, research institutions and private farms. It is the basis for local level decision-making in agriculture, healthcare, food preparation, education, natural-resource management and a host of other activities in rural communities (Warren, 1991). Indigenous knowledge systems are tuned to the needs of local people and the quality and quantity of available resources. They pertain to various cultural norms, social roles, or physical conditions. Their efficiency lies in the capacity to adapt to changing circumstances.

According to Haverkort (1991), indigenous knowledge is the actual knowledge of a given population that reflects the experiences based on traditions and includes more recent experiences with modern technologies. IK is quite fragmentarily distributed throughout the globe that is, socially clustered. Indigenous knowledge is the systematic body of knowledge acquired by local people through the accumulation of experiences, informal experiments, and intimate understanding of the environment in a given culture (Rajasekaran, 1993).

Indigenous knowledge is the information base for a society, which facilitates communication and decision making. Indigenous information systems are dynamic and are continually influenced by internal activity and experimentation as well as contact with external systems (Flavier *et al.*, 1995). IK refers to the unique, traditional, local knowledge existing within and developed around the specific conditions of women and men indigenous to a particular geographic area (Grenier, 1998). IK is the set of adaptive skills of local people usually derived from many years of experience, which have often been communicated through 'oral traditions' and learned through family members over generations. IK includes trial-and-error problem-solving approaches by groups of people with an objective to meet the challenges they face in their local environments. IK indicates to time-tested agricultural and natural resource management practices, which pave the way for sustainable agriculture. IK is the compilation of strategies and techniques developed by local people to cope with the changes in the socio-cultural and environmental conditions.

Classification of IK

Holistically, IKS could be classified into several sectors (Mondal, 2009). These are like:

- Agriculture.
- Animal husbandry, (+ethno-fishery and poultry).
- Handicrafts, tools and techniques.
- Nutrition, healthcare practices and bio-medicines, psycho-social care.
- Natural and biological resource, management of environmental and bio-diversity resources, disaster mitigation.
- Human resource management, saving and lending, poverty alleviation.
- Community development as well as education and communication each with its respective area and manifestation maintained by folk people within a community that is again stratified on the basis of gender, age group, occupational groups and various personalities like local leaders, shamans, healers, medicine man, Wiseman, chiefdom, priest, magico-religious practitioners, craftsmen, art performers and so on.

Indigenous Knowledge Holders

Local people, including farmers, landless labourers, women, rural artisans, and cattle rarer, are the custodians of indigenous knowledge systems. Moreover, these people are well informed about their own situations, their resources; what works and doesn't work; and how one change impacts other parts of their system. Farmers are not passive consumers, but active problem solvers who develop for themselves most of the technology they use. For many hundreds of years before today's national agricultural research systems were set up, farmers did their own research. And, by integrating technology from different sources and continuing to adapt it on their farms, they still do so today.

Criticism of IK/IKS

Norgaard (1984) mentioned that the traditional knowledge has been viewed as part of a romantic past, as the major obstacle to development, as a necessary starting point, and as a critical component of a cultural alternative to modernisation. Only very rarely, however, is traditional knowledge treated as knowledge *per se* in the mainstream of the agricultural and development and environmental management literature, as knowledge that contributes to our understanding of agricultural production and the maintenance and use of environmental systems.

Indigenous knowledge is chiefly local, oral, set of generation wise intellectual reasoning, result out of informal experimentation by virtue of trial and error, empirical, asymmetrically distributed, spread through informal folk communication, functional, adjusted with repeating tradition, part of unreflective many, shared by many, justified unqualified facts that are not scientifically proved truth or theory but extra-scientific hypothesis, culture-oriented, humanitarian, value-loaded, subjective, static due to dependence on religious laboratory of survival, information base of a given society close to nature, non-separable into rational and non-rational or between technical and non-technical, open-type and hidden both, associated with semantic cognates, capable of providing various public services (pro-people, nature-friendly, sustainable, and low-cost) and prone to be tested in various fields of global science in order to become qualified proved facts, universal truth, theoretical, holistic or situated knowledge and wisdom.

Indigenous Culture (IC)

Culture possessed by indigenous peoples of an indigenous community could be regarded as indigenous culture, whereas indigenous knowledge is an important part of it. The future of our planet depends on saving both the remaining biologically diverse ecosystem and the culturally credible diversity of the tribal peoples of the world. The ancient cultures of native peoples, threatened by modern assimilation are the only known, proven time tested models of the sustainable consumption of the Earth's threatened natural resources. (Ref: http//: www.nativeplanet.org/indigenous/indigenous.shtml)

Challenges in Front of Indigenous Culture

This kind of culture is often suffered by thriving modernity that so far neglect the subordinated indigenous communities, but sustenance of these communities, their indigenous cultures and indigenous knowledge banks are now highly needed and thus to be protected for the proper management of our environment, flora and fauna, eco-systems, bio-diversity, traditional modes of production with feedback as well as sustainable development.

IK and Folk Life

Here, IK targets into the Folk Life maintained by a tribal/aboriginal/indigenous/folk community: folk etymology and chants, folk proverb, folk riddle, folk rime, folk poem, folk song, folk music, folk dance, folk play, folk lore, folk tales or fairy tail, myths and legends, folk literature, folk recreation, folk painting, folk sculpture, folk art and craft, dialectology of folk speech, folk dialect to folk technology, folk customs regarding household affairs and production systems, the notion of time in folk society, weather forecasting, folk cookery, folk settlement and patterns, folk architecture, sense of right and wrong (folk ways), folk norms and values regarding kinship relations and rites-de-passage, superstitions, folk magic, folk religion, ethno-medicinal practices as well as various institutions and organizations (*viz.*, political, economic, religious, and social) that is all the material and the non-material, tangible and intangible, verbal and non-verbal aspects of life of a traditional or better to say, an indigenous community.

The Term Indigenous

'Indigenous' as a term is much conflicting, ambiguous and with strong moral load. It might have similar connotations with 'native' and 'aboriginal' from the view of western society to indicate the folk or tribal. The term indigenous is more acceptable than the other two too much restrictive and confusing with a political condition.

Indigenous and Colonialism

Indigenous though political term is associated with the essence of colonialism by the Westernized. Indigenousness has no universal measuring scale. Indigenous is applied to indigenous knowledge, indigenous knowledge system, indigenous culture, indigenous community, indigenous peoples, indigenous rights and intellectual property rights. Thinking apolitically, indigenous is a term that indicates components close association and prolonged inhabitation with nature.

Indigenousness: 3 Level Approach

The distinction between 'indigenous' and 'non-indigenous' is specific to a regional and again to historical connotations. Treating a community indigenous needs much more ethnographic works. We can go through a three level approach: attachment of the community to nature, quality of its knowledge system, and response to globalisation (or various other international, national, regional issues). There is no universal scale to measure indigenousness, while indigenous being truly political.

Indigenous Rights and Peoples (IR and IP)

ILO has postulated some indigenous rights (IR) on the global basis and not specifically concentrating on a single indigenous community, included all of them under the category of Indigenous Peoples (IP). IR is applicable to all the indigenous communities which are brought under the common umbrella of Indigenous Peoples. The peoples affiliated to Indigenous Rights are known as Indigenous Peoples (IP). IR holders or IP fragmentarily spread all over the world as indigenous communities associated with respective indigenous cultures. They are the inventors of IK/IKS as practical/empirical/functional and again concrete/partial/justified but not qualified/traditional/folk/ traditional ecological and environmental/indigenous technological/culturally embedded/ hypothetical/ethno-scientific knowledge. The Public Services from such IKS can fill in various defaults in Western Knowledge System; make harsh way of unilinear development a pro-people and nature friendly shape, make people aware about nature and natural resources. But still then they are in hypothetical stage, believed after tested in religious laboratory of survival, faith and fear; but not scientifically tested to be qualified as situated universal truth or theory. If one research foundation can separate its technical part from the non-technical one, properly document it and prove its qualification in research lab of pure or bio-sciences; who would be the actual owner of that intellectual property? The community or the foundation!

Practical Problems

Kelkar (2004) has mentioned Inge Kaul, Isabelle Grunberg and Marc Stern (1999) who viewed the rapid developmental activities of the Western-Modern Society in search of a wider global market economy as the root cause of six major problems as pointed out in UNDP report: *(i)* Challenges of global warming, *(ii)* Rapid loss of bio-diversity, *(iii)* Crisis-prone financial market, *(iv)* Growing international inequality, *(v)* Emergence of new-drug resistant disease strains and *(vi)* Genetic engineering. Solution of these problems lies within the IKS which is the summation of all the TKS and not a single TKS of certain locality. Therefore, there is a need for IKS rather than community-specific TKS. Truly, the Article 8(j) of the Convention of Biological Diversity (Rio, 1992) has indicated the importance the noble deed of: "respect, preserve and maintain knowledge, innovations and practices of indigenous and local communities embodying traditional life-styles relevant for the conservation and sustainable use of biological diversity".

Das Gupta and Saha (2009) have discussed the connection between Indigenous Knowledge and Biodiversity. They have tried to characterise Traditional Ecological Knowledge (TEK) as a part of IKS and clarify how this TEK could help in providing global public service in favor of nature and bio-diversity in one hand and on the other, in service of human systems from rural to urban and *vice versa*. Managements of agriculture, animal husbandry and poultry, fishery, folk cookery, handicraft, hunting and gathering, forest resources, soil and water, irrigation, pest control and fertilization, post harvesting practices and disasters are all ensured in a rural life by TEK traits interlinked by well established network. So, proper systematization of TEK would develop themselves into IKS with particular global public service in form of Natural Recourse Management (NRM). Ultimately, the resultant outcome from NRM would facilitate Sustainable Livelihood Development (SLD) in favor of both nature and world humanity.

Co-operatives can play a good role if they are provided with bank and government assistance. That would be helpful for both Micro-Economies as well as traditional economy of rural society – the precious source of IKS. This is actually telling the scope for saving the current globalisation by the virtue of a new one with IKS (Dasgupta, 2010). By capitalizing the collective wisdom of formal and traditional sciences, we shall be able to help people address the problem of declining common property and to manage the risk they face because of the destruction of the resource base and ecological. Not only regarding management of natural resources by regulating modes of exploitation, division of labour, and supernatural faith-fear-belief system in culture/superstructure/cognition; we can get also crucial contributions of the indigenous knowledge holders even in maintaining social, economic, political and religious systems. But so far we exclude this folk people and treated them as being native or excluded.

Study Area

West Bengal state of India comprises of 19 districts of which 6 northern forms North Bengal and 13 southern forms South Bengal. The 6 north are Uttar Dinajpur, Dakshin Dinajpur, Malda, Cooch Behar, Jalpaiguri and Darjeeling. Included from two Himalayan states Bhutan and Sikkim, there are Kalimpong and Darjeeling-Kurseong regions in Darjeeling Himalayas respectively. These along with Siliguri Terai postulate Darjeeling district. Darjeeling district was the first pedestal for inclusion of Sikkim within Federal Structure of India. Sikkim is a state now in India that shares international border with Chumbi Valley of Tibet (China) along with Royal Kingdom of Bhutan.

River Systems

- *Mahananda river system:* Indo-Nepal Himalayas including Darjeeling-Kurseong region of North Bengal→ Siliguri foothill region (Siliguri Terai) of North Bengal and Morang foothill region (Nepal Terai) of Nepal → Thakurganj-Kishanganj-Purnia plains of Bihar state of India → Mahananda-Ganges flood-land in Malda district of North Bengal → Nawabganj region of Rajshahi division of Bangladesh → falling into Padma distributary of Bengal Delta.
- *Teesta-Torsha River System:* Tibet+Indo-Bhutan Himalayas including Bhutan, Indian state Sikkim and Kalimpong region of North Bengal → Alipurduar foothills (Duars) and Jalpaiguri-Cooch Behar plains of North Bengal → Rangpur region of Rajshahi Division of Bangladesh → falling into Jamuna distributary of Jamuna-Brahmaputra mouth.

Darjeeling district comprises of three Himalayan subdivisions, Darjeeling, Kurseong and Kalimpong; and the fourth one being Siliguri sub-division.

Conceptual Framework

Rajbanshis, Nepalis or Gorkha people and Adivasis are living in various pockets of this territory. They often claim that they are amongst the indigenous communities of South Asia or Indian Subcontinent. They claim that they have initiate understanding of nature and folk life covering all sub-structures, structures and superstructures of various pockets of this transnational borderland district of India. Henceforth, they have become indigenous to this land. They should be incorporated into the mainstream. Such inclusion would be good for the Nation.

Discussion

Evidence 1:Rajbanshi of Siliguri Sub-Himalayas (Terai) in Darjeeling District, West Bengal State, India

A century before Rajbanshis did not cultivate paddy varieties throughout the whole year, but only in a specific season; so cultivation is seasonal and not yearly. They preferred rice cultivation in the monsoon season. Rajbanshis then with very low population and minimum need left the cultivation ground for a season or a year or several years and allow the land to regain its productivity. Though they did not know about crop rotation, but applied various techniques regarding highland and lowland cultivations. That Shifting Cultivation was associated with Slash-and-Burn type of crop cultivation. They called it *jhum* cultivation where the bush and trees of the selected area were cut off to let them rotten, provided with sun-treatment, and then burnt with fire before planting the crops. In late winter when soil was covered with deciduous leaves of shorea and teak, they set up fire in order to prepare piles of ash manuring the soil. Light raining in late winter and temperature fall at night made the ash more fertile, and proper situation arose for the earthworms. Under the clear sky pleasant sunshine of autumn, the soil remained free from harmful insects, vectors and pests. Seeds were spread unevenly in late summer or at the pre-monsoon stage when rains just launched in the Himalayan terrains causing flash floods Sub-Himalayan valleys. Soil used to be covered with sand, lime, clay, loam, boulders, conglomerates and gravels; and accordingly they were selected on the basis of their criteria: sloppy, highland, lowland, ditch, mound, bushy terrain, marshy wetland, etc.

Rajbanshis now propagate paddy, jute and other local fiber yielding plants, pineapple, local fruits and flower including gerbera, various vegetables, bamboo, mushroom, spice, kitchen-garden product including medicinal plants and so forth. They are also associated with carrel rearing, fishing, poultry, handicraft, preparation of preserved foods, brewery and carpentry. They also know about mustard, sunflower, tobacco, drug-yielding plants, cow-pea and pulses of different varieties: *maskalai, thakurkalai*, pea, gram, *moog* and *khesari.* They have become settled cultivators as their population size has grown up considerably in a heterogeneous condition. They maintain their small pieces of grazing lands, bamboo bush, sacred groove, fencing, and ponds. In pockets, they have developed continuity of catchment-marshland, ridges and furrow, small irrigations, crop-rotation, alternative cropping, fish-paddy-fodder-fuel system, fish-duck-mollask system, mollask-lime-betel-areca system and a few others. They know about some natural dyes, soap and toxic elements. They are mostly associated with small farm size and mutual labour transactions rather than joint-extended family system (*Jot* system) as before. They have rich knowledge about traditional crop verities and seeds. They can manage well their biodiversity which is their natural resource also. They are very much in favour of organic and sustainable agriculture using their IKS and necessary modern technologies. However, *Amon* or monsoon varieties that they have preferred the most are *Kukra or Kukurjali, Sada Nunia, Kalo Nunia, Tulaipanji, Swarna, Kalam, Kamon/Kaon, Payejam, Mala, Dighe, Banshiraj, Aralia, Baran, Nalach, Kechardam, Harigachhi, Bayaj, Fulbete, Ropa* and so on. Some aush verities are *Pakshiraj, Tepishal, Nayachur, Muktahar, Bhadma, Chapari, Kotki, Shate* and so forth. *Mala* ripens first. Rajbanshis have the concept of six seasons like summer (*Greeshma*), rain (*Varsha*), spring (*Sarat*), foggy (*Hemanta*), clod winter (*Sheet*) and autumn (*Basanta*); each with two months out of total twelve. They also cultivate *Boro* or dwarf winter verities requiring less water along with *Makoi* (Maize) and *Kaon* (wheat supplement). They know the uses of yam, potato, aurum, rhizomes, ginger, banana, edible fern and even sugar cane. They know that Boikunthopur forest region is a watershed that divides Mechi-Mahananda from Teesta. They have also idea about forest management a little. They have developed into caste, but do not shed off dominant community like attitude. Kind of Tribe-Caste Continuum and Status Mobility Processes they know well. They are familiar with mixed deciduous, rainforest and savanna plants. Rajbanshis have several models in mind:

1. Bengal Delta Model.
2. North Bengal Model.
3. Mithilanchala Model.
4. Aryan Settlement Model from Kashmir-Tibet.
5. Koch-Kamboja Model.
6. Odisha-South Bengal Vaishnava Continuity.
7. Pundrabardhana-Bogra Model.
8. Kashyapa clan and the Myth of Parasurama.
9. East India Model.
10. Deccan Model.
11. Extreme South India Model.
12. Shahi Models.
13. British Involvement.
14. Gorkha people in Darjeeling Himalayas.
15. Sikkim-Bhutan-Tibet Model of transnational trade.
16. Agitations and local statehoods.

They are capable of understanding of contemporary situation, globalisation, alternative job, identity issues, indignity, social system, gender issues, migrations and multiculturalism and so many things. Their becoming a caste is very important and itself a kind of division of labour. Rajbanshis know about globalisation, Buddhism, pre-Buddhist versions, Khmer traditions and gold. Many landless of them are working in brick manufacturing outside the district and stone-crushing in and outside the region.

Rajbanshis from earlier time have been living very closer to various Mon, Bodo, Thai and Khmer groups as well as tribal communities like Mech, Dhimal, Rabha, Koch, Khen, Bodo, Garo, Hajoi/Hajong/Hajo as well as with Ahom, Chetia, various Bhot tribes, Limbu, Lepcha, and Kirata ethnic communities of Nepal Himalayas since pre-Gorkha formation there. They cover 18 per cent of total population of North Bengal.

Evidence 2:Oraons in Tea-Garden-Cropland Continuity of Siliguri Terai in Darjeeling District, West Bengal State, India

Oraons in North Bengal are segregated into two religious halves, the Samsara (animists/Tribal Hindu?) and the Christians. Oraon is a tribal community and falls under the Scheduled Tribe category of Indian Constitutional safeguard. The Samsars are more traditional and folk-based, but the Christians are much attached to modern way of life. Even the Christian sect claims to be transformed with the constitutional safeguard of Scheduled Tribe supported by an extra support of the Church.

Bangladesh, North and South Bengal of West Bengal State, Odisha and Bihar are combined treated as East India. Chhotonagpur was shared by Bengal, Bihar and Odisha. Presently, its main segment ancient settlement of *Champa* has been separated from Bihar state of India to form a new state Jharkhand full of mines and ores. This state formation has happened due to long demand of the Austro-Dravidian Adivasi tribal communities, Santal agitation and administrative purpose. Among various Adivasis, Oraon is a good example. They have continuity with Chotonagpur-Nagpur continuity of Deccan. Their majority stays in Ranchi-Palamu.They are praised for their supposed role of introducing irrigation system in Chotonagpur. These people are Dravidians and good overlap with Kolarian-Mundari people. They used to maintain tribal hierarchy claiming a very high position among the Adivasis. Many of them once migrated to Indo-Bangladesh watershed of Dinajpur proper (Rajshahi Division of Bangladesh) whose various pockets are in North Bengal. Many Oraons were introduced as tea garden lobourers during the British India. As a result of this, a considerable amount of Oraons we can find out in and around the tea-gardens in Terai-Duars included foothill Himalayas. Oraons are present Siliguri Terai tea gardens along with other *Adivasis*. Many of them have been shifted over to agriculture. Many become landless day labourers. Some have been shifted over to rururban and semi-urban areas, villages and hamlets. During British India, British Company and British Raj encouraged both civilians and native collaborators in establishing tea estate in included Jalpaiguri-Assam Duars as well as

Darjeeling-Kurseong-Siliguri continuity. In Duars-Terai region, aboriginal Austro-Mundaric *Adivasi* peoples from Nagpur-Chotonagpur as well as Central India-Deccan were introduced as labourers. They along with Nepali groups in tea garden barracks and adjoining regions changed the demography of those included territories. Tea estates plus newly established permanent cultivable grounds and well as establishment of Forest Department in borderlands brought a new kind of economy other than previous forest dwelling, shifting cultivation and transnational trade. Other agrarian tribal communities and various groups in Tribe-Caste Continuum from Chotonagpur-Bihar region sheltered in North Bengal-Rajshahi watershed-wetland areas also.

So, actually the IKS of Oraons here in North Bengal has been hampered and on the other hand along with their non-reflective domains they have accepted many things local. The primmest thing that they would never shed is their Adivasi identity in multicultural situation of Siliguri foothills. They also preserved their food habits, rite-de-passages, alcoholism, and to some extent biodiversity and agricultural knowledge. Their existence is the proof that these transnational regions are integral parts of India.

Change has been noticed not only on religious and political grounds, but also in education, health, exchange of goods, exchange of message, kinship terminologies as well as exchange of women. In few cases, we can get exogamy. With Christians, inter-clan marriage is present, but that is prohibited among Samsars. Both the religious groups have now accepted Oraon as their surname. People of *Lakra* clan, with *Sinha* or Lion as totem, seldom use *Singha* title that is used by Rajbanshis mostly in Mechi-Mahananda basin of Siliguri Terai. Samsars generally avoid beef consumption, whereas Christians are now not consuming mollusk and snails. Rich section or meddle class, especially the Christians, do not consume country rice liquored *Handia* or *Haria*. However, it is customary in Samsar ceremonies where they also practice blood sacrifice of birds and animals. Hunting has been totally lost in semi-urban areas. Witchcraft has been lowered down. Tattoo is however a common attribute. Oraons and other Adivasis are not against west Bengal state machinery, but they consider remote included areas of Terai and Duars foothills as Tribal Lands. Besides Kurux mother tongue, common Adivasi language Sadri, Hindi, other local languages and dialects like Bengali and Nepali and in some cases English are modes of communication here.

Evidence 3:Sentiments of Nepali People of Darjeeling Hills of Siliguri Terai in Darjeeling District, West Bengal State, India

For the three hilly sub-divisions in the Darjeeling districts are dominated by the Nepalis or the Gorkhas overwhelmingly existing there over Lepchas, Bhutias, Tibetans, and somr other Diasporas. However, Subbas of Nepali social fold were originally the Limbus of the place. Lepchas were of two

Box No. 1: Change In Family Pattern with Migration (ORAON)

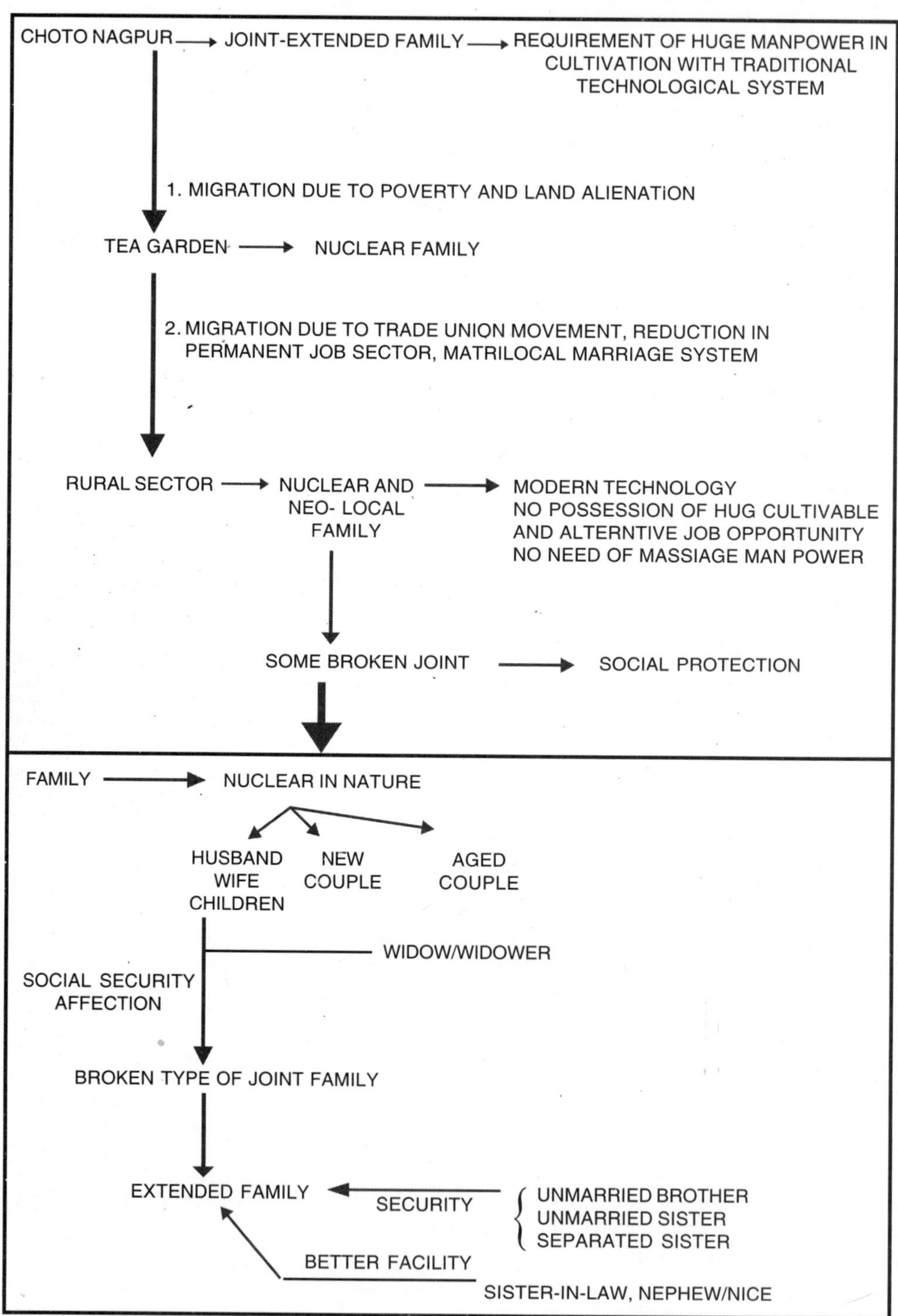

Box No. 2: Effect of Migration of Culture of Oraon Community

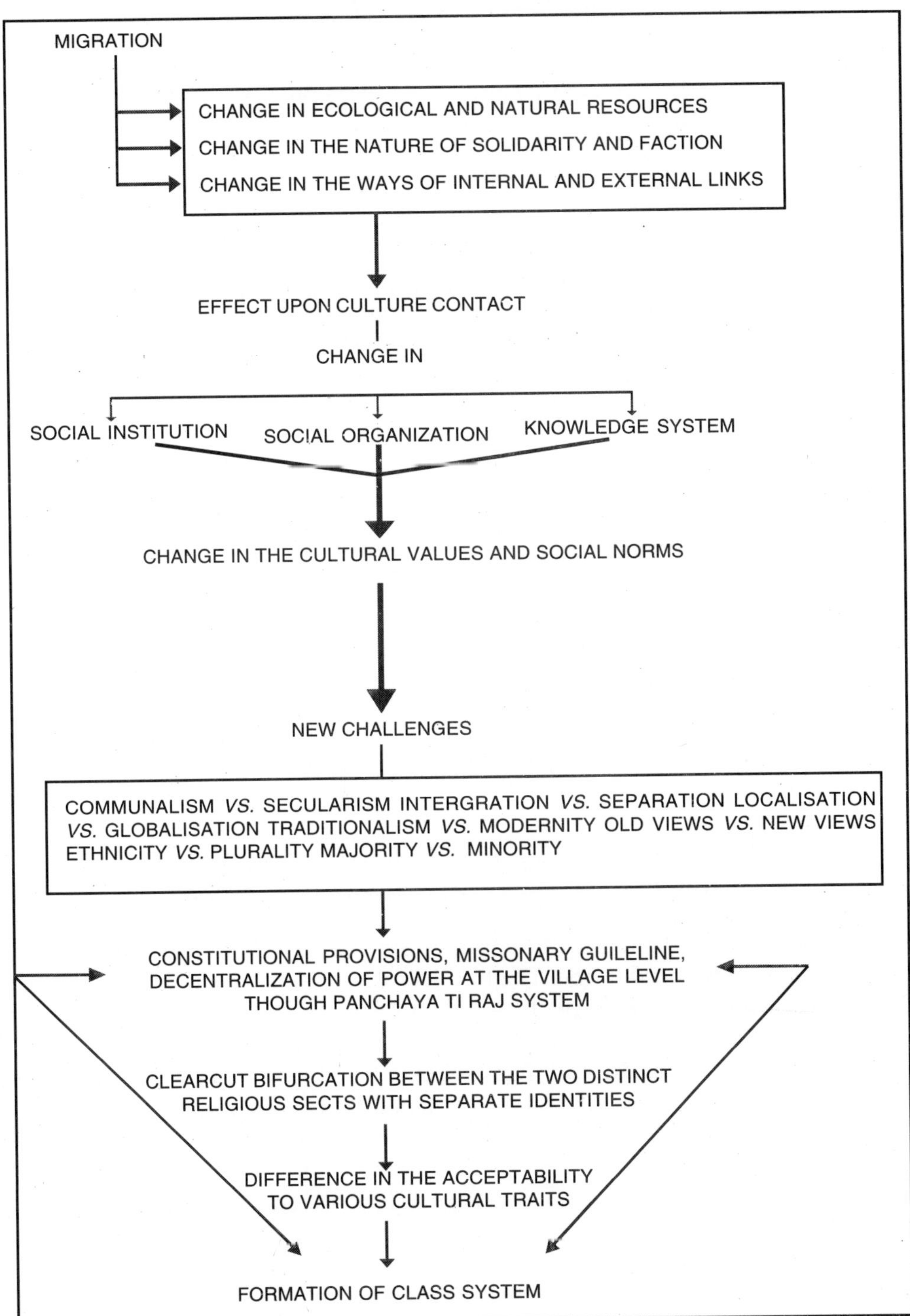

Box No. 3: Change in Family Types: Changes in Occupation and Mode of Production (ORAON)

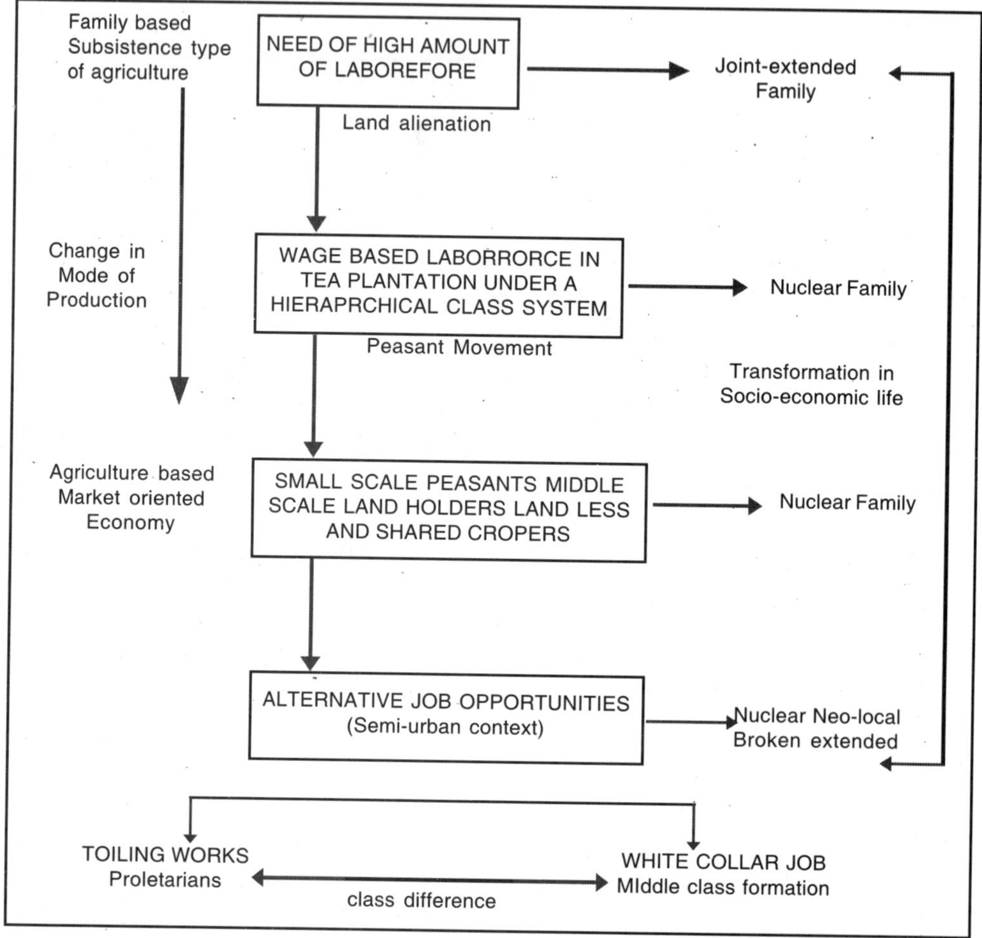

types: *(i)* Nepal and *(ii)* Sikkim. Bhutias of Bhutan are mostly known as Drukpa; but in Tibeto-Nepal border and Tibeto-Sikkim borderline they are known as Sherpa and Denzongpa respectively. Mongor of Nepal and Yalmo plus Kagatiya might have some affinities with them. Sonowar of Nepal are goldsmiths; Baun, Chhettri and Thakuri being of Upper Caste descendants (*Tagadhari*); Karki, Kami and Damai being Scheduled Caste; few Nepali groups like the Bhutias and Tibetans are Buddhist; and few portion being associated with Christianity and additive to Hill Muslims. There are so many ethnic groups of Nepali descendants working in forest department, tea estates, plantation sectors, floriculture sector, terraced cultivable land on hilly slopes, and urban centres such as hill stations full of hotels and restaurants, traveling agencies and vehicles, boarding schools and market.

Box No. 4: Factors Behind Change in Family Structure

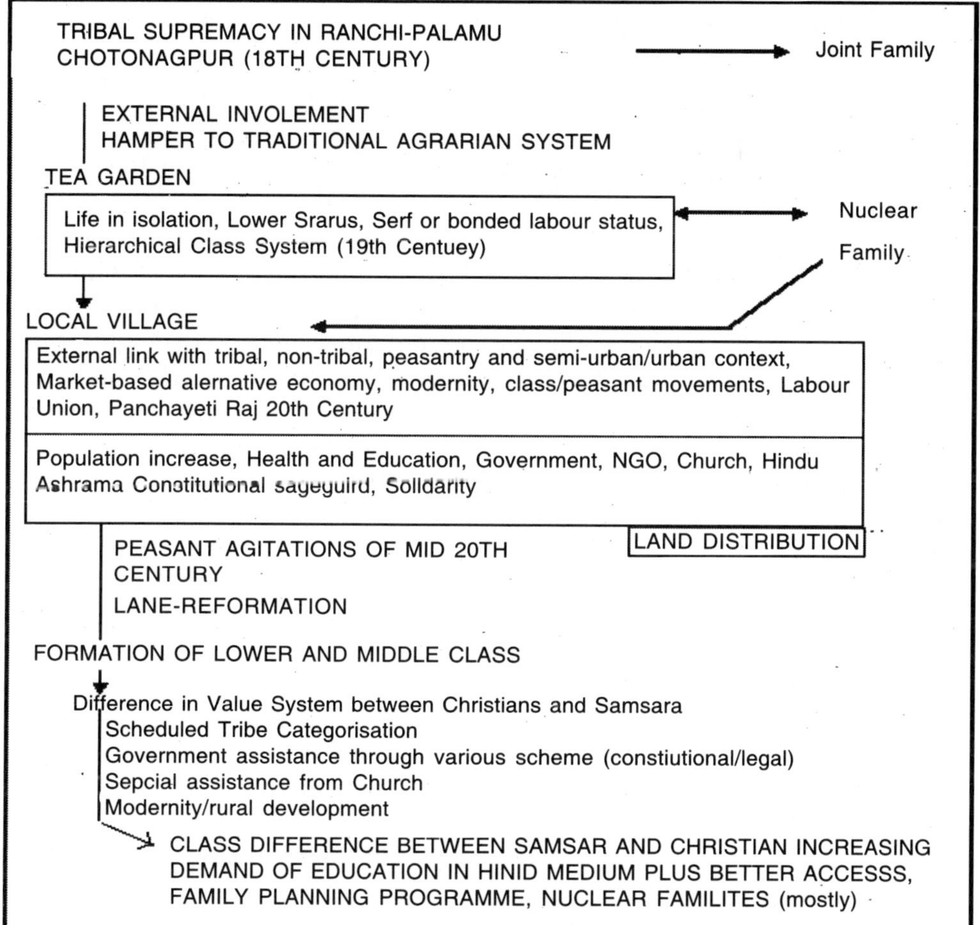

These majority sections of Hill people, mostly in-migrated along with autochthons, are united together with a Gorkha Nationalism. Different opinions are there: autonomous territory, separate state, Union Territory, and pan-Himalayan nationhood. Separate statehood demand has been raised for three hilly subdivisions with further claims to enter entire Siliguri subdivision and Siliguri City, Boikunthopur watershed, and Jalpaiguri Duars.

Hill people have a special aspiration of separate statehood in the name of Gorkhaland. This is mainly demanded by the Nepali population spread throughout the tea garden belt of Doors-Terai-Hill. The Nepali people are mostly concentrated in the hill areas and have other alternatives like Gorkha Regiment and various other jobs in different parts of the world. Like Mogul-Rajput alliance in 16-mid19th century AD; the Gorkha Shahi of Nepal took the policy of Pan-Himalayan statehood. But it could not get into Bhutan,

Sikkim, Tibet or Western Himalayan and also failed to pierce into the *Terai* areas of Bihar and Utter Pradesh, India.

Gorkha Shahi kept good relation with the British in India and out-migrated a lot from Nepal in the newly formed Darjeeling and Jalpaiguri tea zones. Their maximum concentration is now in hill areas of Darjeeling district along with several pockets in gateway of Nepal from Terai and in the gateway to Bhutan from Duars. They have become the human shield for this entire border region.

However, hills of Darjeeling district are famous for tea, timber, tourism and boarding schools. Illegal logging, illegal mining of coal, small dams on rivers, unplanned construction, water scarcity, landslide and unemployment are other issues for the hills. Rapid improvement can be noticed in neighboring Himalayan state Sikkim in both educational and economic sectors since its inclusion in Indian Federal Structure during 1970s. Population pressure in the foothills is there due to large scale of emigration from Bangladesh (formerly East Pakistan) since independence. Indo-Nepal friendly relation also helped the Gorkha people to come and stay in Darjeeling, other pockets of included regions and even in North East India. The Nepalis hate to be addressed as Toiling Class and foreigners in Indian Territory. Nepalis are basically Hill people of Nepalese population. They are more likely to stay here in North Bengal's extreme pockets as Gorkhas and not by their pre-Gorkha designation. Therefore, they have refused to accepr Sixth Schedule of Indian Constitution. Their ultimate claim is Gorkhaland which is like a Utopia for them. Otherwise, they could deal with West Bengal state in form of any set-up that would not wound their Gorkhahood. They believe in Gorkha regimen and wish to keep close contact with the Central Government from New Delhi that still seems to be the Mogul-Rajput Shahi. They always remember certain things:

1. Racism like *Kirata* and *Yaksha*, magico-religious issues like *Mashan*, Buddhism and Jainism emerged at ancient *Mithilanchala* in Indo-Nepal border of Bihar famous since *Ramayana*, story of Parashurama and Kashyapa, Aryan innovation from Irano-Afghanistan and sub-Himalayas, such innovations from Kashmir-Tibet region, various religious reforms, Katmandu and Gorkha Shahi.
2. Mogul-Rajput Dynasty in Indian Subcontinent, semi-autonomous pockets, self-reliance of peoples at extreme south of Indian peninsula, and the British rule.
3. World Wars and Florence Nightingale.
4. Burma and Bay of Bengal.
5. Jinnah and his First World attachment, Kashmiri Diaspora in Darjeeling, Gandhi and his Swadeshi Movement.

6. Gorkha Regiment in British Army.
7. World Wars.
8. Indo-China War on Indo-Tibet border.
9. Indo-Pak war on Kashmir.
10. Independence War of Bangladesh at Bogra (Rajshahi Division, North West Bangladesh attached to North Bengal).
11. Nehru's policy of Panchasheel, Non-Alliance of the Third World, Silk and Spice Routes, and emergence of Naxalbari Movement in Siliguri Terai.
12. Cold War, inclusion of Sikkim, proxy war in Kashmir, separatist activities in North East India, and assassination of Indira Gandhi.
13. Macro-economic Nationalisation and Micro-financing while India within Second World.
14. Labour Movement in tea plantations in Terai-Duars, and so forth.

They have managed themselves of being with Shahi cognate, the First World, Neo-liberalism, USA; mobile phones and SMS, Global Market, gold, urbanisation, global recession, New Delhi and Mumbai; Islamic activities, growing influence of China in various sectors like ASEAN and BRICS, Maoist activities, Look East Policy, re-juvenilation of ancient Silk and Spice routes, opening of Nathula pass in Sikkim-Chumbi transnational region and so forth.

A number of Nepalis live in Siliguri municipality along with majority Bengali and others. Siliguri the second largest municipal corporation of the state is the knot of National Highway 31, NH 31A, NH 52, and a number of major state highways (SH-2, 12A). It is rightly the Gateway of the North-Eastern States. The entire road and train traffic to the North East India is passing through the narrow corridor of Siliguri Terai of Darjeeling district which links it to the rest of India. Its proximity to the international borders of Nepal, Bhutan, Bangladesh and China further increases its strategic and economic importance. It is now considered the second capital of West Bengal. It has petroleum refineries of Indian Oil Corporation. Rapid urbanisation in Matigara block is another fact. Siliguri is the headquarters of FOCIN (Federation of Chamber of Commerce and Industry of North Bengal). Opening of shopping and entertainment malls like COSMOS, ORBIT and City Centre has affected a change in lifestyle. The city recently also witnessed the arrival of its first set of multiplexes – CINEMAX, INOX at ORBIT and Big Cinemas. The rapidly growing city also has showrooms of numerous automobile companies such as Maruti Suzuki, Honda Siel, Toyota Kirloskar, Ford, Tata, JCB, Mahindra and Mahindra, Hyundai, Skoda, General Motors, Fiat, Mahindra Renault, Chevourlet, Eicher, Ashok Leyland, Sonalika etc. There are numerous two wheeler showrooms also of companies: Hero Honda, Kinetic, Honda scooters, Yamaha, TVS, Suzuki, Bajaj, and LML. A large number of retail jewelers have opened showrooms in Siliguri: Tanisq, P. C. Chandra, M. P. Jewellers, Senco Gold, etc. With the growing commercial transactions there have opened up some major banks in the city namely Standard Chartered, HDFC, ICICI, Allahabad, State Bank of India, Axis Bank, UCO, Vijaya, IDBI and UBKG bank. There are also some other banks such as Bank of Maharastra, Bank of Baroda, Canara Bank, Andhra Bank, PNB, Indusind Bank, Sonali Bank etc. They keep their close eyes on rapid urbanisation surrounding Siliguri. And after all these things, they still maintain their IKS regarding agriculture, ethno-medicine and other productive systems. They put extra emphasis on migrations, cognitive aspects, gender, culture, empirical facts and local-to-international issues.

Conclusion

From the elaborate three discussions, it is clear that social exclusion of populations with Indigenous Knowledge is Crisis to the Nation. We have to keep out eyes always clear. And with micro-level studies, anthropologists can contribute here. We should not confine indigenous populations within modes of production, but will explore their divisions of labour, polity, economy, social and religious aspirations, cognition and culture, empirical facts, local to national and internationalism, gender and migration. Being human resource, they can really contribute to the Nation. That would not only be certain production-oriented IKS delivering a few public services to mitigate environmental problems and pollution due to unsustainable modernity. IKS be really the other side of modernity and not its opposition. Globalisation and Global Village could run side by side. IKS also teach us about how to live in a time of crisis.

REFERENCES

Agrawal, A. 2004. Indigenous and Scientific Knowledge: Some Critical Comments. *IK Monitor 3(3)* http://www.nuffic.nl/ciran/ikdm/3-3/articles/agrawal.html

Banarjee, S., Basu, D., Biswas, D. and Goswami, R. 2006. *Indigenous Knowledge Dissemination Through Farmers' Network: Exploring Farmer-to-Farmer Communication* in Choudhuri, B. and Choudhuri, S. (ed.) 2007. *Indigenous People: Traditional Wisdom and Sustainable Development,* IUAES Intercongress on Mega Urbanisation Multi-Ethnic Society Human Rights and Development (Vol. 4). New Delhi: Inter-India Publications.

Banrjee, D., D. Basu and R. Goswami. 2009. *Farmers' Knowledge and Scientists' Knowledge: Myths, Mutualities and Synergies.* In: Das Gupta, D. (ed.) 2009. *Indigenous Knowledge Systems and Common People's Rights.* Jodhpur: Agrobios (India).

Booth and Rhoades (1982), Chambers *et al.*, (1989), Colfer *et al.* (1988), Haverkort and Zeeuw, (1992), Jorgensen (1989), Tripp and Woolley (1989), and Warren, (1992) in Rajasekaran, B. 1993. *A Framework for Incorporating Indigenous Knowledge Systems into Agricultural Research, Extension, and NGOs for Sustainable*

Agricultural Development. Studies in Technology and Social Change No. 21. Ames, IA: Technology and Social Change Programme, Iowa State University.

Brokensha, D., Warren, D.M., Werner, O. 1980. *Indigenous Knowledge Systems and Development*, University Press of America, Washington, D.C.

Brush, S. B. 1989 Rethinking Crop Genetic Resource Conservation. *Conservation Biology* 3 (1): 19-29.

Census of India. 2001. Provisional Population Totals: India. Census of India 2001 [paper 1 of 2001] New Delhi: Office of the Registrar General, India www.censusindia.net

Chambers, R., A. Pacey and L.A. Thrupp (eds.). 1989. *Farmers First: Farmer Innovation and Agricultural Research*. Intermediate Technology Publications, London, pp. 218.

Chowdhuri, S. and C.K. Panda. 2009. Intellectual Property Rights and Indigenous Knowledge: A Major Challenge for the Rural People. In: Das Gupta, D. (ed.) 2009. *Indigenous Knowledge Systems and Common People's Rights*. Jodhpur: Agrobios (India).

Chowdhuri, S. and P. Ray. 2009. Incorporating Indigenous Technical Knowledge in Integrated Pest management Programmes: A Participatory Technology Development approach. In: Das Gupta, D. (ed.) 2009. *Indigenous Knowledge Systems and Common People's Rights*. Jodhpur: Agrobios (India).

Das Gupta, Ashok. 2010a. Rajbansi Festivals Decoding Indigenous Knowledge System, *Antrocom Online Journal of Anthropology*, 2010, Vol. 6, No. 2, pp. 249-261, ISSN 1973-2880, DOAJ Indexed, Peer Reviewed.

Das Gupta, A. 2010b. *The Relevance of 'Indigenous Peoples': A Case Study of the Rajbansi Community of North Bengal*. In R. K. Sen, A. Mukherjee and P. K. Pal (eds.). Environment and Sustainable Development in India, Deep and Deep Publications, Delhi, India, pp. 137-156, ISBN: 978-81-8450-280-0.

Das Gupta, Ashok 2010c. *Conceptualizing Identity Movements in India,* Indiascapes: Reflections of Contemporary India (W119), European Association of Social Aanthropologists (EASA) Conferences, 11th Biennial Conferences: Maynooth, Ireland 24-27th August 2010: Crisis and Imagination, Member of World Council of Anthropological associations (WCAA).

Das Gupta, Ashok 2011. Does Indigenous Knowledge have Anything to Deal with Sustainable Development? *Antrocom Online Journal of Anthropology*, 2011, Vol. 7, No. 1, pp. 57-68, ISSN 1973-2880, DOAJ Indexed, Peer Reviewed.

Das Gupta, D. and A. Saha. 2009. Indigenous Knowledge Vis-a-Vis Bio-diversity Conservation. In: Das Gupta, D. (ed.) 2009. *Indigenous Knowledge Systems and Common People's Rights*. Jodhpur: Agrobios (India).

Davis, S. H. and K. Ebbe (eds.), 1993. Traditional Knowledge and Sustainable Development. *Environmentally Sustainable Development Proceedings* Series No. 4. The World Bank, Washington D. C.

Ellen, R. and Harris, H. 1996. *Concepts of Indigenous Technical Knowledge in Scientific and Developmental Studies Literature: A Critical Assessment*, Internet Search on Indigenous Knowledge System. www.worldbank.org/afr/ik/basic.htm_68k

Flavier, J.M. *et al.* 1995. The Regional Programme for the Promotion of Indigenous Knowledge in Asia, pp. 479-487 in Warren, D.M., L.J. Slikkerveer and D. Brokensha (eds) *The Cultural Dimension of Development: Indigenous Knowledge Systems*. London: Intermediate Technology Publications.

International Labour Organization. 1991. Convention No. 169 (Concerning Indigenous and Tribal Peoples in Independent Countries, 1989) in *International Labour Conventions and Recommendations* Vol. 2 (1919-91). Geneva: International Labour Office.

Jorgensen. 1989. In: Rajasekaran, B. 1993. A framework for Incorporating Indigenous Knowledge Systems into Agricultural Research, Extension, and NGOs for Sustainable Agricultural Development. Studies in Technology and Social Change No. 21. Ames, IA: Technology and Social Change Programme, Iowa State University.

Grenier, L. 1998. *Working with Indigenous Knowledge – A Guide for Researchers*, IDRC, Ottawa.

Hobsbawm, E. and T. Ranger (eds.) 1983. *The Invention of Tradition;* Cambridge University Press, Cambridge.

Indian Journal of Traditional Knowledge

Inge Kaul, Isabelle Grunberg and Marc Stern, 1999 in Kelkar, G. Nathan, D. and Walter, P. (ed.) 2004. *Globalisation and Indigenous Peoples in Asia – Changing the Local-Global Interference,* Sage Publication: New Delhi\Thousand Oaks\London

Mondal, S.R. 2009. Biodiversity Management and Sustainable Development – The Issues of Indigenous Knowledge System and the Rights of Indigenous People with Particular Reference to North Eastern Himalayas of India. In: Das Gupta, D. (ed.) 2009. *Indigenous Knowledge Systems and Common People's Rights.* Jodhpur: Agrobios (India).

Muchena, O.N. and Williams, D.L. Utilising Indigenous Knowledge Systems in Agricultural Education to Promote Sustainable Agriculture. *Journal of Agricultural Education*. 1991/ Winter: p. 54.

Rajsekaran, B. and Warren, D.M. 1991. Utilising and Integrating Indigenous Knowledge Systems for Agricultural and Rural Development: Training Manual and Guide for Extension Workers. Ames, Lowa: CIKARD, Lowa State University.

Rajasekaran, B. and Whiteford M. B. 1992. Rice-Crab Production in South India: The Role of Indigenous Knowledge in Designing Food Security Policies. *Food Policy* 18 (3): 237-247.

Rajsekaran, B. and Warren, D.M. 1993. Putting Local Knowledge to Good use. *International Agricultural Development* 13 (4): 8-10.

Rajasekaran, B. 1993. *Indigenous Technical Practices in a Rice-based Farming System.* Ames, IA: Centre for Indigenous Knowledge for Agriculture and Rural Development. Draft.

SECTION – III

Indigenous Population

Extremism, Displacement and Education

13

Insurgency in the State of Manipur

From Ethnic Contest to Societal Exclusion

***Sonkhogin Haokip**

ABSTRACT

Manipur with a population of 30,23,141 (2002 census) is perhaps, the state with the highest per capita 'tutilizerrorist organization' not only in India but the whole world. Of the 28 militant Organizations branded as 'Terrorist' in India under POTA, ten are from the Northeast region out of which again six are from Manipur. At present, there are about (thirty) 30 insurgent groups operating in Manipur some of which have an ideology whereas majority of them are allegedly purely extortionist groups that use the underground façade to their own advantage.

This paper attempts to highlight the fact that 'Insurgency' in Manipur is the offshoot of ethnic contests reflected in the form of 'dominant ethnic groups versus non-dominant ethnic groups' where the former submerges and excludes the latter from social, political and economic advantages. The paper also attempts to highlight the fact that civil society along with a wide variety of economic activities that were integral to the lives of the people of Manipur have been 'criminalized', forcing otherwise law abiding

* Assistant Professor, Department of Political Science and Development Administration, Gandhigram Rural University - Gandhigram, E-mail: lhingneinemhaokip@gmail.com

citizens into a collusive relationship with militants within their areas of influence (be it the dominant ethnic groups, or non-dominant ethnic groups).

Eventually, the paper concludes by saying that the strong and deep-rooted nexus between the Militants, Politician, and Bureaucrats has eventually excluded people by and large (irrespective of the ethnic group they belong to) from social, political and economic advantages.

Keywords: Insurgency, Manipur, Ethnic contest, Exclusion.

Manipur has been witnessing insurgency for the last 40 years, commencing with the Federal Government of Nagaland (FGN). The FGN insurgency was initiated in the Naga Hills district of Assam in 1956. It naturally spilled over into the four Naga-dominated districts of Manipur.[1] The base of the FGN was in Ukhrul district, but Senapati and Tamenglong districts also provided good support. A majority of the cadres and leaders were from the Thangkhuls of Ukhrul, the Maos, Poumeis and Marams from Senapati district and the Zeliangs from Tamenglong district. Ukhrul district has a 140 km unguarded border with Myanmar. To a depth of 20 km from the border there are virtually no roads. The Yomadung and Angouching are the last north south ranges along the border. Across are the Somra tracts, also populated by the Thangkhuls. The slopes of Yomadung and Angouching are thickly forested and do not offer easy access for conventional troops. All along the border there is only one fair weather dirt road of Second World War vintage from Kamjong to the Chindwin valley. Terrain wise, Ukhrul was a good district for the Naga underground army of the FGN. So were the districts of Senapati and Tamenglong, both thickly forested and with hardly any roads.

Later, with the signing of the Shillong Accord,[2] peace returned to the four districts of Manipur. This peace was, however, short-lived as Thuingaleng Muivah and Isak Chisi Swu,[3] who was not a party to the Shillong Accord, formed the Nationalist Socialist Council of Nagaland (NSCN) along with S. S. Khaplang, a Hemi Naga from north Myanmar. By 1980, the NSCN was operating in all the four Naga districts of Manipur. Later in 1988, the NSCN split in Myanmar and became two units, the National Socialist Council of Nagaland – Isak-Muivah (NSCN-IM) led by Muivah and Isak Swu and the National Socialist Council of Nagaland – Khaplang (NSCN-K) led by S. S. Khaplang. The NSCN-IM did not lose much time in setting up their units in all the four Naga districts of Manipur.

Insurgency made its first appearance in the valley districts of Manipur in 1960s in the form of a shadowy Pan-Mongoloid movement and the Revolutionary Government of Manipur. These groups preceded the creation of the United National Liberation Front (UNLF)[4] of Manipur in November 1964. The People's Revolutionary Party of Kangleipak (PREPAK), a chauvinist and revolutionary group was set up on October 9, 1977, by R. K. Tulachandra.[5] The People's Liberation Army (PLA) was raised on September 25, 1978 by the late N. Bisheswar Singh.[6] The reasons for the raising of these three organizations are not far to seek. Meitei pseudo-intellectuals never reconciled to the accession of Manipur in 1949 nearly two years after India attained independence. Manipur, an ancient kingdom with a 2000-year-old recorded history and a magnificent culture, was made a Part C State[7] – a Union Territory. Then in 1962, as a step to appease the secessionist FGN, the Naga Hills district of Assam was made a State. Manipur continued to be a Union Territory for another ten years, before being granted Statehood. Manipuri, an ancient language spoken and written by all the Meiteis and tribals, was not included in the Eighth Schedule of the Indian Constitution for years. The bureaucrats who came from Delhi and other States in 1949 were by and large not sympathetic to the Meiteis and the tribals. With a few exceptions, they did not win the confidence of the Manipuris. The worst was the policy of the party in power at Delhi, as a result of which the North East was flooded with funds, indirectly encouraging corruption, on the premise that this would make the people soft and finish off insurgency. On the contrary, it had just the opposite effect, driving home the truth that it is neither good nor expedient to tamper with the self-respect of a people. A coterie of contractors, all followers of the party in power at Delhi, was created, and later came to be called the 'Delhi Durbar'. This coterie secured most of the government contracts in the North eastern states. This infamous band of contractors took 95 per cent of the development funds allocated by Delhi back to private coffers in Delhi. Hundreds of km of roads were built on paper and even annually maintained on paper. Food grains from the public distribution system were siphoned off wholesale into the black market. The politicians and bureaucrats of Manipur quickly adapted to this system.

The raising of the PLA, the UNLF, and the PREPAK was a direct reaction to these factors. The PLA, raised in 1978, grew rapidly and was in full cry in the Valley by 1979. A Meitei chauvinist group, its fierce leftist ideology and integrity attracted a cross-section of the educated youth. Many bright Meitei students from national universities left their studies and joined the organization. A series of dacoities and ambushes committed in 1978 and 1979 were attributed to the PLA and the PREPAK. The object was to snatch arms from the security forces and collect money for purchasing arms.

The heart of the business community is the Thengal and Paona *bazaars*, home of the *Marwaris* and outside traders. They were key participants in the siphoning of essential goods into the black market. They naturally became a prime target of the PLA and the PREPAK in extorting money. This extended to the coterie of outside contractors who had cornered the bigger contracts in the State and from them to the corrupt politicians and bureaucrats was a natural step. The unholy nexus of the politician, bureaucrat and contractor in siphoning funds led to a fourth channel – the insurgent, who now claimed the biggest share at the point of the gun.

Terrain is a crucial factor in any insurgency and the terrain of Manipur entirely favoured the insurgent. The hill ranges of Manipur are roughly north-south and peter off into the valley in the centre in a series of low hills. The hills are thickly forested, but for three national highways traversing them, are bereft of roads. Of the five hill districts, Ukhrul to the east is exclusively Thangkhul Naga, with a few Kuki villages on the eastern border with Myanmar. National Highway 150 (NH 150) bisects Ukhrul, coming from Jessamie in the north and, turning west, enters the valley at Yanganpokpi. The Border Roads Organization (BRO) has recently constructed a road from Shangshak near Ukhrul to Kasamkhullen in the south, crossing into Chandel district connecting Tengnoupal. In the north, Senapati district is bisected by National Highway 39 (NH 39), coming from Kohima. There are two lateral roads to the west connecting Kangpokpi to Tamenglong and Maram to Paren and one to the east from Tadubi to Ukhrul. In Tamenglong, a road links the district headquarters to Khongsang on National Highway 53 coming from Imphal to Jiribam and to Silchar. From Churachandpur, National Highway 150 was extended to Tipaimukh. This road has been abandoned for the last 10 years. In Chandel district, NH 39 connects Pallel to Moreh. The Tengnoupal New Samtal road constructed by the Border Roads has been abandoned. The interiors of Chandel and Churachandpur districts are the sanctuaries of the PLA, PREPAK, UNLF, the Kangleipak Communist Party (KCP),[8] and the myriad Kuki-Chin-Mizo underground groups. This is the hinterland from which they operate, and the main base camps and training areas of the PLA and the UNLF are in these two districts.

The PLA and the UNLF initially had their hideouts in the Meitei villages in the valley, but established camps for training their cadres deep inside Chandel district and also inside Myanmar[9] into which they crossed easily, as the border was not policed. Initially, weapons were purchased from the Myanmar Army, but a clandestine arms market gradually developed across the border of Chandel district. The breakup of the Khmer Rouge in Cambodia and the later peace agreement between the Shan State and Myanmar released a whole lot of Russian and US army weapons into the arms market. In the nineteen seventies, when the PLA and PREPAK were raised, arms were not easily available. Their arsenal was built up by looting arms from the police and para-military forces and buying from the poorly paid Myanmar's soldiers deployed across India's borders.

The Indian Army operated extensively against the PLA in the early nineteen eighties. In a series of swift operations, they were able to capture the PLA chief, N. Bisheswar and kill a number of top ranking leaders.[10] The

PLA was halted in its tracks. Upon his release, Bisheswar took to politics and became a Member of the Legislative Assembly (MLA). Although dormant, however, the hard core of the PLA remained intact. Later, after eliminating Bisheswar for changing track, the organization regrouped and along with the NSCN and the United Liberation Front of Asom (ULFA), sought help from the Kachin Independent Army (KIA) in northern Myanmar, to arm and train its cadres.[11] All three groups secured adequate training but not much by way of arms. Except for a few Chinese M-22, the equivalent of the AK-47, they only got G-3 rifles and old weapons captured from the Myanmar army. In 1990, Bransen, the KIA leader, withdrew support to the NSCN, PLA and ULFA and all three turned to Bangladesh for sanctuary. Here, they secured support beyond measure from the Bangladesh government and the Inter Services Intelligence (ISI), Pakistan's external intelligence agency, at the Pakistan Embassy in Dacca. It was around this time that the Khmer Rogue broke up in Cambodia releasing a number of AK-47s, RPD 7.62 LMGs and RPG-7 rocket launchers into the clandestine arms market of South East Asia. The ISI seized this opportunity to sponsor the North Eastern insurgent groups. The first consignment of arms purchased in Thailand was landed in Cox's Bazaar in 1991, where a group of 240 NSCN cadres were waiting to receive them. It was carried overland, via Bandarban, Parva, the eastern border of Mizoram, along the Tiddim road into Churachandpur district, then over the hills to Tamenglong and then into the Paren sub-division of Nagaland. All the major insurgent groups linked with the NSCN got their weapons through this channel. In January 1996, the drug lord, Khun Sa surrendered to the Myanmarese government.[12] This led to the release of more arms to the clandestine arms market. Groups like the UNLF, the KCP and the different Kuki militant outfits discovered that they could procure arms from across the border from Chandel district.

Areambam Samrendra Singh founded the other main valley group, the UNLF, on November 24, 1964, initially as a social organization. It was the culmination of several movements like the Pan-Mongoloid Movement and the Revolutionary Nationalist Party, which raised the banner of independence in 1953. The UNLF took to arms only in the late nineteen eighties. The self-styled chief of this group, Rajkumar Meghen alias Sana Yaima, has royal lineage and was linked to the NSCN. It is reported that Meghen was aware of Khaplang's plans to attack Muivah and Isak Swu and their followers in northern Myanmar, but did not alert Muivah, as a result of which many of his followers were killed and Muivah himself barely escaped with his life. Since then the NSCN-IM severed all links with the UNLF. Rajkumar Meghen continues his close links with the NSCN-K.

By the nineteen nineties, some of the PLA cadres left the group, came overground and joined politics, and after the elections to the State Legislative

Assembly in the year 2000, even became ministers. Today, the PLA and the UNLF maintain that they do not believe in elections conducted by India. The smaller groups, particularly the myriad Kuki outfits, each supported candidates of different parties who hired them. This included all the main national parties, except the Communist parties. They openly used arms to rig the State-level elections both in 2000 and 2002.[13]

The FGN was the first to introduce extortion to Manipur. The NSCN-IM took over where the FGN left off and systematised it into an annual 'house tax' and 'ration tax'.[14] Additionally, they taxed all buses and trucks and contractors. At times, their subordinate formations muscled in on development funds, applying coercive tactics to intimidate Deputy Commissioners. The UNLF and PLA initially sought donations for their social activities, but these were gradually transformed into extortion demands. The primary target was, of course, the unholy trio of the politician, the bureaucrat and the businessman. Later, they spread to the salaried government servant. By the nineteen nineties, the entire system had become institutionalised. Cashiers of different government departments were directed to deduct certain percentages according to the rank of the official, and pay the amount to the underground organization. Traders and businessmen were, similarly and regularly 'taxed'. Tankers carrying petrol, diesel and kerosene oil were diverted from the big authorised dealers and sold in the black market by all the major underground groups. These groups also diverted rice from the Public Distribution System (PDS) from all the dealers, with a part taken for supplying the underground camps. Rice, kerosene, petrol and diesel were also sold in the black market. Against the quota of five litres per family per month of kerosene oil, most people were getting only one or two litres in Imphal, while in the interior towns and villages; there was no penetration of the PDS supply at all. In the interiors of Chandel and Churachandpur districts, the PLA and UNLF sold rice and kerosene at absurdly low rates to the villagers near their camps to secure a 'Robin Hood image'. In Imphal, both the PLA and UNLF had well oiled 'finance wings' working. Their records were computerised and they had up-to-date information of the receipt of development grants in the different government departments. They had full knowledge of the bank accounts of all government officers, doctors and engineers. Extortion demands were served accordingly. While there were standard deductions from all the government servants, doctors who also had good earnings from private practice got proportionate extortion demand notes. Officers dealing with development grants were forced to divert substantial sums to all the underground groups. Worse still, Chief Engineers were forced to award contracts to cadres of the main insurgent groups at gunpoint. The members of the 'Finance wing' of the different groups had free access to all government offices. Very often, senior officials were summoned to chosen rendezvous on the outskirts of Imphal where they were forced at gunpoint to do the biddings of the groups. During the reign of the People's Front government of 2000, the nexus between the PLA and the UNLF with the politicians reached its peak.

All this could come about because of the trend set by politicians in siphoning out money in collusion with spineless bureaucrats. Money was collected from government servants for enhancing the pay scales. Large-scale diversion of development funds took place at the level of politicians and bureaucrats. It was only then that the insurgent groups intervened and started taking a major share in these deals. Most of the non-governmental organizations (NGOs) in Manipur are run by politicians in the names of their hangers-on. Grants obtained by them from the Union government for schemes like housing for the rural poor, watershed projects, etc., were largely siphoned off by these politicians. Only a trickle of approximately five per cent reached the people. Against this background, the development of this extensive extortion network is not a surprising development.

Of the five major valley underground groups, the UNLF is the one whose ideology is by and large intact. The PLA is better organized but there are narratives of PLA cadres constructing large houses in Imphal. However, the senior leadership is well educated and has a good organizational control. The lower level cadres are primarily dropouts from schools and colleges. The poor quality of education and the lack of jobs and entrepreneurial opportunities produce a pool of youth readymade for the insurgent groups. Of the five groups, the KCP and Kanglei Yawol Kunna Lup (KYKL)[15] exist mainly for extortion. The PLA, UNLF and PREPAK have a loose collaboration and have worked out space allotments in the hinterland and operational areas. The KYKL, formed by N. Oken, established links with the NSCN- IM, the first and only penetration of the valley underground by an outside group. KYKL has a junior but extensive role in the extortion net in the valley and operates along with the NSCN-IM cadres giving a share to them. The KYKL had split into two factions in 1994[16] due to differences between Oken and Achou Toijamba, who linked up with the NSCN-K. Recently in year 2002, the two factions have patched up. Presumably, the NSCN-IM has won another round with Toijamba's link with NSCN-K severed.

Till the nineteen nineties, the valley groups had operated only in the valley. They did use the secluded hills and jungles of Chandel district as their hinterland and had base camps and training areas there. This changed when the Kuki National Organization (KNO) and the Kuki National Army (KNA) were set up in 1992-93 in Tamu across the border town of Moreh. The Nagas and Kukis were ancient enemies. The Kukis were the most enterprising of the Kuki-Chin-Mizo group and had not restricted themselves to Churachandpur district where they had presumably first migrated. In their wanderings, they occupied areas in Naga country in Ukhrul, Tamenglong and Senapati districts and even occupied areas in the Naga hills and North Cachar Hills districts of Assam. The Kukis were used as a buffer against the Nagas both by the Meitei kings and the British. The KNO and the KNA were raised probably taking a leaf from history to again act as a buffer against the Nagas, now in the shape of the NSCN-IM. Chandel district has a number of smaller tribes – Maring, Anal, Chothe, Kom, whom the Kukis claimed to be part of the Kuki-Chin-Mizo group, but with the rise of the FGN and later the NSCN, these tribes claimed that they were part of the Naga group. Irrespective of their origin, these small Naga tribes were numerically more than the Kukis in Chandel district. This district is roughly bisected into two by the Pallel-Moreh road. The eastern part adjoining Ukhrul is majority Naga. The area around Moreh is however dominated by the Kukis. And Moreh is a smuggler's town with enormous profits to whoever controlled it. The NSCN-IM had for long been eyeing it. The bait given to the Kukis in raising the KNO and the KNA was control of the rich spoils of smuggling through Moreh. Fierce clashes occurred between the KNA and the NSCN-IM as they attacked each other's camps. Soon, they were attacking each other's villages and both Naga and Kuki villages went up in flames. The NSCN-IM were better trained, equipped and much more experienced. With years of fighting the Indian army, they were better motivated. There ensued an ethnic cleansing of the Kukis in Ukhrul, Tamenglong and Senapati districts. The Kukis, realising that they could not fight the battle on their own, sought assistance from all their brother sub-tribes in the Churachandpur district. Some of the sub-tribes responded positively but the Paites, one of the larger and more prosperous of the Kuki-Chin-Mizo group refused to help and berated the Kukis for sticking their neck out unnecessarily. This angered the Kukis and they attacked the Paites in a fratricidal war. The Kuki-Paite clashes were bitterly fought and several Kuki and Paite villages were burnt.[17] The Paites were not well armed and naturally took a beating. They lived generally along the southern areas of Churachandpur district and many fled across the border into Myanmar where they ran into the NSCN-IM, who sympathised with them and soon developed an axis with them. They gave them arms, equipped and trained them. A new underground group primarily for the defence of the Paites was formed – the Zomi Reunification Army (ZRA). The Zhou, a sister group was dragged in by the Paites as a reluctant partner. For the NSCN-IM, it was a major breakthrough – they had penetrated the Kuki-Chin-Mizo group.

The PLA and the UNLF never had any bases in Churachandpur district. They had for long been eyeing the sparsely inhabited vast tract of hills and jungle from Churachandpur to Senvon, Tipaimukh, in the south, the Thangjing hills to the east, and the Tipaimukh-Jiribam road to the west and NH 53 to the north. This was a vast rectangle of hills and forests with only tracks connecting the isolated lonely villages. NH 150 constructed by the BRO had been virtually abandoned. This was classical guerilla country. The PLA and the UNLF with admirable foresight, taking advantage of the ethnic clashes between the Nagas and the Kukis, extended help to the Kukis in rehabilitating hundreds of Kuki families rendered homeless, providing money, food and building materials. The Kuki chiefs were grateful and could not refuse the PLA and the UNLF when they asked for permission to purchase land. Hundreds of acres of land were purchased by both these valley groups in Churachandpur district. They had now secured a foothold in the Kuki-Chin-Mizo area. Recruitment to the main valley groups was opened up to the Kukis and related sub tribes. Some axis between the groups also developed, such as the links between the PREPAK and the Hmar Peoples Convention Democratic (HPCD), a Mizoram underground group.

The worst fallout was the leadership squabbles, which soon followed in the KNO and the KNA. Out of the KNA emerged the Kuki National Front (KNF),[18] which later split into the KNF – Military Council and the KNF – Presidential. The latter again split into two further factions. Although these myriad Kuki militant groups were ostensibly for the protection of their community, they were, in reality, only extorting money from the people in the form of 'donations' from traders and contractors and even from government departments. They had soon aligned themselves with different politicians of national parties. In the elections of year 2000, the different groups were hired by politicians of all hues, both State and national. The groups freely used their guns to intimidate voters and the elections were completely rigged. This was the case again in the elections of 2002, with the different groups firing at each other on polling days with abandon on behalf of their candidates. It is even reported that the leaders of some of these groups stay in the houses of senior politicians of the State in New Delhi. The KNO, when first formed, talked of Zalengam, a homeland for the Kukis. However, this idea has long been abandoned. The myriad Kuki groups now have only one objective – extortion and hiring themselves to the highest bidder.

In the year 2000 elections, two Kuki lower level leaders, unhappy at not being given tickets for the State Legislative Assembly elections, had each left with some followers and linked with the NSCN-IM who armed and trained them. These constituted the United Kuki Liberation Front (UKLF), who now operate on the Churachandpur, Chandel axis and the Kuki Revolutionary Army (KRA), who operate in the Saikul valley. Earlier, still another group had broken off from the KNO, the Kuki Liberation Organization and the Kuki Liberation Army.

This is the unhappy state of affairs in Manipur. Can something be done to restore normalcy? A very determined effort will be required to stabilize the politics and administration of the State. The effort has to be a civil-military co-ordinated manoeuver. The Union government has always had a standard reaction to any insurgent situation – send a couple of battalions of central para military forces (CPMF) or if there is a critical scenario, send in the army. Not in any insurgent situation have we analysed the causes of why an insurgent situation has developed, of why a group of people have taken to arms and is fighting the state. In the State of Bihar, when the Ranbir Sena, a private army of landlords, had massacred 35 Dalit (scheduled castes) sympathizers of the Maoist Communist Centre (MCC),[19] on June 16, 2000,[20] a series of meetings were held in the Home Ministry and several battalions of CPMF were sent to Bihar. After some time, when the situation was reviewed, it was found that the forces sent were deployed to hunt for the MCC and not for the Ranbir Sena. No one talked of the unlawful and unequal distribution of land and the denial of land to peasants because of their caste.

In any insurgent situation, the causes must be first dispassionately analysed. This must be left to professional economists, sociologists, judges, professional police officers and professional administrators. The emphasis on the prefix 'professional', qualifying 'police officers' and 'administrators' should be specially noted. In the last 30 years, the concept of 'committed bureaucracy' has become deep rooted. It is of no use to leave the judgement of an insurgent situation to a police officer or administrator who is aligned to any political party and has earned his promotions by patronage.

Once this has been accomplished, a blue print for counter-insurgency should be drawn up. The effort has to be a combined civil and military effort with the civil at the forefront. This has to be clearly emphasised. There should be no question of the armed forces ever having the leadership in an insurgent situation. Heavy deployment of army or paramilitary forces is bound to cause excesses. This is unavoidable. And when this happens, without redressing the conditions of the population, which has in the first place led to the resort to arms by a section of the population, they are bound to get further alienated. It is imperative therefore that the civil effort should be at the forefront and supported by the military effort.

The first step in the kind of situation we are faced with in Manipur, where there is an undercurrent of secession, rampant corruption led by the politicians and tamely abetted by the bureaucrats, and a complete failure by the state to protect the few upright government servants, is to list out the local civil, judicial and police officers and identify the few who have not been tainted by chauvinism and corruption and who, if protected, are likely to stand up against intimidation. The second step is to post these officials in all crucial posts. The first preference should be for local officers. Where reliable local officers are not available, specially selected outside officers should be brought in and posted. The third step is to ensure that reliable judicial officers are posted. This is a sphere, which is invariably neglected, after the 1973 amendment of the Criminal Procedure Code (CPC), separating prosecution from investigation. The police now forget the case after the chargesheet is filed. It is necessary that every hearing be followed to ensure that the underground is not taking advantage of the police failure to follow the course of the case, to get their cadres released. The judicial officers posted should be equally strict to the prosecution and to the defence, in fact more so to the prosecution. In every insurgency, the underground always uses the judiciary, primarily because it is always local, except for the Chief Justice. Also, the judiciary does not get the kind of protection – the guards and escorts – that the executive gets. There is no reason why the Judges from the Sessions up to the High court cannot be from outside. Their security should be more stringent than that of the field officers. The Jammu and Kashmir judge, who sentenced Maqbool Butt to death, was not protected, and he was killed later.[21] After this, no judge would have dared to sentence any insurgent to imprisonment, let alone death.

Special attention should also be paid towards strengthening the police. The Manipur Rifles was a very fine force but has degenerated because of very poor officering and lack of finance, resulting in a situation where the riflemen are forced to buy their own uniforms. Pay is never regular and as a result, the men have to borrow from the unit *bania* canteen. A soldier who lives like this loses his self respect and cannot be expected to fight. The first step to be taken is to see that the ration of the riflemen is equated to that of the CPMF and to ensure that he is paid on time, equipped well and trained rigorously. The command of the battalions should be given to officers of the CPMF. The civil police must also immediately be reorganised and strengthened. Some of the districts have only about 200 personnel with no reserve lines and miserable barracks, which have not been repaired for years. All sub-inspectors and above should be put through in-service courses in investigation, interrogation and intelligence tradecraft.

There are pitfalls into which the police can easily fall when involved in counter-insurgency operations. Fortunately, we have examples at close hand. In Punjab, we saw the police picking up innocent boys saying that they were terrorists and releasing them after taking money. This happened in Jammu and Kashmir too. In Assam, Hiteswar Saikia, the then Chief Minister, created a mafia after securing the surrender of known ULFA criminals, who had murder cases pending against them, and forming them into mafia gangs, extorting money from coal transporters. The surrendered ULFA (SULFA) boys were allowed to keep their weapons and operate as gangs under unofficial patronage.[22] In all these cases, the victims were the very people who were to be won over to the government side and who were to be weaned away from the insurgents. The end result was an indignant populace, who were further alienated and a police force who had become terrorists themselves.

In Manipur, civil policemen and officers were selected and trained as commandos. Although they did a very good job initially, they soon deteriorated into a state terrorist force due to faulty leadership. They started extorting money from the business community, picking a leaf out of the insurgent's book. What were the consequences for the hapless public? Here were five to six underground groups extorting money from the traders and here was a special wing of the police force, set up to arrest the under ground, who also demanded their share of the extortion pool. To whom could the people now turn? These are lessons before us and that is why it is imperative that, in all such situations, the leadership of the police force should be very carefully chosen.

The same rules apply to the civil administration. We have seen the way politicians and bureaucrats siphoned away development funds, diverted essential commodities to the black market and built roads on paper. It is very necessary to screen all the civil servants in such a situation and list out the personnel who are honest and not tainted with underground sympathies. One of the most important steps to be undertaken is to ensure that all essential commodities of the PDS are made available to the public in the remotest villages at correct prices. This is not too difficult a task as was demonstrated by an experiment undertaken during the recent phase of President's rule in the State. When President's rule was declared in June 2001, kerosene oil was being sold at Rs. 25 to Rs. 30 in Imphal and consumers were getting merely one or two litres per month. The condition was much worse in the districts and in remote villages where the PDS was defunct. Of the approximately 100 tankers of petrol, diesel and kerosene oil coming to Imphal weekly, approximately 30 tankers of kerosene oil would not even report at the Indian Oil Corporation (IOC) depot, but would drive to the dealers, who would divert most of the supply to the black market. The huge storage reservoirs of the IOC depot were empty for many months. The main valley underground groups, of course, had their share in this diversion. The PLA, UNLF, PREPAK and others regularly took two to three tankers of kerosene oil and sold them in the black market. The traders did the rest of the black marketing. However, when the Central Reserve Police Force (CRPF) was deployed in the IOC depot and movement of unauthorised personnel strictly restricted, the members of the 'finance wing' of the underground groups found that they had no access to the depot. All tankers coming from Dimapur were stopped at Mao on the Manipur border, the challans (receipts) taken from them and escorted to Imphal by the Manipur Rifles. In Imphal, they were parked in the Manipur Rifles campus for the night and escorted to the depot in groups. There, storage tanks were filled for the first time in several months. From the depot, the Manipur Rifles escorted kerosene oil tankers to the district dealers. In Imphal, 50 per cent of the dealer's quota was directed to be sold in mobile sale directly by the dealer to the public on ration cards – ten liters per family, at Rs. 8 per litre. This was supervised. Long queues of women and children were a familiar sight and consequently, people secured kerosene oil at the correct price. There were some attempts by the underground to disrupt the sale. However, no one had the courage to buck the public when the government was doing a correct job. Within a month, the black market price of kerosene oil had come down to Rs. 11 to Rs. 12 per litre in the city. It was reliably learnt that one or two underground groups diverted two to three tankers of kerosene oil from some of the dealers, but sheepishly returned them, as they could not find any buyers. In the districts where the Deputy Commissioners were honest, they were able to get kerosene oil to the interior villages by escorting the tankers or by carrying the kerosene oil in drums. Very effectively, both the traders and the underground were defeated. Not giving up the fight, one of the underground groups served a notice on the IOC depot to pay Rs. 10 lakhs to them. The staff sensibly reported this to the police. The staff quarters were adjacent to the storage depot and were guarded by the CRPF and several telephone calls were made to the IOC manager. He was told not to respond to the calls and to confine himself to his quarters after work. The CRPF was directed to enhance their vigil and always escort the manager and his staff. The IOC management was contacted and requested to post personnel for two months at a time to the depot at Imphal. They co-operated. There was one attempt to abduct the manager when he crossed from one depot to the other, but two CRPF guards who were alert escorted him and the group gave up the attempt even before they could get started. After several more futile calls, the group gave up the attempt. Constant monitoring and visits by senior officers thwarted the attempt of the underground in this case.

It is very necessary to ensure that all civil police and judicial officers are guarded both at office and in their residences. For this the Union Home Ministry must set apart two to three battalions of the CRPF and direct the State police to see that they guard the offices, residences and escort all these officials. In the case of engineers, forest officers and officers of development departments, all of them should be escorted to their work sites. The counter-insurgency grid must, therefore, visualize a sizeable force. The main area for extortions is, of course, Imphal. Extensive coverage of the city is absolutely necessary. Continual cordon and search operations are also unavoidable. It must be ensured that all such operations are done in the presence of magistrates. While all this is done, it should be ensured that the civil administration has been cleaned up and the public is getting essential commodities at correct prices and does not have to pay to get recruited or promoted. If the people feel that the government is responsible they will tolerate the inconvenience and indignity of cordon and searches. But, if it is the same corrupt government, then they will only be further alienated. One way to ensure positive results is to see that officers at the highest levels are accessible to the public.

One sphere in which the State has done well is that of agriculture. Currently the valley, with approximately 20 per cent double cropping, produces enough rice to feed 80 per cent of the population of the whole State. This can easily be improved by concentrating on minor irrigation schemes, and with double cropping brought upto 80 per cent. Within two to three years, Manipur can be made a surplus State in rice. In the hills, there is tremendous scope for horticulture, piggery, fisheries, poultry farming and dairy farming. It will also be necessary to take up conversion of slash and burn agriculture to terrace farming. A number of roads will have to be constructed to link the interiors with market towns. The beautiful Khoupum valley produces excellent oranges, which are wasted as the road to Bishnupur has been abandoned. The construction of roads into the interior should be co-ordinated with the setting up of the counter-insurgency grid in the hills.

The main concentration of deployment in the hills should be in the districts of Chandel and Churachandpur, the hinterland of the main valley groups. A careful study will show that most of the tracks in the hills are along the ridgelines or along the river valleys. It is imperative, therefore, to deploy along all the ridgelines in these two districts. Extensive use of helicopters for logistics is unavoidable. Once this is done, the groups will have no choice but to slip into Myanmar. Once this happens and the ridgelines and valleys in these two districts are held, it will be necessary to deploy the Border Security Force (BSF) on the Arunachal Pradesh, Nagaland, Manipur and Mizoram international border with Myanmar. Although this is an expensive proposition, it is imperative that such measures are undertaken.

In the hills, the counter-insurgency operations must first concentrate on the rebel Kuki groups, like the United Kuki Liberation Front (UKLF), the KRA and the Zomi Revolutionary Army (ZRA) who have links with the NSCN-IM. There is always the tendency to use one group against the other. This has been done in Jammu and Kashmir, in Assam using the SULFA against the ULFA, and in Manipur using groups like the ZRA against the PLA. Such a strategy should never be resorted to. It is not only immoral and unethical but also counter-productive to arm any group or allow it to keep arms. There should be no question of anyone having unlicensed arms. The aim of the counter-insurgency operations should be to see that not a single unlicensed arm remains with anyone. There should be no question of any group feeling insecure, and consequently buying arms for their security. The NSCN-IM should not be allowed to keep any arms in Manipur and such a measure should be strictly enforced. This group has been pampered beyond measure.

After the smaller groups are de-fanged, the major valley groups should be taken on. In the hills, particularly in Chandel and Churachandpur, the ridgelines should be occupied and the main camps taken on in the river valleys. While these operations are being conducted, the valley areas should be carefully cordoned so that the groups do not filter back. This will force the groups to go to Myanmar and then to Bangladesh. The deployment of BSF on the borders should now be taken up. Simultaneously, the BRO should take up extensive construction of roads on the borders. As and when the interior areas are cleared, the civil effort should follow on the heels of the armed forces. The armed forces deployment should continue till the roads are constructed, water supply schemes implemented, electricity conductors and substations set up, health centres opened, horticultural and other schemes taken up. While this is being done, the government should gradually privatize. There are many spheres where the government should disengage, like in the spheres of collection of power tariff, irrigation, cess, etc. Government can also disengage in the field of education and health care. This should be given increasingly to the missionary institutions.

During the counter-insurgency operations, magistrates and police should be associated with all cordon and search operations. Suspects picked up by the armed forces should be handed over to joint interrogation centres immediately. All cadres from whom weapons are recovered should be detained under the National Security Act (NSA) and their trials under the Arms Act or other special acts should be closely monitored. Special courts should be set up for such purposes. Whenever interim stay orders are granted, the higher courts must be appealed to and the stays vacated. Special day-to-day hearings should be carried out in all-important cases.

It must be borne in mind that India's powerful neighbour China is not far from Manipur and the North East. All the major insurgent groups in the North East have at one time or the other met the Chinese government and secured arms from them. Currently, the Myanmar's government has become heavily dependent on them. The Myanmar army is equipped with Chinese arms. It is reliably learnt that arms from the Chinese ordnance factories are trickling into the clandestine arms market in Myanmar. Recently, the Myanmar special unit NA-SA-KA (Border Control Unit), is reported to have arrested 36 cadres of the valley insurgents from Kalemyo and seized 1600 weapons from them.[23] It is learnt that the cadres were released after payment of heavy fines. The Myanmar army retained the weapons. All the weapons were reported to be of Chinese origin. The question is, were the weapons released to the arms market by accident or by design?

One must clearly understand that Manipur is geographically, ethnically and linguistically South East Asian. We have neglected this beautiful land and beautiful people too long. Instead of nurturing this Frontier State we have allowed its politics and administration to degenerate. Despite all this, the people are remarkably patient. When one visits remote villages with an inaccessible dirt road, no water supply, no electricity, no primary health centre and a dilapidated primary or middle school without any teachers, one is astonished by the warmth of the welcome given by the people for just visiting their village. One feels ashamed. The State is so small and population so limited, it is not difficult to usher in progress. All that one requires is the will.

With three major ethnic groups in Manipur, its insurgency is also primarily divided into insurgent groups of Meitei, Naga and Kuki. While the Meitei insurgents' prime objective is to free their pre-British territorial boundary from "Indian occupation", the Naga insurgents of Manipur support the demand of sovereign 'Nagalim' (Greater Nagaland) comprising of Nagaland along with the Naga majority areas of Manipur, Assam, Arunachal Pradesh and Burma (Myanmar). The Kukis on the other hand support the demand of separate Kukiland for which Kukis of Burma are also fighting.

Encouraged with the growth of Naga insurgency, a section of Meitei youths under the leadership of Hijam Irabot, a local communist leader opposed the merger of Manipur in Indian Union and set-up Manipur Red Guard with a view to wage war for liberation of this state from Indian occupation. This first symptom of secessionist tendency among the Meiteis gave birth to ethnicisation of politics in this state. The revolt though, failed to draw mass support and gradually fizzled out particularly after the death of Irabot, ethnic politics remained the focal point in the state, which even continues today.

The insurgency in Manipur like other states of northeast began with an ideology for restoration of the pre-British politico-ethnic supremacy of the Meiteis, later turned into ethnic conflict and finally entered into a cross-current of socio-political whirlpool due to individualised interest of the multiplying leaders of its respective insurgent groups. The Meiteis in the valley viewed the growth of Naga militancy in Nagaland and its close link with the Nagas of Manipur as danger to their political supremacy in the state. With a view to restore their pre-British pride some of the educated Meitei youths known to be the followers of Irabot regrouped and formed United National Liberation Front (UNLF) in 1964 under the leadership of Arambam Somorendra Singh and launched an underground movement. With sustained anti-Indian campaign a breakaway group of UNLF later established an underground government called Revolutionary Government of Manipur (RGM) under the leadership of Oinam Sudhir Kumar with its headquarter in erstwhile East Pakistan.

The Nagas and the Kukis of Manipur initially remained indifferent to the Meitei rebels to their obsession to respective ethnic politics. The Nagas of Manipur were supporting the movement of National Socialist Council of

Nagaland (NSCN) demanding a sovereign 'Nagalim' (greater Nagaland) including the Naga inhabited territory of Assam, Manipur, Arunachal Pradesh and Burma. The Kukis, who live side by side with the Nagas however, never supported the latter instead often clashed with them and formed underground group to fight for their separate sovereign identity. The Kukis were getting support from Kuki National Organization (KNO) and Kuki National Army (KNA) the insurgent groups in Burma. Similar to the demand of separate Kukiland in Burma, the Kukis of Manipur too came up with a demand for separate Kuki district and subsequently for a separate Kuki state.

Defeat of Pakistan in Indo-Pak war of 1971 and emergence of Bangladesh was a great set back to Meitei insurgents operating from the pre-war East Pakistan. Indian security forces arrested a number of insurgents but most of them were gradually released and the secessionist movement apparently subsided for a while. However, by late 1970s and early eighties the UNLF cadres, who were reportedly trained in erstwhile East Pakistan and China regrouped and revived their movement with the objective of 'liberating Manipur from Indian occupation through armed struggle'. The insurgents asserted that their territory was forcibly merged with India and therefore, they had waged armed struggle for restoration of Manipur's independence (Encyclopaedia of Northeast India – H. M. Barek, 2001). They founded a number of underground organizations prominently Peoples Liberation Army (PLA) led by Nameirakpam Bisheshwar allegedly a China trained rebel in 1978, People's Revolutionary Party of Kangleipak (PREPAK) led by R. K. Tulachandra in 1977, Kangleipak Communist Party (KCP) in 1980 etc. They started lawless violence in Manipur valley and indulged in looting of banks, raiding police stations, killing of police personnel, snatching their arms and so on.

The first violent incident in the post-statehood history of Manipur was noticed on July 17, 1978 when, a Manipur Sub-Inspector of police along with a constable was shot dead in Imphal, which shocked the unprepared state police. The rebels escaped with the revolver of the deceased. The state later was placed under President's rule and the Government declared a number of insurgents organizations as unlawful associations under Unlawful Activities (Preventing) Act 1967. With declaration of entire Manipur Valley as disturbed area and imposition of Armed Forces (Special Power) Act, 1958, the security forces took strong actions and succeeded in killing almost all the front ranking insurgent leaders in encounter. They also arrested Bisheswar the founder leader of PLA and contained the insurgency to a great extent.

By late 1980s PLA cadres regrouped again and revived their activities. It formed Revolutionary People's Front (RPF) as its political front and also a united front of Meitei rebel organizations under the banner of Revolutionary Joint Committee (RJC). Indo-Burma Revolutionary Front comprising of various northeast ethnic insurgent groups including ULFA of Assam, NCSN (K) of Nagas and KNA of Kukis was also formed in 1990 though, it failed to make any significant dent in the movement. Later the Meitei rebels formed Manipur People's Liberation Front (MPLF) incorporating UNLF, PLA and PREPAK. Now the avowed objective of the PLA is to organize a revolutionary front covering the entire northeast and unite all ethnic groups, including the Meiteis, Nagas and Kukis to liberate Manipur. PLA, though, a Meitei outfit claims itself to be a trans-tribal organization seeking to lead the non-Meiteis as well. It is alleged that the PLA has a government in exile in Sylhet district of Bangladesh with two training camps and five camps in Myanmar.

By mid nineties, the insurgents also raised the issue of outsiders (Mayangs) and the Muslims (Pangals). A clash between Meiteis and Pangals in 1993 resulted in large number of deaths. Following the massacre of Muslims some militant Islamic outfits like Northeast Minority Front (NEMF), Islamic National Front (INF), Islamic Revolutionary Front (IRF), United Islamic Liberation Army (UILA), Islamic Liberation Front (ILF), People's United Liberation Front (PULF) were founded in Manipur valley to counter the challenge of Meitei insurgents.

Insurgents, their Strength and Ethnic Loyalty

By the end of last millennium the estimated strength of the cadres of various insurgent groups operating in hills and valley of Manipur reached around twenty thousand. According to an intelligence report, 19,590 insurgents and extremists were operating both in valley and hill areas of Manipur by 2001 (Bleeding Manipur by Phanjoubam Tarapot, Har Anand Publication, New Delhi, 2003, page 178). Another book (Insurgency or Ethnic Conflict by S. C. Sharma, Magnum, 2000, page 217-18) listed emergence of 34 insurgent groups including ten inactive in the state. Leaving apart the ten inactive groups the list includes the following: Peoples Liberation Army (PLA), United National Liberation Front (UNLF), Revolutionary Peoples Front (RPF), People's Revolutionary Party of Kangleipak (PREPAK), Manipur Liberation Front Army (MLFA), Kanglei Yawol Khnna Lup (KYKL), Revolutionary Joint Committee (RJC), Kangleipak Communist Party (KCP), Peoples United Liberation Front (PULF), National Socialist Council of Nagaland (NSCN-K), National Socialist Council of Nagaland (NSCN-I/M), Naga Lim Guard (NLG), Kuki National Front (KNF), Kuki National Army (KNA), Kuki Defence Force (KDF), Kuki Democratic Movement (KDM), Kuki National Organization (KNO), Kuki Security Force (KSF), Chin Kuki Revolutionary Front (CKRF), Kom Rem Peoples Convention (KRPC), Zomi Revolutionary Volunteers (ZRV), Zomi Revolutionary Army (ZRA), Zomi Reunification Organization (ZRO), and Hmar Peoples Convention (HPC).

Among over thirty militant groups, three Meitei militant outfits namely UNLF, PLA and PREPAK are most active in Manipur valley. They are presently under a unified platform namely Manipur People's Liberation Front which they had formed in 1999 with Rajkumar Meghen @ Sanayaima (Chairman of UNLF) as convener but maintaining their independent identity with their respective strength which is as under:

- UNLF – Rajkumar Meghen @ Sanayaima (Chairman), Khundongbam Tomba @ Sunil or Pambi (General Secretary), A. Wangpa (Secretary), M. Nongyai (Secretary Organization) and N. Thabal (Secretary of Publicity). With Manipur People's Army (MPA) as its armed wing and estimated cadre strength of 2500 it also maintains link with RPF, NSCN-K, ULFA, KNF, KYKL-T, National Liberation Front of Tripura (NLFT) besides PLA and PREPAK.
- PLA – Irengbam Bhorot @ Chaoren (Chairman), Manoharmayum (Vice-Chairman) and estimated cadre strength of 3000. Apart from UNLF and PREPAK it is also maintaining link with KCP, NSCN – K, ULFA, Tripura People's Democratic Front (TPDF), and Kachin Independent Army (KIA) of Myanmmar. It reportedly also received weapons from KIA. It is known to have largest following among the Meiteis.
- PREPAK – Achamba Singh @ Subhas (Chairman), Palliba Singh (General Secretary) and Tajila (C-in-C) With estimated cadre strength of 1500, it also maintains link with KYKL-T and NSCN – I/M which trained its activists. It also received arms from KIA.

All the three groups have common objective to free Manipur from Indian occupation. All of them are having their training camps in neighbouring Burma and Bangladesh. Apart from these three most active groups KYKL-O, KYKL – T and KCP are also operating in the valley though their strength is relatively much less. Both the factions of NSCN, and Kuki outfits are actively operating in the Hills of Manipur. While the estimated strength of NSCN-I/M in Manipur is 6000, NSCN-K's strength is 3500.

Most of these underground organizations waged war either for sovereign Manipur state or for forming different smaller independent states by dividing the present Manipur. Government of India being common target of all the insurgent groups of entire northeast however worked as a common link between them, which they have been maintaining even today. As per a survey report (Survey of Conflict and Resolution in India's Northeast – Ajai Sahni) cumulative total of fatalities in insurgencies in Manipur between 1992 to April 2002 was 3090. The deaths include Civilians, security forces and militants.

Corruption, Drug Running and Nexus between Militants and Politicians

The sequence of events shows that the core ideology of all the insurgent groups moved around their respective distinct ethnic identity. With number of splinter groups due to individualised interest and personal ambition of the leaders, factional feud among them coupled with, realignment with different insurgent groups of entire northeast, and their support link with various foreign powers pushed the insurgency in a cross-current of strange socio-political whirlpool. Inter ethnic clashes over control in drug trafficking added another dimension to insurgency. This also encouraged other smaller tribes like Paite, Vaiphei and Hmar in establishing their respective armed groups. Criminalisation of insurgency, clandestine link of its leaders with various political parties, NGOs, Government officials and their pressure on allotment of Government contract works made the process of peace initiative more complicated.

Notwithstanding the continuous native rule by democratically elected successive governments after the departure of colonial power, frequent defection by opportunist, selfish and corrupt political leaders for sharing power put the state under socio-political confusion and the common people are facing the brunt of the ongoing turmoil in the state.

Protracted deployment of security forces in the state to handle the situation caused lot of inconvenience to common citizens and lawless violence perpetrated by the insurgents not merely disrupted the socio-economic development of the people but pushed them to the economic backwardness. This gave rise to compounding unemployment problem leading to involvement of youths in drug trafficking for easy money. The political leaders of the state irrespective of their political affiliation due to individualised interests are more bothered to share political power than to find out a peaceful solution to the problem of insurgency. They do not approve any strong action by Government of India to deal with the situation. They often sabotaged the peace initiative by the Government with any insurgent group due to their vested interests. The national leadership in the country too is more interested in power politics than to have a lasting solution to the problem, which has perhaps left the people in disarray.

Common citizens who want a normal and peaceful life are fed up with the no-win situation and their recent outburst in November 2004 over the custodial death of Manorama, a local lady was the frustrations of the people against the Government. This has again surcharged the atmosphere of Manipur valley thick and heavy. They wanted withdrawal of the Armed Forces (Special Power) Act and indulged in lawless violence in the region. Sensing the mood of the people, the state Government decided to de-notify this Act without concurrence of the Union Government. This shows a perceptual difference between state and centre in assessing the situation, which would adversely affect the ongoing peace initiative in the region.

Factors that Sustained Insurgency

Peace initiative by the Government of India ever since the insurgency began – failed to bring any negotiated settlement due to many factors such as:

- Failure of the national leadership in constitutional and cultural integration of the various ethnic groups of isolated northeast with the rest of diverse Indian society.
- Multiplicity of insurgent organizations.
- Top leaders of prominent insurgent groups are seldom interested in negotiated peace as "their children study in the best schools abroad and their family live in luxury" (Insurgency or Ethnic Conflict by S. C. Sharma, 2000, page 215).
- Obstacle by Drug Traffickers, who control huge amount of underground economy with their money-spinning strength. Return of normalcy will hamper their unlawful business.
- Higher levels of corruption in State agencies, which are responsible for utilisation of substantial fund allocated by the centre for developmental programmes. Central Government has been bearing about 90 per cent of the state budget but economic and industrial development is negligible.
- Negligible benefit to the common people through developmental programmes alienated them from the centre.
- Connivance between corrupts officials and the insurgents created underground economy under the control of the secessionists.
- It is alleged that the insurgent organizations collect monthly donations from government employees. "Going by the sources, the collection of money by various underground groups was nearly 100 crores of rupees a year" (Bleeding Manipur by Phanjoubam Tarapot, Har Anand Publication, New Delhi, 2003, page 54).
- Prolonged stay of security forces in the region has annoyed the people.
- Poor generation of employment opportunity for educated youths.
- Constant external support to all the insurgent groups.
- Liberalised trans-border movements with weak neighbours like Burma and Bangladesh wherefrom the insurgents operate conveniently.
- Demographic imbalance due to unabated illegal infiltration from Bangladesh, which has not been tackled by the Central Government effectively. The central leadership placed party interest above of the nation due to vote bank politics. Lt. Gen. (Retd.) S. K. Sinha, PVSM, Governor of Jammu and Kashmir in his foreword in ACDIS (Arms Control, Disarmament, and International Security) Paper written by Jaideep Saikia quoted B. K. Nehru, Governor of Assam in late sixties saying: "The East Bengal Muslim was the main vote bank of the Congress party in Assam. Chaliha (then Chief Minister of Assam) doing as he did from the days of freedom struggle, was governed by the value of that time. He placed the national interest above those of the party. But the High Command thought otherwise. The party interests

were paramount. Chaliha was ordered to stop the nonsense forthwith. This was of course welcomed by the Government of Pakistan. It had always pretended, as Bangladesh does now, that there is no migration from its territory to Assam". The present Muslim population in Manipur has increased to about 8 per cent of total state population, which were only around 4 per cent in 1901. Sinha also quoted Lt. Gen. Jameel Mahmood, the then GOC-in-C, Eastern Command telling him in 1992 that "unabated illegal migration from Bangladesh into Assam and Bengal has been posing a serious problem for our national security".

- Political leadership at centre has failed to instil confidence among the natives regarding its peace initiative since 1997. The ongoing peace-talk with NSCN (I/M) has aggravated their apprehension that the government might concede the demand of underground Naga militants for 'Nagalim' (Greater Nagaland) by unification of Nagaland with the Naga majority areas of Assam, Manipur, Arunachal Pradesh and Myanmar.
- Non-Naga populations of Manipur do not like the idea of any territorial division of Manipur. Ever since the peace initiative by the government with a selected group of insurgents (NSCN-I/M) they organized protest rallies time to time. A huge rally of over five lakh people in the state capital Imphal on 1st August 1997 under the banner of All Manipur United Club Organization (AIMUCO), a non-political body appeared to be a mass upsurge to oppose any such attempt. Similar rally was also organized in September 2000 as well as in June 2001.
- Extension of ceasefire agreement between Government of India and NSCN (I/M) was never liked by the Non-Nagas of Manipur.

A close examination of the situation shows that the goals of the insurgents in Manipur are in conflict, which in long run will doom their own people if they ignore the ground reality. The scenario reflects the uncertain, anarchic and chaotic future of the state. With about 350 km of international border and people of hostile attitude the ongoing insurgency is a not only a matter of security concern but is also relevant in the context of national unity.

FOOTNOTES

1. The National Socialist Council of Nagaland — Isak-Muivah (NSCN-IM)'s Vision of a 'Greater Nagaland' Includes four Districts of Manipur – Senapati, Ukhrul, Chandel and Tamenglong.
2. The Governor of Nagaland, L. P. Singh, representing the Government of India and the Underground Leadership Represented by Assa and Kevi Yalley, signed the Shillong Accord on November 11, 1975, at Shillong in Meghalaya. See http://nagaland.nic.in/history/shillong.htm.

3. Thuingaleng Muivah and Isak Chi Swu are the General Secretary and Chairman Respectively of the NSCN-IM
4. For a Profile of UNLF, see South Asia Terrorism Portal; Countries; India; States; Manipur; Terrorist Outfits; UNLF; www.satp.org.
5. For a Profile of the PREPAK, see South Asia Terrorism Portal; Countries India; States; Manipur; Terrorist Outfits; PREPAK; www.satp.org.
6. For a Profile of the PLA, see South Asia Terrorism Portal; Countries India; States; Manipur; Terrorist Outfits; PLA; www.satp.org.
7. 61 out of 552 Indian States that integrated into India after independence were the centrally administered areas under the 1949 Original Constitution, which formed Part C States. This categorisation was a part of the effort to create administratively viable units and integrate the Indian States *i.e.*, princely States, which had accepted British 'paramountcy', but were not under direct British rule as were the British India Provinces before independence into the dominion of India. See Durga Das Basu, *Introduction to the Constitution of India*, New Delhi: Prentice Hall of India, 1997, pp. 44-48 and 429.
8. Kangleipak Communist Party was formed under the leadership of Ibohanbi on April 14, 1980. Like PREPAK, its major demand has been the ouster of outsiders.
9. Based on Indian intelligence reports, the Myanmar Army is reported to have destroyed certain UNLF camps. See www.nenanews.com/NEE%20Jan.7%20%2021,%20%2002/GuestC.htm.
10. See "Insurgent groupsin Northeast India", http://www. larouchepub.com/other/1995/2241_ne_india_groups.html.
11. "The Rediff Interview/Luhit Deuri, former ULFA militant", www.rediff.com/news/2001/jan/22inter.htm.
12. Also see "Armed Conflicts Reports 2001", www.ploughshares.ca/content/ACR/ACR00/ACR00-Burma.html
13. Also see "Armed Conflicts Reports 2001", www.ploughshares.ca/content/ACR/ACR00/ACR00-Burma.html
14. See "Democracy at gunpoint", *Frontline*, Chennai, Vol. 19, No. 6, March 16-29, 2002.
15. Speaking to media at Dimapur, Nagaland in July 2001, a senior NSCN-IM leader and convenor of the cease-fire monitoring cell, Phunting Shimrang said, "We collect nominal taxes from individuals as well as business establishments based in Naga-inhabited areas as a contribution towards the Naga cause". According to Shimrang, while the armed wing of the GPRN, the Naga army, collects Rs. 100 per individual per annum as 'ration tax', the GPRN itself levies 24 per cent of an individual's annual income as royalty tax and Rs. 10 as house tax. See "NSCN (I-M) likely to go on a fresh offensive".
16. http://home.nycap.rr.com/nagaland/nnews47.html. Also see "Dy. Chief Minister admits tax collection by Naga insurgents", http://www.nenanews.com/OT%20Jan%207-20Jan%2021,%2000/oh15.htm

17. A Meitei underground group called the Kanglei Yawol Kunna Lup (KYKL), meaning "the Organization to save the revolutionary movement in Manipur" was formed in January 1994 after the merger of the Oken faction of the UNLF, the Meiraba faction of the PREPAK and Ibo Pishak faction of the KCP. For profile of the KYKL, see South Asia Terrorism Portal; Countries; India; States; Manipur; Terrorist Outfits; KYKL;www.satp.org
18. "Insurgent on parole", http://www.northeastvigil.com/newsarch/01121999i.htm.
19. Based on Indian intelligence reports, the Myanmar Army is reported to have destroyed certain UNLF camps. See www.nenanews.com/NEE%20Jan.7%20%2021,%20%2002/GuestC.htm.
20. Kuki National Front was formed under the leadership of Ranco Thangboi Kuki on May 18, 1988. See South Asia Terrorism Portal; Countries; India; States; Manipur; Terrorist Outfits; KNF; www.satp.org.
21. The MCC, a Left-wing Extremist group came into existence, in its earlier version, on October 20, 1969, as *Dakshin Desh*. When the Communist Party of India (Marxist-Leninist) was formed with the merger of several Maoist groups in 1969, one left-wing extremist group, *Dakshin Desh*, did not join and decided to retain its independent identity. In 1975, the outfit was renamed as the Maoist Communist Centre. Currently, the MCC has a presence in the States of Bihar and Jharkhand. See South Asia Terrorism Portal; Countries; India; Terrorist Outfits; MCC; www.satp.org.
22. "Striking at the roots", *The Week*, Cochi, July 2, 2000.
23. In Jammu and Kashmir, one of the first terrorist acts was the killing of District and Sessions Judge Neel Kanth Ganjoo on November 4, 1989. Ganjoo had sentenced Jammu and Kashmir Liberation Front (JKLF) chief Maqbool Butt to death for killing an Indian diplomat in London.

REFERENCES

Dutta, 2001. *Armed Conflicts Reports*, www.ploughshares.ca/content/ACR/ACR00/ACR00-Dutta, 1992. *Autonomy Movement in Assam* .New Delhi: Omsons Publications.

Phanjoubam Tarapot, 2003. *"Bleeding Manipur"*. New Delhi: Har Anand Publications.

Sajal Nag, 2002. *Contesting Marginality*. New Delhi: Manohar Publications..

Democracy at Gunpoint, *Frontline* Vol. 19, No. 6, March 16-29, 2002. Chennai.

Durga Das Basu, *Introduction to the Constitution of India*, New Delhi: Prentice Hall of India, 1997, pp. 44-48 and 429.

Khanna, S. K., 1999. *Encyclopaedia of Northeast*. Indian Publishers.

Bareh, H. M., 2001. *Encyclopaedia of North East India*. New Delhi: Mittal Publications.

Das, N. K., 1989. *Ethnic Identity Ethnicity and Social Stratification in North East India –* Inter – New Delhi: India Publications.

Sareen, H. K., 1980. *Insurgency in North East India*. New Delhi: Sterling Publishers Private Ltd.

Sharma, S. C., 2000. *Insurgency or Ethnic Conflict.* New Delhi: Magnum.

Sanajaoba, N., 2003. *Manipur: A British Anthology. Vol. I.* New Delhi: Akansha Publishing House.

Singh Chandrika, 2004. *Naga Politics: A Critical Account.* New Delhi: Mittal Publications.

Kuhoi Zhimomi, K., 2004. *Politics and Militancy in Nagaland.* New Delhi: Deep and Deep Publications Private Ltd.

Coch, 2000. Striking at the roots. *The Week,* July 2.

Lokendra Singh, N., 1998. *Unquiet Valley.* New Delhi: Mittal Publications.

14

Rise of Extremism in Adivasis (Tribal People) of Kerala

A Close Look on Muthanga Incident

*N. Sumesh

ABSTRACT

Adivasis – meaning original inhabitants – are the indigenous communities that have been living in the forested highlands of Kerala since time immemorial. They are heterogeneous communities that have had historically different relations to land and forests. On this background we can look into the Muthanga incident. On the one side it was a mass struggle for land and life but in the other side the nature of the agitation also got an extremist character.

The unexpected turn of events that led to the Muthanga tragedy was the culmination of the State's inaction on the Adivasis' just demands for a homeland. The State Government failed to keep its promise on the distribution of land to the landless Adivasis as a result hundreds of them 'encroached' upon the Muthanga wild life sanctuary on 5th January, 2003. Days later, policemen fired indiscriminately at the tribal group that included women and children. One tribal was killed in the police firing, while many others were wounded. A policeman who was held hostage by the tribals was also killed in the fight.

* Research Scholar, Department of Political Science, University of Kerala.

The gory incidents in Muthanga attracted international condemnation. The world at large came to know about the kind of hardships the tribals had been undergoing for their very survival. Here the study discusses the questions, why the Tribal (Adivasis) turned this kind of Land agitation? What is the social and political reason behind the rising up of extremism among the Tribals? Will it happen tomorrow? Weather Political parties have any role on that? Why the State behaves like this? We can't consider it as an isolated incident as the agitations are still going on with extremist trends. At the same time the tribal's rightful claim for land still remains unfulfilled even as the State government goes on with its empty promises.

Keywords: Extrimism; Adivasis; Muthanga struggle.

Introduction

Adivasis – meaning original inhabitants – are the indigenous communities that have beening living in the forested highlands of Kerala since time immemorial. Colonial anthropologists and administrators chose to describe these communities as tribes in the process of 'othering' them and the post-colonial state created a 'Scheduled Tribe' slot to include the min the Constitution for affirmative action purpose.[1] There are 84.3 million tribal people (also known as Scheduled Tribes) in India according to the census of 2001. They are present in all the States except Punjab, Haryana, Delhi and the Union Territories of Pondicherry and Chandigarh, and are located mostly in hilly and forest areas. The architects of the Constitution, being conscious of the distinct identity of the tribal communities and their habitat, provided certain articles exclusively devoted to the cause of the tribal people, including Articles 244, 244A, 275(1), 342, 338(A) and 339. Following these provisions in the Constitution aimed at ensuring social, economic and political equity, several specific legislations have been enacted by the Central and State Governments for the welfare and protection of tribal people and their tribal domain.

In general, the contradiction between the tribal community and the State itself has become sharper, translating itself into open conflict in many areas. Almost all over the tribal areas, including Nagaland, Manipur, Tripura, Assam, Jharkhand, Orissa, Chhattisgarh, Maharashtra, Andhra Pradesh and Kerala, tribal people seem to feel a deep sense of exclusion and alienation, which has been manifesting itself in different forms. The Report of the Expert Group on Prevention of Alienation of Tribal Land and its Restoration (October 2004) pointed out that the socio-economic infrastructure among the tribal people is inadequate, thereby contributing to their disempowerment and deprivation. Apart from poverty and deprivation in general, the causes of the tribal movements are many: the most important among them are absence of self-governance, forest policy, excise policy, land related issues, multifaceted forms of exploitation, cultural humiliation and political marginnalisation. Land alienation, forced evictions from land and dispalcement also added to unrest. Failure to implement protective regulations in Scheduled Areas, absence of credit mechanism leading to dependence on money lenders and consequent loss of land and often even violence by the State functionaries added to the problem.[2] The unexpected turn of events that led to the Muthanga tragedy was the culmination of the State's inaction on the Adivasis' just demands for a homeland. When the State government failed to keep its promise on the distribution of land to the landless Adivasis, hundreds of them 'encroached' upon the Muthanga wild life sanctuary on 5th January 2003. Days later, policemen fired indiscriminately at the tribal group that included women and children. One tribal was killed in the police firing, while many others were wounded. A policeman who was held hostage by the tribals was also killed in the fight.

The mainstream media and the State government tried to demonise the tribals by alleging that they were connected with militant groups like the LTTE. There were even attempts to connect the tribals' agitation to Naxal groups. But all these all egations have proved to be groundless as none of these sabre-rattlers or media analysts couldn't establish any terrorist connection. The Chief Minister A. K. Antony had defended the police action by saying that what had happened in Muthanga was an 'armed rebellion'. The gory incidents in Muthanga attracted international condemnation. The world at large came to know about the kind of hardships the tribals had been undergoing for their very survival. The National Human Rights Commission dismissed the reports of both the police and the State government on the incident, and suggested an enquiry by an independent agency like the CBI. Even though the government ordered a CBI enquiry, justice continues to elude the tribals. Worse, the CBI officials have pinned the blame on the Adivasis. Some of the tribals were reportedly even beaten up by the CBI officials during interrogation. The wounds, both physical and psychological, caused by last year's bloody events remain unhealed. Lots of tribals who were wounded in the police action are struggling to get back to normal life. They are the living martyrs of State brutality. Like Velayudhan. After being injured in the police firing, he lives the life of a recluse, cocooned in the darkness of his hut.

This is the first time in the history of Kerala that the Adivasis, who have always been driven from pillar to post, became the target of police firing and brutality which ostensibly resulted in the death of many and maiming of hundreds. Surprising it may be, the casualties consequent upon the police firing are still shrouded in mystery. The fact that the State government has categorically ruled out the possibility of a judicial enquiry on the whole question strengthens the suspicion whether the government has too many skeletons on the cupboard. One still wonders as to why the media personnel were forcibly locked out when the operation got under way against the retreating tribals. During the witch-hunt, which lasted for almost 18 hours, the police cordoned off the entire area creating a panicky situation. Many tribals and human rights activists believe that the police as they went berserk within the forest area would have buried all evidences of its brutality.

Muthanga Struggle: A Legal Background

The tribal people have become more assertive about their rights and the nature of their demands has undergone a subtle transformation. The year 1975 once seemed a crucial one for the marginalised tribal people of the State. Although they did not have a powerful presence in the State, their plight had struck a chord and they had found themselves being offered the protection of a law that promised to end exploitation by non-tribal settlers and forest encroachers, and lack of livelihoods. In April 1975, the State Assembly unanimously adopted the Kerala Scheduled Tribes (Restriction on Transfer of Lands and Restoration of Alienated Lands) Act, which sought to prevent the lands of the tribal people from falling into the hands of non-tribal people. The Act also sought to restore to the tribal people their previously alienated lands. To a large extent, post-Independence governments were responsible for the Adivasis losing their lands. Non-tribal settlers made their plight worse as the pressure on land increased in the plains. The land-people ratio is very high in the State.

In the majority of cases, the ignorance and innocence of the Adivasis were used to the hilt by the non-tribal settler 'farmers'. Either by using force or inducements such as a bundle of tobacco, or by offering a low price, they made the Adivasis part with their 'ancestral land'. In most cases there was no document validating such transfers and some tribal persons were even forced to sign on blank sheets of paper. The non-tribal people who got possession of the lands gradually became the virtual owners. Over the years, alienation from their land of birth pushed the Adivasis into poverty and dependence and forced them to search for other forest land for food and shelter. At the same time the non-tribal society trying to transform the tribal people into their own image.[3] However, the same process was repeated in the new stretches of forest land, and these too became the farmlands of non-tribal settlers. Political parties and successive governments turned a blind eye to the process, as more settlers meant more votes. (The Adivasis, who number 3.21 lakhs, account for only 1.1 per cent of the population of the State.) The social and ecological implications of this were serious. When the 1975 Act got the presidential assent in November that year and was subsequently included in the Ninth Schedule of the Constitution (which ensured that the Act would not be challenged in any court of law), it seemed a dream come true for the Adivasis. But it was not to be. Successive governments allowed more than a decade to pass (during which the encroachments continued, especially in the tribal areas of Palakkad and Wayanad districts) before framing the rules to implement the Act. When the State government finally formulated the rules in 1986, it specified that the Act would come into effect retrospectively from January 1, 1982.

The rules made all transfer of property 'possessed, enjoyed or owned' by Adivasis to non-tribal people between January 1, 1960 and January 1, 1982 'invalid' and directed that the 'possession or enjoyment' of property so transferred be restored to the Adivasis concerned. However, the Act required that the Adivasi return the amount, if any, they had received during the original transaction and pay compensation for any improvements made on the land by the non-tribal occupants. The government was to advance this amount to the tribal people as loans and recover it from them in 20 years. Only about 8,500 applications seeking restoration were received from the tribal people, because most of them were either unaware of the new law or afraid to accept the offer of loans or were cheated by the corrupt encroacher-official nexus. Hence, even after the framing of the rules, the general atmosphere helped only to encourage the encroachers to continue to occupy tribal land and successive governments took no action to implement fully the 1975 Act. This triggered the second important phase of the Adivasi struggle. In 1986, Dr. Nalla Thampi Thera, a non-tribal person from Wayanad district, approached the Kerala High Court seeking a direction to the State government to implement the 1975 Act. It took five years for the court to give a verdict – a favourable one – on the public interest petition. In October 1993, the court ordered the government to implement the Act within six months. Yet the case dragged on for two and a half years with the government continuing to seek extensions of deadline to implement the Act.

Finally, in 1996 the court fixed a final deadline of September 30, 1996 to evict the non-tribal occupants, if necessary with the help of the police, and threatened the officials concerned with contempt of court proceedings if they failed to implement the court directive. However, the government responded with yet another controversial act of amending the 1975 Act. Meanwhile as the non-tribal settlers where getting entrenched in the alienated land of the tribal people, the tribal people themselves were getting increasingly disillusioned with the ability of the government and the courts to find a remedy for their plight. Hence, although government programmes had helped improve the lot of many tribal people, the majority of them continued to be landless, had no means of livelihood, and became more dependent on the non-tribal settlers for work and wages.

As a large section of the landless tribal people had not filed applications and were hence outside the purview of the 1975 Act, they were ineligible for a piece of land even if the Act was implemented in toto. By the early 1990s, the first signs of discontent were already becoming evident in the Adivasi-inhabited areas, especially in Wayanad district, where some extremist groups had been active for a long time. On the other hand, most of the land from which the settlers were to be evicted under the 1975 Act had by the 1990s been in their possession for 15 to 30 years. They were cultivating the land and had constructed buildings and other structures on them. In several cases, the next generation of the original encroachers was in possession of the lands. When the State government could get no more extensions of the deadline from the High Court, the politically and economically powerful settler-farmers activated their organizations and raised the demand to amend the 'impractical provisions' of the 1975 Act.

To the consternation of the tribal people, successive governments started to give in to the demands of the settlers. Two ordinances seeking to amend the 1975 Act, introduced by the United Democratic Front government during early 1996 and later by the Left Democratic Front government, which came to power in May 1996, did not get the Governor's approval. As pressure from the court mounted on the government to evict encroachers by September 30, 1996, the government hastily introduced an amendment Bill in the State Assembly. Whatever may have been the justification for it – the impracticality of the provisions of the 1975 Act perhaps being the most important one – it must have been an eye-opener for the mushrooming tribal organizations in Kerala to see the 140-member State Assembly pass the Kerala Scheduled Tribes (Restriction on Transfer of Land and Restoration of Alienated Lands) Amendment Bill, 1996 almost unanimously (there was only one dissenting vote).

Adivasi Land Struggle: An Extrimistic Turn

The 1996 Amendment Bill dashed all hopes of the Adivasis. Most important, it made legal all transactions of tribal land up to January 24, 1986. In other words, the government made the need for the restoration of alienated land (as per the 1975 Act) unnecessary. According to the government, it was the only practical alternative, given the turmoil and the political repercussions that would have been created had it tried to evict the non-tribal settlers. However, the tribal people felt that the government was trying to give legal sanctity to the alienation of their land. The agitation in front of the State Assembly, with the Adivasis, led by their leader from Wayanad C. K. Janu, trying to enter the State legislature, supported by a group of Communist Party of India (Marxist-Leninist) volunteers, was perhaps an early indication of the gradual transformation of the agitation.

This was soon followed by one of the best known incidents in the struggle. On October 4, 1996, a so-far unknown extremist group named 'Ayyankali Pada' (named after a Dalit leader from Kerala), stormed the Palakkad Collectorate and held Collector W. R. Reddy hostage for over nine hours. The incident invited a strong response from the government against growing signs of radicalism among Adivasis and also in a way prevented the agitation from taking a turn for the worse. Later, the President refused to give assent to the 1996 Amendment Bill passed by the State Assembly on the grounds that the 1975 Act had been included in the Ninth Schedule of the Constitution. However, to bypass this difficulty, yet another Bill was passed unanimously by the State Assembly in 1999. The Kerala Restriction on Transfer by and Restoration of Lands to Scheduled Tribes Bill, 1999, defined 'land' as 'agricultural land' (a State subject) in order to try and get over the need to send it for presidential assent. The new Bill also had a controversial provision to repeal the 1975 Act.

As per the 1999 Act, only alienated land in excess of two hectares possessed by encroachers would be restored, while alternative land, in lieu of the alienated land not exceeding two hectares, would be given elsewhere. The thinking was that the number of applicants claiming land in excess of two hectares would be negligible, making restoration unnecessary. The new Bill also had a provision to provide up to 40 acres (16 hectares) to other landless tribal people – a new set of beneficiaries – within two years. The government said that it estimated that there were about 11,000 such families in the State. However, the High Court rejected both the 1996 and 1999 Amendment Bills and declared the provisions under them illegal. The State government, in turn, went on appeal to the Supreme Court and obtained stay orders. Several appeals against the stay orders were pending before the Supreme Court.[4]

It was in this context that starvation deaths were reported from the Adivasi-inhabited areas in the State from July 2001. The outside world came to know about it only after a group of tribal people, supported by some naxalite groups, waylaid a mobile store run by the State Department of Civil Supplies and took away its contents. They distributed the foodstuffs and encouraged the tribal people who gathered there to take home the rest of it.

Conclusion

It was on 19 February, 2003: the day when a ruthless State with all its brutal force suppressed the genuine cause of the weak and the marginalised The events that led to the Muthanga was the culmination of the State's inaction on the Adivasis' just demands for a homeland. But the unrestful agitation by the Tribal was not favoring extrimistic way for justice. It may, must have political and social reasons.

C. K. Janu, Chairperson Adivasi Gothra Maha Sabha and President Adivasi Rashtriya Maha Sabha, said that, "First the government pretended that not sufficient land was available to distribute among all the adivasis. But the AGMS (Adivasi gothra Maha Sabha) corroborated it by evidence and facts. At present 11 lakhs hectares of land is under the unofficial custody of the governmentt in the state and even if it is distributed among the 3.5

lakhs adivasis only 1.5 lakh hectare is needed for this purpose. Then the Government came forward made an agreement with AGMS. Accordingly every Adivasi family would get 1 to 5 acres of land, as per the availability of land in the state. The govt agreed that this process would start within the allotted term of five years of this government. But other than making this agreement the government did not heed any interest to implement it. Initially they allotted land to 3000 families. After that gradually they stopped it. So in order to compel the government to implement the agreement the adivasis encroached the forest land at Muthanga, made hutments and agitated there for 43 days". While then Chief Minister A. K. Antony claimed that his government was more sympathetic to the tribal people's cause than the previous government, other leaders of the ruling coalition said there were vested interests behind the agitation. There are also allegations that organizations and political parties more sympathetic to the interests of the settler farmers are now supporting the tribal people in order to prevent them from demanding the restoration of alienated land, especially when the legality of the amendments striking down the 1975 Act is coming up as an issue before the Supreme Court. But as Janu told Kerala's Adivasis are not fighting the settler farmers any longer. However, the Adivasi agitation is overshadowed by another one – the shift in demand will genuinely help the tribal people's cause. Who are responsible in making extrimistic mode of agitation among the tribals? Both the successive fronts are answerable, tribals arec the victims of either government or extristic political supporters. Obviously it is State's responsibilty to provide land and shelter to the indigeneous poulation. The indigenous peoples' articulation of identity as *adivasis* and the re-articulation of their sub-identities as particular communities with specific spiritual and material attachment to place can be viewed as conjunctural positionings that would serve them well in their struggle for land without an exrtimist identity, and the State can redefine them with social inclusion by giving constitution guarantees.

REFERENCES

1. Jose Kjosavik, Darley Articulating Identities in the Struggle for Land: The Case of the Indigenous People (*Adivasis)* of Highland Kerala, South India p. 1.
2. Government of India (2004), *Report of the Expert Group on Prevention of Alienation of Tribal Land and its Restoration* (New Delhi: Ministry of Rural Development).
3. A. K. Singh, (1984), Tribal Development in India, New Delhi, p. 5.
4. R. Krishnakumar, The Adivasi struggle in Front Line, October 13 - 26, 2001 Volume 18 - Issue 21.

15

Displaced Massai

A Study on An Ethnic Group in East Africa

*Fr. I. Sekar

ABSTRACT

Africa is the second largest continent in the World and it covers 20.4 per cent of total surface of earth and 14.72 per cent of population. It constitutes 56 sovereign states and number of Islands. There are hundreds of ethnic groups in each states and unity in diversity is the nature of Africa. The study focuses on Massai tribe in East Africa who are well known for their cultural heritage and migration. They keep migrating since from 15th Century starting from North Africa, along the Nile valley to Northern Kenya and boarding Tanzania and Kenya. They count nearly one million population and for centuries known as nomadic pastoralist living in the forest. Their economy is centered on cattles, which are the sign of wealth. The traders exploit the Massai in paying low price and make huge margin in urban. With all that the frequent drought chased the Massai from place to place. And in 19th Century British land allotment for developmental activities in Kenya and Tanzanian Government creation of wildlife reserves and national parks alienated.

* Research Scholar, Department of Applied Research, Gandhigram Rural University, GRI, Gandhigram.

Today Massai live in surrounding to game reserves in Kenya and Tanzania. Modern Maasai's known for their beadwork and ornamentation of the body. Often the non-Massai and tourist get attracted and pay for this service. The centauries nomadic pastoralist turned to be of bead workers, watchman in urban areas and small traders are the consequences of civilization and deforestation. The Governments don't have proper rehabilitation programmes for them. Historic research design is used in this study. The study describes the richness of Massai tribe in East Africa, their struggle for survival and their contribution to the national tourism. It enables the policy-makers to make proper rehabilitation programme for the affected tribes while carrying out activities like mining and construction of dams.

Keywords: Massai tribe; cultural heritage; economy; religion.

Introduction

Africa is the second largest continent in the World and it covers 20.4 per cent of total surface of earth and 14.72 per cent of population. It constitutes 56 sovereign states and number of Islands. There are hundreds of ethnic groups in each states and unity in diversity is the nature of Africa. The study focuses on Massai tribe in East Africa who are well known for their cultural heritage and migration. They keep migrating since from 15th Century starting from North Africa, along the Nile valley to Northern Kenya and boarding Tanzania and Kenya. They count nearly one million population and for centuries known as nomadic pastoralist living in the forest. Their economy is centered on cattles, which are the sign of wealth. The traders exploit the Massai in paying low price and make huge margin in urban. With all that the frequent drought chased the Massai from place to place. And in 19th Century British land allotment for developmental activities in Kenya and Tanzanian Government creation of wildlife reserves and national parks alienated.

Today Massai live in surrounding to game reserves in Kenya and Tanzania. Modern Maasai's known for their beadwork and ornamentation of the body. Often the non Massai and tourist get attracted and pay for this service. The centauries nomadic pastoralist turned to be of bead workers, watchman in urban areas and small traders are the consequences of civilization and deforestation. The Governments don't have proper rehabilitation programmes for them. Historic research design is used in this study. The study describes the richness of Massai tribe in East Africa, their struggle for survival and their contribution to the national tourism. It enables the policy-makers to make proper rehabilitation programme for the affected tribes while carrying out activities like mining and construction of dams.

Significance of Africa

Africa is the second largest continent in the World and it covers 20.4 per cent of total surface of earth and 14.72 per cent of population. African population is much smaller than in Asia, but the growth rate is highest of any continent. Africa constitutes 56 sovereign states and number of Islands. There are hundreds of ethnic groups in each states and unity in diversity is nature of Africa. The outer world understands Africa as a dark continent, a jungle, a wildlife park, a place of disease, famine, ignorance, debt, corruption, mismanagement and dictatorship etc. Partially it may be true that Africa is the poorest, least developed, most exploited, worst suffering area on the earth. At the same time globally when we look at unless Africa is prosperous, the world as a whole cannot be prosperous. Therefore if the World needs to be developed then Africa need to be developed. Among the problems that Africa is facing climate change and problems that are related to climate change are the major problems. It can be spelled out as global warming, deforestation, environmental destruction, lack of water, change of pastoralist, urbanization and etc. The continent of Africa is very much affected and it is Africans that pay for the price of global warming very often. Since Africans depend very much on nature and their whole economy and development is centered on nature. Africans are both pastoralists and agriculturist and majority of them have their own cultivate land. At this juncture of climate change, drought and famine it is very much fitting to study an ethnic group like Massai in East Africa. Since Massai an ethnic group in East Africa is purely pastoralist and migrating from 15th century. In history Millions of Massai died due to famine and drought and today's Massai settle in urban areas leaving out their identity in order to survive. This study on Massai a major ethnic group in East Africa helps to know them better and enables the policy-makers to make proper policies and programmes when developmental activities take place in tribal land.

History of Maasai

It is thought that the Maasai ancestors originated in North Africa, migrating south along the Nile Valley and arriving in Northern Kenya in the middle of the 15th century. They continued southward, conquering all of the tribes in their path, extending through the Rift Valley and arriving in Tanzania at the end of 19th century. As they migrated, they attacked their neighbors and raided cattle. By the end of their journey, the Massai had taken over almost all of the land in the Rift Valley as well as the adjacent land from Mount

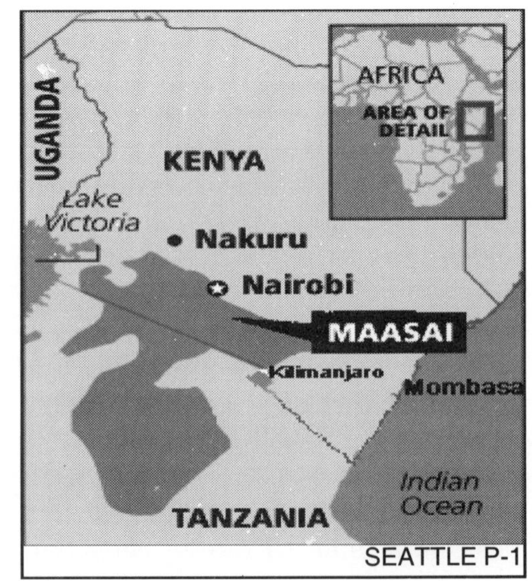

Marsabit to Dodoma, where they settled to graze their cattle. Massai people reside in both Kenya and Tanzania, living along the border of the two countries. They are a smaller tribe, accounting for only about 0.7 per cent of Kenya's population, with a similar number living in Tanzania. And it is estimated that all together there are 1 million Massai live in Kenya and Tanzania.

Historical Change in Life Style of Massai

Land is life for any Ethnic group and the Massai are not exempted from it. Since Massai keep migrating from 15th century onwards, in the course of time they last their land, life and identity. This factor can be seen in all walks of their life.

1. Anglo-Massai Agreements

The period of British colonial rule in Kenya was the major contributing factor for Massai alienation. During which the ruling colonial Government felt that the pastoralist Massai wander simply, destroy the forest land and wanted to bring them under control. And most part of the land was unused and wanted to make use of them. In view of this 10th Aug 1904 "Anglo Massai agreement was made and it says that; *"The Masai leaders 'of our own free will', decided that it is for our best interests to remove our people, flocks, and herds into definite reservations away from the railway line, and away from any land that may be thrown open to European settlement" (New York Times August 25, 2004).* Thus slowly the Anglo Massai agreement began to alienate Massai from their soil. At the course of century tragedy struck the Massai: An epidemic of deadly diseases attacked and killed large numbers of the Massai animals. This was quickly followed by severe drought that lasted years. Over half of the Massai and their animals perished during this period. Soon after, more than two thirds of the Massai land in Kenya was taken away by the British and the Kenyan government to create both ranches for settlers and Kenya and Tanzania's wildlife reserves and national parks. The Amboseli National Park, Nairobi National Park, Masai Mara Game Reserve, Samburu, Lake Nakuru, and Tsavo National Parks in Kenya and the Manyara, Ngorongoro, Tarangire and Serengeti parks in Tanzania all stand on what was once the territory of the Massai tribe. Today, the Massai people live on a smaller piece of land in the Kajiado and Narok districts, surrounded by Kenya's fine game reserves. Many practice nomadic pastoralism, while others have been absorbed into modern day jobs working in tourism where they showcase their culture to visiting tourists.

2. Cultural Heritage of Massai

It is hard to find the real cultural heritage of Massai. Their constant migration on account of drought and urbanization made lot of changes in their language, religion, diet, homestead and labour, economy, private ownership and political system.

3. ***Language: Massai Speak Maa***

A Nilotic ethnic language from their origin in the Nile region of North Africa and now due to urbanization adopt all languages where ever they are in Tanzania and Kenya.

4. ***Massai Religion***

Massai are the worshipers of nature. And the cow is slaughtered as an offering during important ceremonies marking completed passage through one age-grade and movement to the next. When warriors (moran – *are the same peer group on account of circumcision*) complete this cycle of life, they exhibit outward signs of sadness, crying over the loss of their youth and adventurous lifestyles. Maasai diviners (laibon) are consulted whenever misfortune arises. They also serve as healers, dispensing their herbal remedies to treat physical ailment and ritual treatments to absolve social and moral transgressions. In recent years Maasai laibon have earned a reputation as the best healers in Tanzania. Even as western biomedicine gains ground, people also continually search out more traditional remedies. Maasai are often portrayed as people who have not forgotten the importance of the past, and as such their knowledge of traditional healing ways has earned them respect. Laibons are easily found peddling their knowledge and herbs in the urban centres of Tanzania and Kenya.

5. ***Massai the Hunters of Lion***

One myth about the Massai is that each young man is supposed to kill a lion before he is circumcised. Lion hunting was an activity of the past, but in today it has been banned in East Africa – yet lions are still hunted when they maul Massai livestock, and young warriors who engage in traditional lion killing do not face significant consequences Nevertheless, killing a lion gives one great value and celebrity status in the community.

6. ***Female Circumcision in Massai***

Young men undergo circumcision and just like young women also undergo excision ('female circumcision' or emorata). It is as part of an elaborate rite of passage ritual in which they are given instructions and advice pertaining to their new role, as they are then said to have come of age and become women, ready for marriage. In Kenya female circumcision is practiced by 38 per cent of the population. The most common form is clitorectomy. These circumcisions are usually performed by an invited 'practitioner' who is often not Maasai, usually from a Dorobo group. The knives and blades which make the cut are fashioned by blacksmiths, il-kunono, who are avoided by the Maasai because they make weapons of death (knives, short swords (ol alem), spears, etc.). Similar to the young men, women who will be circumcised wear dark clothing, paint their faces with markings, and then cover their faces on completion of the ceremony.

7. ***Homestead and Labour of Massai***

The Maasai live in Kraals arranged in a circular fashion. The fence around the kraal is made of acacia thorns, which prevent lions from attacking the cattle. It is a man's responsibility to fence the kraal while women construct the houses. Traditionally, kraals are shared by an extended family. However, due to the new land management system in the Maasai region, it is not uncommon to see a kraal occupied by a single family. But in these days the modern Massai adopt themselves to any type of houses. Normally the houses are provided by the NGOs and the government.

8. ***Massai Economy***

Cattle are central to Maasai economy. They are rarely killed, but instead are accumulated as a sign of wealth and traded or sold to settle debts. Their traditional grazing lands span from central Kenya into central Tanzania. Young men are responsible for tending to the herds and often live in small camps, moving frequently in the constant search for water and good grazing lands. Maasai are ruthless capitalists and due to past behaviour have become notorious as cattle rustlers. At one time young Maasai warriors set off in groups with the express purpose of acquiring illegal cattle. Maasai often travel into towns and cities to purchase goods and supplies and to sell their cattle at regional markets. Maasai also sell their beautiful beadwork to the tourists with whom they share their grazing land.

9. ***Private Ownership in Massai***

The concept of private ownership was, until recently, a foreign concept to the Massai. However, in the 1960s and 1980s, a programme of commercializing livestock and land was forced on Massai initially by the British and later by the government of Kenya. Since then, the land has been sub-divided into group and individual ranches. In other parts of Massai land people sub-divided their individual ranches into small plots, which are sold to private developers.

The new land management system of individual ranches has economically polarized the Massai; some Massai as well as outside wealthy individuals, have substantially increased their wealth at the expense of others. The largest loss of land, however, has been to national parks and reserves, in which the Massai are restricted from accessing critical water sources, pasture, and salt lick. Sub-division of Massai land reduced land size for cattle herding, reduced the number of cows per household, and reduced food production. As a result, the Massai society, which once was a proud and self-sufficient society, is now facing many social-economic and political challenges. The level of poverty among the Massai people is beyond conceivable height. It is sad to see a society that had a long tradition of pride being a beggar for relief food because of imposed foreign concepts of development. The future of the Massai is uncertain at this point.

10. Massai Political System

Massai community politics are embedded in age-grade systems which separate young men and prepubescent girls from the elder men and their wives and children. When a young woman reaches puberty she is usually married immediately to an older man. Until this time, however, she may live and have sex with the youthful warriors. Often women maintain close ties, both social and sexual, with their former boyfriends, even after they are married. In order for men to marry they must first acquire wealth, a process that takes time. Women, on the other hand, are married at the onset of puberty to prevent children being born out of wedlock. All children, whether legitimate are not, are recognised as the property of the woman's husband and his family.

11. Maasai Diet

Traditionally, the Massai rely on meat, milk and blood from cattle for protein and caloric needs. People drink blood on special occasions and it is given to a circumcised person (o/esipolioi), woman who gave birth to a child (entomononi) and the sick (oltamueyiai). Also, on a regular basis drunken elders, ilamerak, use the blood to alleviate intoxication and hangovers. Blood is very rich in protein and is good for the immune system. However, its use in the traditional diet is waning due to the reduction of livestock numbers.

More recently, the Maasai have grown dependent on food produced in other areas such as maize meal (unga wa mahindi), rice, potatoes, cabbage (known to the Massai as goat leaves), etc. The Maasai who live near crop farmers have engaged in cultivation as their primary mode of subsistence. In these areas, plot sizes are generally not large enough to accommodate herds of animals; thus the Massai are forced to farm. Our people traditionally frown upon this. Massai believe that utilising the land for crop farming is a crime against nature. Once you cultivate the land, it is no longer suitable for grazing.

Consequences of Life Style Changes

The life style changes in Massai bring positive and negative impact in the society.

The Positive Impact

- To an extent the cultural heritage is maintained.
- The modern Massai are able to read and write.
- Due to education civilization is taking place among the Massai.
- Massai are involved in National tourism and bring revenue to the government.

The Negative Aspects

- The migrated Massai have lost their culture and heritage.
- The Massai who settle in urban areas get infected with HIV and AIDS and as they come back to the community infect others.
- The migration has brought loss to the government in terms of pastoralist income.
- The Massai who settle in urban areas are exploited and women are sexually abused.

Conclusion

The study on Massai an Ethnic group in East Africa is most relevant for the developing county like India since development is at its pick moment. At the moment in India lot of developmental activities such as mining, construction of dams, establishment of hydro electric power units, industries and etc., are going on. In this juncture the developmental activities should not alienation the indigenous people and their life style. Their life style is to be preserved and they are to be compensated. It is the primary duty of the Government to bring strict legislation and policies to safe guard the life and livelihood of the affected people.

REFERENCES

http://www.gregvogl.net/views/importan.htm downloaded on 22-12-2011.

Adams, J. S. and McShane, T. O. (1996), The Myth of Wild Africa: Conservation Without Illusion, Berkeley, Los Angeles and London: University of California Press (First Published in 1992).

Ake, C. (1986) 'Kenya', in Adedeji, A. (ed.): Indigenization of African Economies, New York: Africana.

Babu, A. M. (1981), African Socialism or Socialist Africa? Dar es Salaam: TPH and London: Zed Press.

Chachage, C.S.L. (2000), Environment; Aid and Politics in Zanzibar, Dar es Salaam: Dar es Salaam University Press (1996) Ltd.

Chambers, R. (1983), Rural Development: Putting the Last First, Harlow: Longman Group Ltd.

Dietz, A. J. and Mohamed Salih, M.A. (1997), Pastoral Development in East Africa: Policy Review, Options and Alternatives, Second Revised Edition Report for I/C Consult, Zeist (for Bilance) Amsterdam and The Hague.

16

Strategies to Overcome Barriers in Education of Maasai Girls in Kenya

*H. Magara Robinson Makori
**Nyangwencha M. Jeridah

ABSTRACT

Maasai girls who do enroll in primary school attend public day schools which are free. But all students in Kenya are required to wear uniforms, and many families cannot afford even the uniform needed for their child to go to school. Public primary boarding schools, which offer many advantages, are prohibitively expensive for most Maasai families. The quality of education in these rural day schools is rarely adequate to prepare students for the national tests, which are required to go on to secondary school, because these schools are underfunded and woefully overcrowded, with a student-teacher ratio as high as 100 to 1.

For the exceptional girl who does pass the national test to graduate from primary school, all secondary schools in Kenya are boarding schools, and the annual cost is prohibitive for most Maasai but, if economically feasible, sons are always given priority. The Maasai Girls Education Fund has developed a multi-faceted strategy to overcome the obstacles Maasai girls

* Research Scholar, Department of Gandhian Thought and Peace Science, GRI, Gandhigram.

** Research Scholar, Centre for Women Studies, GRI, Gandhigram.

must overcome to get an education. These strategies focus on increasing enrollment, reducing early marriages and circumcision, providing the means for economic independence, and promoting cultural acceptance of educating girls and its economic benefits.

This paper will focus on barriers and Strategies to overcome the barriers in education. Strategies help to improve the educational level of the Maasai girls in Kenya.

Keywords: Education; Maasai; Social Exclusion; Nomadic Lifestyle.

Introduction

Kenya is situated in the Eastern part of Africa with a Total population of 41,070,934 (July 2011) and the age structure is as follows 0-14 years: 42.2 per cent (male 8,730,845/female 8,603,270) 15-64 years: 55.1 per cent (male 11,373,997/female 11,260,402) 65 years and over: 2.7 per cent (male 497,389/ female 605,031) (2011.) with Population growth rate 2.462 per cent (2011).

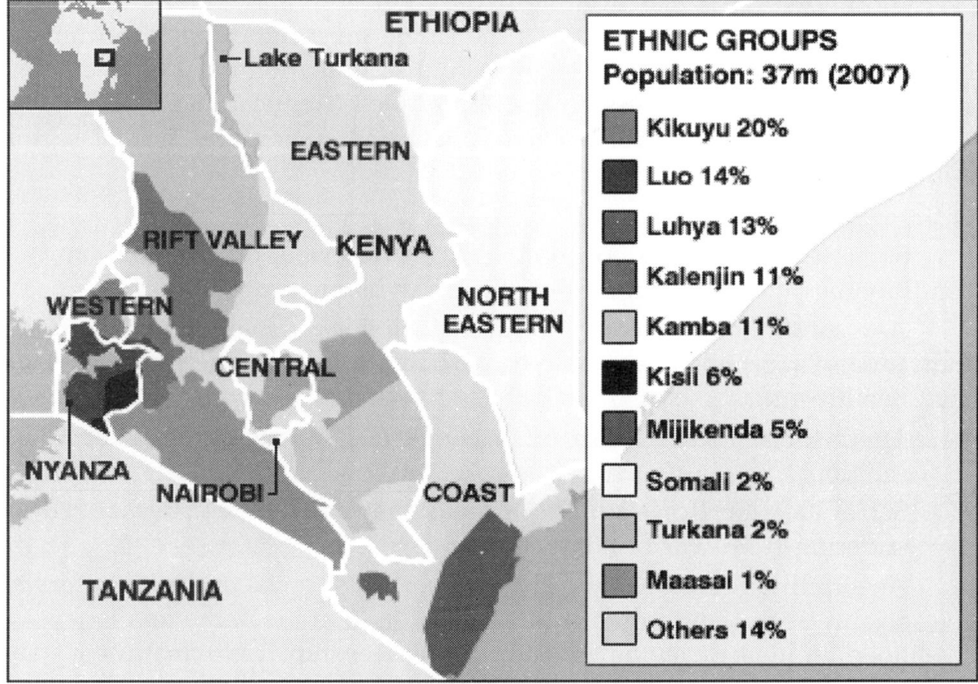

Source: CIA, UK Foreign Office, Africa Studies Centre

The concept of social exclusion emanated from European dissatisfaction with perceived failures of the welfare system in the face of persistent poverty and slow eco-nomic growth in the early 1990s. It mirrors concern in the late 1970s in the United States regarding the emergence of an underclass that appeared unable to climb out of poverty. The socially excluded are those who receive inadequate support from public institutions and whose opportunities remain constrained due to structural and cultural factors.

Exclusion arises from multiple sources, some endogenous and some exogenous. Social exclusion from immutable factors, such as gender, ethnicity, and race, contributes to low educational participation for girls and members of subgroups. Social exclusion from external factors, such as poverty, contributes to low educational participation and to a cycle of exclusion based on poverty.

Gender discrimination in education among the Maasai in Kenya is recognised as the number one cause of persistent poverty and all of its consequences, especially to health and nutrition of the Maasai people. "Illiteracy has emerged as the number one root cause of poverty in the district. Education is a means of overcoming poverty, increasing income, improving nutrition and health, reducing family size as well a raising people's self-confidence and enriching the quality of their lives." ..."the gender gap in education however comes at a high cost to growth and development. For example, the mother's education is the single most important determinant of a family's health and nutrition. Female discrimination must be overcome through increased awareness on the importance of education for all, and in particular, increased female participation in education and formal sector employment"...

Defining Social Exclusion

Social exclusion is a concept that can describe, on the one hand, a condition or outcome, and, on the other, a dynamic process.

As a condition or outcome, social exclusion is a state in which excluded individuals or groups are unable to participate fully in their society. This may result from:

- Their social identity (for example race, gender, ethnicity, caste or religion).
- Social location (for example in areas that are remote, stigmatized or suffering from war or conflict).

As a multidimensional and dynamic process, social exclusion refers to the social relations and organizational barriers that block the attainment of livelihoods, human development and equal citizenship. It can create or sustain poverty and inequality, and can restrict social participation. As a dynamic process, social exclusion is governed by:

- Social and political relations.
- Access to organizations and institutional sites of power.

The abbreviated working definition of social exclusion used in this report is as follows:

Social exclusion is a process and a state that prevents individuals or groups from full participation in social, economic and political life and from asserting their rights. It derives from exclusionary relationships based on power and marginalization of the poor by the wealthy, perpetuating the cycle of poverty due to limited economic and social mobility.

Socially Excluded Groups

Socially excluded groups are defined as cultural subgroups that are marginalized due to one or more of the following phenomena:

- Stigmatization by recent historical trauma at the hands of the majority population.
- Ethnic differences, including differences in ethnic group, language, and religion.
- Low status, such as caste, as excluded groups are 'ranked' or subordinated in the social hierarchy below the majority population.

Social exclusion sidelines certain population groups, preventing them from receiving the social rights and protections meant to be extended to all citizens and restricting their economic mobility. Discrimination against such groups by the majority population excludes them to varying degrees from mainstream activities, such as education and employment.

Girls in excluded groups suffer not only as members of the excluded group but also as girls. Whether exclusion is additive or multiplicative is not known. Some sociological research suggests that it is additive (Ridgeway and Erickson 2000; Ridgeway 1991), and the studies in this volume provide limited evidence of interaction effects. All studies indicate a severe education disadvantage from multiple sources of exclusion: girls from impoverished families, girls from tribal, ethnic, or linguistic 'minority' communities, girls living in remote settings, and girls from lower castes are less likely to participate in education and more likely to stay in school only briefly if they enroll at all (Lewis and Lockheed 2006). The extent of their disadvantage can be seen in primary schooling.

Social exclusion of groups is rare, albeit not unknown, in homogeneous societies (Meerman 2005). It is common in heterogeneous, stratified societies, across ethnic groups, languages, and customs, with groups sometimes separated by geography. What distinguishes social exclusion from simple separatism are the invidious social evaluations (in terms of differences in honor, respect, esteem, and the like) that are accorded the excluded group by a dominant social group and that may even be shared by the excluded group .These evaluations lead to differences in expectations for a range of behaviours, including those related to education.

Barriers to Education for Maasai Girls

Maasai girls must face many obstacles to get an education, and most of those are related to the high level of poverty among the Maasai. The cost of education is prohibitive for most families, and the promise of a dowry is a powerful incentive for arranging a daughter's marriage as soon as she 'crosses the childhood bridge'. But cultural factors also contribute to preventing girls from getting and education.

MGEF Challenges

Just 48 per cent of Maasai girls enroll in school, and only 5 per cent of those who enroll will make it to secondary school. 90 per cent of Maasai girls undergo female genital mutilation. Girls between the ages of 15 to 24 are four to six times more likely to become infected with HIV than their male peers. The average life expectancy for a Maasai woman is 45 years.

Economic, Cultural and Physical Barriers

The economic, cultural and physical factors that combine to deny education to Maasai girls in Kenya are numerous and, taken together, almost impossible for all but the most determined girls to overcome. Even when possible, Maasai girls have the added impediment of cultural beliefs that prevent many from enrolling or completing school.

- Economic incentives for early marriage, such as cattle and cash dowries.
- The belief that the biological family does not benefit from educating a daughter, since the girl becomes a member of her husband's family when she marries, and they will reap the benefits.
- Family and peer pressure for early marriage, as women are valued by the number of children they have.
- Fear of early pregnancy, which is a disgrace prior to marriage and lowers the bride price, which perpetuates the practice of early marriage.
- The distances that a girl must walk to the nearest school make it unsafe and even impossible for a nursery-school-age child.

Cost of Education

Maasai girls who do enroll in primary school attend public day schools which are free. But all students in Kenya are required to wear uniforms, and many families cannot afford even the uniform needed for their child to go to school. Public primary boarding schools, which offer many advantages, are prohibitively expensive for most Maasai families. The quality of education in these rural day schools is rarely adequate to prepare students for the national tests, which are required to go on to secondary school, because these schools are under funded and woefully overcrowded, with a student-teacher ratio as high as 100 to 1.

For the exceptional girl who does pass the national test to graduate from primary school, all secondary schools in Kenya are boarding schools, and the annual cost is prohibitive for most Maasai but, if economically feasible, sons are always given priority.

Economic Barriers

- Economic incentives for early marriage, such as cattle and cash dowries.
- The belief that the biological family does not benefit from educating a daughter, since the girl becomes a member of her husband's family when she marries, and they will reap the benefits.
- Family and peer pressure for early marriage, as women are valued by the number of children they have.
- Fear of early pregnancy, which is a disgrace prior to marriage and lowers the bride price, which perpetuates the practice of early marriage.
- The distances that a girl must walk to the nearest school make it unsafe and even impossible for a nursery-school-age child.

A daughter's marriage increases the wealth of Maasai girl's family through combined cattle and cash dowries and, since a girl joins her husband's family upon marriage, her father is relieved of the economic burden of supporting her. The practice of early marriage is also worsened by the increasing poverty of the Maasai people, which leads Maasai fathers to marry their daughters off at increasingly young ages. Return on investment. For those few families that are able to pay education costs, there is a widespread cultural preference for educating sons first. This stems from the tradition that Maasai girls leave their parents' village and become a member of the husband's family upon marriage. Maasai fathers tend, therefore, to believe that their family will not benefit from investing in their daughter's education.

Cultural Barriers

Family and peer pressure for early marriage. Early marriage is the most often cited reason that Maasai girls drop out of school. Maasai girls are taught that circumcision is a rite of passage into womanhood that accompanies puberty and an immediate precursor to marriage. Once circumcised, they are ridiculed by their peers if they continue their education, since school is for children. Further escalating the pressure for early marriage is the reality that in the Maasai culture women are traditionally valued on the basis of how many children they can produce for their husbands, not by how educated or economically successful they might become.

Fear of early pregnancy. Pregnancy is the second most frequent reason that girls drop out of school. In the Maasai culture, children as young as nine years old are not allowed to stay in the same house with their father, and instead sleep in a separate house without supervision. In addition, girls are not told how a woman becomes pregnant. This combined lack of supervision and ignorance make girls highly vulnerable to becoming pregnant, and pregnancy before marriage brings disgrace and a reduced bride price. Fear of premarital pregnancy is a common reason for parents to insist that their daughters leave school and marry early.

Physical Barriers

Walking distance. Since the pastoral Maasai require significant land resources to graze their cattle, their villages are constructed far apart from each other. As a result, one school must serve several villages typically within a 15-20 km radius. There are no cars, buses, horses, or even bicycles available to Maasai children, so they must walk this great distance. Many girls are denied an education solely because of parental concerns for their safety during these long walks. Even for those who make it to school, the long walks undermine education. Not surprisingly, teachers report that children who have spent two to five hours walking to school in the morning, often without having had anything to eat, are tired, and their ability to concentrate is impaired. Also, it is often late when children arrive home after such long walks, and they are still required to do chores. Even if they still have the desire and energy to study after they have finished with their responsibilities at home, it is dark and there is no electricity or artificial light.

The Nomadic Maasai Lifestyle

The Maasai are a pastoral, nomadic society, and circumstances sometimes require that families move in order to find water and grass for their cattle. In drought conditions, a child's education is often interrupted or halted until the rains come, causing them to fall behind in their school work, or to stop attending school altogether.

Strategies for Overcoming Barriers

The Maasai Girls Education Fund has developed a multi-faceted strategy to overcome the obstacles Maasai girls must overcome to get an education. These strategies focus on increasing enrollment, reducing early marriages and circumcision, providing the means for economic independence, and promoting cultural acceptance of educating girls and its economic benefits.

1. Increasing Enrollment

MGEF, through a volunteer network of community advocates for girls' education, identifies young Maasai girls who will never have an opportunity to go to school and, after obtaining permission from parents, enrolls them in a boarding school with proven high standards of performance. Equally important is sustaining the number of girls who are already enrolled in school that would be forced to drop out against their wishes because of cultural reasons, such as early marriage or the belief that girls do not need to be educated, or because their parents cannot afford the cost. Community advocates and educators are vigilant in their effort to identify these girls in time to keep them in school.

2. ***Enrollment in Boarding Schools***

Physical barriers are removed and cultural barriers are weakened by placing girls only in boarding schools. Physical barriers include the long, walks to local schools, which may be as far as 15 km from a girl's village, and disruptions of education caused by droughts and related tribal migrations of this pastoral culture. Boarding schools also mitigate the cultural barriers by giving girls a place to escape the relentless pressure for early marriage and motherhood to an environment supportive of girls' education. In addition, boarding schools provide regular, nutritious meals, health care, structured time for study, and a housing option for girls who have reached puberty and are at risk of being married off.

3. ***Making a Long-term Commitment***

MGEF is committed to the complete education of its students, from nursery school to post-secondary education, because our mission is to provide opportunities for economic independence, which requires that each student has the knowledge and skills to enter the workforce in Kenya, whether through vocational training or college. Our strategy is to ensure that MGEF-sponsored students remain in school as long as their desire and ability allow, including a post-secondary education in their chosen fields, but only where there is a viable job market in Kenya.

4. ***Maximizing the Impact***

MGEF selects students based on family and geographic diversity by limiting sponsorship to one child per family, except under special hardship circumstances, and following a formula that ensures equitable selection among the five Divisions in the Kajiado District, the Loitokitok District, and the Ngong District. This strategy increases the reach of the benefits of educating our students and, therefore, the impact on the next generation will be greater.

5. ***Applying Geographic and Ethnic Focus***

MGEF is concentrating its effort in the Kajiado, Loitokitok, and Ngong Districts of Kenya, where approximately two-thirds of Kenya's Maasai population lives. This area, which is about the size of the state of New Jersey, has one of the lowest school enrollment levels and highest poverty rates in Kenya, and education of women is the single, most effective way to alleviate poverty. By focusing on the Maasai, MGEF can address their unique cultural belief systems that prevent girls from being educated.

6. ***Partnering with the Community***

MGEF is structured to maximize community participation. MGEF works in co-operation with a community-based organization and members of the community throughout the Kajiado, Loitokitok and Ngong Districts of Kenya to accomplish its goals. By involving the community, MGEF is able to incorporate the Maasai cultural perspective and local concerns into our strategies, and by doing so, gain greater acceptance of our mission, among men as well as women.

7. Empowering Rural Women

MGEF is developing a series of seminars for rural Maasai women who have no formal education, which focus on practical skills in areas such as healthcare, nutrition, agriculture, and business. Through this effort, the mothers, grandmothers, aunts, and sisters of our students will be gaining knowledge that will improve their lives and the lives of their families and communities. At the same time, the benefits of educating girls will be demonstrated directly and immediately, thus accelerating an increase in community support for education of girls.

8. Educating the Community

MGEF's Scholarships Programme offsets many of the barriers to girls' education, but not all. In addition to economic and cultural barriers, the spread of HIV, female genital mutilation, and teen pregnancy also contribute to girls dropping out of school. MGEF has created a Life Skills Programme for girls, boys, mothers, and chiefs and elders to address the myths, misinformation, and customs about HIV and FGM, the social structure that makes girls vulnerable to teen pregnancy, and the benefits of educating girls.

Kenya Constitution and Exclusion

- *No. 43 (1):* Every person has the right to free education.
- *No 53:* Every child has the right to free and compulsory basic education.
- *No. 54 (1)*: A person with any disability is entitled (b) to access educational institutions and facilities for persons with disabilities that are integrated into society to the extent compatible with the interests of the person.
- *No. 55:* The State shall take measures, including affirmative action programmes, to ensure that the youth (a) access relevant education and training.
- *No. 56:* The State shall put in place affirmative action programmes designed to ensure that minorities and marginalized groups (b) are provided special opportunities in educational and economic fields.

Impact on the Community

MGEF scholarships, workshops, and community partnerships are empowering women and promising a better future for all Maasai. The MGEF scholarship programme offers every student an opportunity to attend vocational school, college or university, as their interest and ability allow. The MGEF alumni are educated and employed. They are helping their families and communities, and they are role models in a world where there are few educated women. They are shown great respect in their communities, and even the status of their families has risen because they have educated daughters who help their family and community. The workshops are helping girls to stay in school by addressing barriers to education, such as teen pregnancy, early marriage, FGM, and the spread of HIV. The community partnership is helping to build an independent organization in Kenya that will in time be able to support itself.

Conclusion

Gender discrimination in education among the Maasai in Kenya is recognised as the number one cause of persistent poverty and all of its consequences, especially to health and nutrition of the Maasai people. Illiteracy has emerged as the number one root cause of poverty in the district. Education is a means of overcoming poverty, increasing income, improving nutrition and health, reducing family size as well a raising people's self-confidence and enriching the quality of their lives. However, the incidence of gender discrimination in education is high. Most women tend to be illiterate, especially in rural areas. Chances of a girl child, as compared with the boy child being in school are proportionately lower and the discrimination continues. The gender gap in education however comes at a high cost to growth and development. For example, the mother's education is the single most important determinant of a family's health and nutrition. Female discrimination must be overcome through increased awareness on the importance of education for all, and in particular, increased female participation in education and formal sector employment.

REFERENCES

Books

Public Procurement Manual for Schools and Colleges from PPOA For Development.

Erickson H. Erick , "Childhood and Society" Pergium Dorks Ltd., 1969.

George G Thompson , "Child Psychology", Times of Indian Press, 1965.

Paul Hendry Mussen, *et al.* "Child Development and Personality", Edition Two, Harpher and Row, New York, 1977.

Websites

http://www.maasaigirlseducation.org/the-need/value-of-educating-maasai-women/the-need-to-eliminate-gender-discrimination.

http://www.worlded.org/WEIInternet/projects/ListProjects.cfm?Select=Topic&ID=16&ShowProjects=No&gclid=CJ2Dt4ebs60CFY4a6wodEnBCmw.

http://www.maasaigirlseducation.org/how-you-can-help.

http://www.smilefoundationindia.org/girls-education.asp

17

A Study on the Educational Status of Tribal Children

With Special Reference to Kuttakarai Village Jawadhi Hills, Thiruvannamalai District Tamil Nadu

*F. Jayachandran
**Dr. P. B. Shankar Narayan

ABSTRACT

The Tribal communities occupy a unique position in Indian Society. Unfortunately their isolation has kept them out of the mainstream and made them easy prey to exploitation. Education in the tribal areas has always been a matter of great concern and the lack of it has had a negative impact on the development of tribal people. The specific objectives are:

(i) To analyse socio-economic causes for educational backwardness.
(ii) To study the problems faced by students in school and at home.
(iii) To study their interest in pursuing higher education.
(iv) To study the reasons for dropouts.

The researcher has chosen *Descriptive Research Design* for the present study. The *universe* of this study is the *tribal children aged between 6 to 14 years in Kuttakarai village* of Jawadhu hills. *60 samples* were collected using *Simple random sampling*. The major findings of this study are 32 per cent of the respondents are dropouts, 23 per cent of the school going students are

* M. Phil, Department of Social Work, Pondicherry University.
** Assistant Professor, Department of Social Work, Pondicherry University, Puducherry.

not interested in studies, 42 per cent of the respondents are not able to understand the subjects, there is no proper playground and play material in schools, no toilet facility in kuttakarai primary school, teachers are not regular to school, and students are not receiving proper mid-day meals.

Keywords: Educational Status; Scheduled Tribe; Jawadhi Hills.

Introduction

The word 'Education' is derived from the Latin word *educare,* which means 'to bring up'. There is yet another Latin word 'educare', which means 'to bring forth'. Education does not merely mean the acquisition of knowledge or experience but it means the development of habits, attitudes and skills which help a man to lead a full and worthwhile life. Scheduled Tribes are one of the most deprived and marginalized groups with respect to education, a host of programmes and measures were initiated ever since the Independence. Elementary education is a priority area in the Tribal sub-plans from the 5th Five-year Plan. Education of ST children is considered important, not only because of the Constitutional obligation but also as a crucial input for total development of tribal communities. Another important development in the policy towards education of tribal's is the National Policy on Education (NPE), 1986 which specified among other things the following:

- Priority will be accorded to opening primary schools in tribal areas.
- There is need to develop curriculum and devise instructional material in tribal language at the initial stages with arrangements for switchover to regional languages.
- ST youths will be encouraged to take up teaching in tribal areas.
- Ashram schools/residential schools will be established on a large scale in tribal areas.
- Incentive schemes will be formulated for the STs, keeping in view their special needs and lifestyle.

NPE, 1986 and Programme of Action (POA), 1992 recognised the heterogeneity and diversity of the tribal areas, besides underlining the importance of instruction through the mother tongue and the need for preparing teaching/learning material in the tribal languages. Working group on Elementary and Adult Education for Xth Five-year Plan (2002-07) emphasised the need to improve the quality of education of tribal children and ensuring equity, besides further improving the access.

The Tribal Community

The Tribal communities occupy a unique position in Indian Society. Being the earliest inhabitants of the country, they have maintained a distinctive life style for centuries. Unfortunately their isolation has kept them out of the mainstream and made the easy prey to exploitation. Since independence the tribal communities have become the concern of the government.

A lot has been said on educational planning, as an integrated part of all over all social and economic planning. The Right to free and compulsory education 2009 provides free education for all children until they complete 14 years. Article 16 says that "the state shall promote with special care the education and economic interest of weaker section of the society and in particular, of the schedule caste and the schedule tribes and shall protect them from social injustice and all forms of exploitation.

Mishra (2002), defines Scheduled tribes as people who:

(i) claim themselves as indigenous to the soil;

(ii) generally inhabit forest and hilly regions;

(iii) largely pursue a subsistence level economy;

(iv) have grate regard for traditional religious and cultural practices;

(v) believe in common ancestry; and

(vi) have strong group ties. However, all characteristics do not apply to all tribal communities.

Scheduled Tribes and their Education in India

The Indian Constitution assigns special status to the Scheduled Tribes (STs). STs constitute about 8 per cent of the Indian population. There are 573 Scheduled Tribes living in different parts of the country, having their own languages different from the one mostly spoken in the State where they live. There are more than 270 such languages in India. Education in the tribal areas has always been a matter of great concern and the lack of it has had a negative impact on the development of tribal people. Primary education as well as continuation of education in high schools in the rural and remote areas has suffered due to lack of institutional facilities, non-availability and absence of teachers in the primary schools, lack of text books and other physical facilities in the primary, secondary and High schools. Literacy rate among the boys and girls in predominantly tribal areas has always been governed by two major factors that are: *(i)* the poor socio-economic conditions of tribal people; and *(ii)* the lack of political and administrative will in such remote tribal belts. One of the challenges in providing education to tribal children is with respect to setting up schooling facilities in small, scattered and remote tribal habitations. The majority of the Scheduled Tribes live in sparsely populated habitations in interior and inaccessible hilly and forest areas of the country. Nearly 22 per cent of the tribal habitations have population less than 100 while more than 40 per cent have population of 100 to 300. The rest have population of 300 to 500 (Sujatha, 2000).

Telesara (1994), in his book 'social background of tribal girl student' says the role of education for the scheduled tribes in more specific. The scheduled tribes who have been living in forest and hilly region for centuries did not get any education. Lack of education not only kept them away from the fruit of education but also landed them to exploitation, ignorance, poverty and above all general backwardness. They did not have any idea of nutritional food. It entrapped them to excessive drinking. Their personal hygiene also became very unscientific. A number of diseases victimized them owing to their lack of education.

Kailash (1994), in his book 'tribal education and occupation' he says that the low level of education as well as the prevailing illiteracy often seen as the main reasons for preventing the tribal's from getting better employment and better opportunities. A study conducted by shri Kailash for his doctorate from Jawaharlal Nehru University in 1994, entitled "the impact of education on the occupation challenges of tribes in Jhabua district of Madhya Pradesh" In this study the researcher attempted to analyse the impact of education on occupational diversification of inter generation levels. The study seeks education as only independent variable which patronizes the changes among occupation in different sectors.

Shukla and Sharma (2000) mentioned about the literacy of the tribal and non-tribals in the studies conducted by them. They emphasise on the educational attainment of the tribal and non-tribal. They state that tribals may not be highly educated or not interested in higher education due to low economic condition, lack of awareness, lack of educational facilities provided and their educational attainment is also low in comparison to that of the non-tribal. They suggested that the government should increase the infrastructure for education and should try to motivate them through awareness campaign regarding the importance of formal education.

According to Aggarwal (2000), "The large share of SC and ST population in DPEP (District Primary Education Programme) II districts is also associated with low literacy rates in these districts. It was observed that out of a total of 30 districts in which the ST population was more than 5 per cent, as many as 11 districts showed less than 10 per cent female ST literacy (1991 Census). In the 66 districts where share of SC population was more than 5 per cent, as many as 29 districts had female literacy varying between 10 and 25 per cent (1991 Census). Thus most of the school-going children, especially the girls, in these districts will be first generation learners" given that the proportion of government schools with a larger concentration of SC and ST students has been steadily increasing, such schools invariably have large numbers of first generation learners and require more experienced teachers.

The Household Survey (2005), conducted in all the district has captured not only the number of out-of school children but also the reasons for their remaining out of school. The survey has identified that there are 6 major reasons for children who have remained out of school. They have been classified as lack of interest, lack of access, involved in household work, migration, earning compulsion, failure.

Research Methodology

The main objective is to study the educational status of tribal children. The specific objectives are:

(i) To analyse socio-economic causes for educational backwardness.

(ii) To study the problems faced by students in school and at home.

(iii) To study their interest in pursuing higher education.

(iv) To study the reasons for dropouts.

The researcher had chosen 'Descriptive Research Design' for the present study. The universe for this study was the tribal children aged between 6 to 14 years in Jawadhu hillls block. The study population for this study was tribal children aged 6 to 14 in Kuttakarai village of Jawadhu hills. 62 samples were collected from kuttakarai village using survey method. Structured Interview Schedule was used to collect the data.

Findings

- Majority of the respondents (66%) are in the age group of 5-10 years.
- 52 per cent of the respondents are female.
- Only 68 per cent of the respondents are going to school at present.
- All the respondents told that there is no playground and sufficient play material in their school.
- All the respondents told that they have no physical education teacher in their school.
- There is no toilet facility in Kuttakarai primary school.
- 23 per cent of the respondents who are studying in Pattaraikadu, Government high school told that they have toilet in their school but they are not allowed to use it, it will be locked always.
- All the respondents told that they have no library facility in their school.
- All the respondents told that special classes were not taken for educationally poor students.
- 32 per cent of the respondents are droupouts.
- 23 per cent of the respondents told that they are not interested in studies.
- Majority of the droupout students (19%) are just roaming in the village.
- 55 per cent of the respondents told that they are really interested in studies.
- 26 per cent of the respondents told that they are afraid of facing the exams.
- Only 3 per cent of the respondents told that they will freely share the problems faced in studies with their teachers.
- 39 per cent of the respondents told that teachers are not regular to school.

- Respondents who are studying in Pattaraikadu Government high school (23%) told that they are getting rice, curry and egg for 3 days in a week in their mid-day meals.
- Respondents who are studying in Kuttakarai Government primary school (45%) told that they get only rice, no curry and egg is twice in a week in their mid-day meals.
- The researcher was pity to see that all the respondents told that the food items they get in mid-day meals is good, without knowing that they have to get curry in every meals and egg in all the five working days of a week.
- 22 of the female respondents told that they will be doing most of the works at home like Cooking, cleaning the house, washing the vessels, fetching water and collecting firewood.
- Majority of the male respondents (28 male respondents) told that they will be Roaming in the forest with friends, hunting birds and watching T.V.
- Only 48 per cent of the respondents told that they are interest in going to high school.
- Only 24 per cent of the respondents told that they are interested in going to college.

Suggestions

Education is the most effective instrument for ensuring equality of opportunity keeping in view of this assumption the government has been making several efforts to educate by extending special educational facilities and reservation of seat in educational institutions .But the development of education is one of the important problems in the case of tribals of the study area. For solving that problem researcher expresses some suggestions:

- Appropriate awareness campaign should be organized to create awareness, about the existing programmes regarding education and schemes and the importance of education in Jawadhu hills block and its villages.
- The attitude of the tribal parents toward education should be improved through proper counselling and guidance.
- A frequent parents and teachers interaction will enhance student enrolment and attendance rate.
- Special attention should be given to the children who are weak and not interest in studies by the teacher.
- The quality of mid-day meals needs to be improved which will attract the children to come to school.
- The higher officials must often check the quality of the mid-day meals provided in the school.

- Proper awareness should be given to the students about their rights, so that students may avail all the facilities at proper time.
- Higher officials should check the functioning of schools frequently relating to the teaching methods, working hours, days of the school and attendance registers of the teachers.
- Residential facilities with all amenities should be provided to teachers and other staff members. In this way they will also cop up with the situation.
- Merit scholarship, attendance scholarship, and more initiatives should be taken to attract the students and to encourage them.
- Livelihood activities should be promoted for the parents of tribal children in order to reduce the migration.
- In order to have better functioning of the school one monitoring group has to be started in each village that will monitor the activities of the school, and this monitoring group must consist of the school head master, village Panchayat members and youths of the village.
- Educated tribal youth should be recruited as teachers and posted in tribal areas, so that they can help other youth to get better education and also through this the upcoming generation will get interest in studying.
- Most of the tribal students will be the first generation learners so the teachers have to be more experienced and trained.

Conclusion

The researcher, in this study aimed to find out the educational status of tribal children. The objectives of this study were framed with this aim and at the end of the project the researcher could achieve his objectives and could bring out suggestions to improve the educational status of tribal children in Jawadhu hills.

At present, India is attaining advancement in science and technology and is capable to compete with the developed countries in respect of science and technology, energy and many other such fields. But the people of Jawadhu hills are facing various problems like: poverty, lack of literacy and lack of employment because of low literacy rate. Majority of the people in this block are living below in poverty line even after 64 years of independence. The level of education is often viewed as an indicator of the development of any country. The main reason for the low level of education among tribes is the peculiar nature of their habitations. The social and economic conditions prevailing in the tribal settlements are not conducive for better education. Lack of sufficient number of educational institutions in tribal areas, poverty, and inability to attract children from primary level, are some of the reasons for low literacy rate among Scheduled Tribes. Moreover, the parents of the tribal children being generally illiterate cannot insist on their children to attend classes regularly. In order to improve education among Scheduled Tribes, the primary efforts should be on eradication of poverty. The parents of the tribal children have to be provided with regular employment for earning income to meet their day-to-day requirement, which will help to send their children to school.

REFERENCES

A. Kumar. (2002), *Tribal Development in India.* New Delhi: Sarup and Sons.

Adidravider. (n.d.), Retrieved March 28, 2011, from Tamil Nadu Government: http://www.tn.gov.in/deptst/AdiDravidar.pdf

Aggarwal, Y. ((2000), *'An Assessment of Trends in Access and Retention'.* New Delh: National Institute of Educational Planning and Administration.

Darling, J. (1994), *Child Centre Education and Its Critics.* London: Paul Chapman Publishing Ltd.

Hazar, A. (2010, September), Rural Litaracy in India. *Kurukshetra,* pp. 3-5.

Kailash. (1994), *Tribal Education and Occupation.* New Delhi: Manak Publications Pvt. Ltd.

Angford, G. (1985), *Education Person and Society a Philosophical Enquiry.* London: Macmillan Publishers Ltd.

Mehta, P. C. (2004), *Ethnographic Atlas of Indian Tribes.* Discovery Publishing House.

Pradhan, D. K. (2010, September), Problem of Tribal Eduaction in India. *Kurukshetra,* pp. 29-33.

R. P. Mohanty, and D. N. Biswal. (2009), *Elementary Education in Tribal India.* New Delhi: A Mittal Publication.

Rao, V. S. (2009, Feb 13), Lack of Community Participation in the Sarva Shiksha Abhiyan: A Case Study. *Economic and Political Weekly,* pp. 61-62.

Reddy, P. (1994), *Education of Tribal Women.* Delhi: Anmol Publication Pvt. Ltd.

Swamy, R. N. (2010, November), Tribal Education as a Tool for Rural Transformation. *Kurukshetra,* p. 15-19.

Talesara, H. (1994), *Social Background of Tribal Girl Student.* Delhi: Himanshu Publications.

Taneja, V. (2005), *Socio-Philosophical Approach to Education.* Atlantic Publishers and Dist.

Taneja, V. R. (1995), *Educational Thought and Practice.* Sterling Publishers Pvt. Ltd.

Times of India. (2010, July 26), *Education is my Legal Right.* Retrieved April 12, 2011, from Times of India: http://articles.timesofindia.indiatimes.com/2010-07-26/education/28302755_1_compulsory-education-muslim-girls-education-act

18

Education and Social Equity

With a Special Focus on Scheduled Castes and Scheduled Tribes in Elementary Education in India

*C. Praba

ABSTRACT

Scheduled Castes and Scheduled Tribes are the terms of reference listed in the Indian Constitution, and in government, legal and scholarly writing, particularly of the colonial period. The terms SC and ST are now used to refer to the communities listed in the Government Schedule as 'outcastes' and 'tribal's', respectively. The notion of 'outcastes' is premised upon the Hindu caste system, which divides society into the four broad categories of Brahmins (priests), Kshatriyas (warriors), Vaishyas (traders), and Shudras (menial workers). The castes of Ati Shudras (performing the most menial tasks) were designated as outside the fourfold caste system and it is these 'outcastes' that are today referred to as Scheduled Castes. Scheduled Castes have also been referred to as 'Untouchables' by Hindu caste society and as 'Harijans' (children of God), a term popularised by Mahatma Gandhi. These terms were deemed unconstitutional in Independent India, and rejected as derogatory and paternalistic by the Scheduled Castes themselves.

* Ph.D Scholar, Department of Economics, University of Madras, Chennai - 05.

Scheduled Tribes are similarly distinct from mainstream Hindu society, with lifestyles, languages and cultural practices different from the known religions of India. There are numerous tribal communities in India, with a population numbering more than 80 million, and who live mostly in forested, hilly and mountainous areas. In the colonial period, they were self-governed and therefore isolated from the rest of Indian society. However, the British administration (motivated primarily by their proximity to rich natural resources) sought to control these areas and communities and bring them into mainstream society. The term 'Adivasi' (meaning original inhabitants) has been self-consciously adopted by the tribal communities in an effort to reclaim their history and a unique place in Indian society. In this paper, I examine both shared issues concerning school access and equity for Scheduled Caste and Scheduled Tribe groups and also highlight their unique problems, which may require divergent policy responses.

Keywords: Education; Social Exclusion; Gender Equity; Incentive Schemes.

Introduction

Scheduled Castes and Scheduled Tribes are the terms of reference listed in the Indian Constitution, and in government, legal and scholarly writing, particularly of the colonial period, terms such as 'depressed classes' and 'backward classes' were also used historically, but these were eventually replaced. The terms SC and ST are now used to refer to the communities listed in the Government Schedule as 'outcastes' and 'tribal's', respectively. The notion of 'outcastes' is premised upon the Hindu caste system, which divides society into the four broad categories of Brahmins (priests), Kshatriyas (warriors), Vaishyas (traders), and Shudras (menial workers). The castes of Ati Shudras (performing the most menial tasks) were designated as outside the fourfold caste system, and it is these 'outcastes' that are today referred to as Scheduled Castes. Scheduled Castes have also been referred to as 'Untouchables' by Hindu caste society and as 'Harijans' (children of God), a term popularised by Mahatma Gandhi. These terms were deemed unconstitutional in Independent India, and rejected as derogatory and paternalistic by the Scheduled Castes themselves. The term 'Dalit' (meaning broken, oppressed, downtrodden) emerged from within the Scheduled Caste community to highlight their oppressed status and establish their unique identity and consciousness as the 'Other' within Hindu society. Scheduled Tribes are similarly distinct from mainstream Hindu society, with lifestyles, languages and cultural practices different from the known religions of India. There are numerous tribal communities in India, with a population numbering more than 80 million, and who live mostly in forested, hilly and mountainous areas. In the colonial period, they were self-governed and therefore isolated from the rest of Indian society. However, the British administration (motivated primarily by their proximity to rich natural resources) sought to control these areas and communities and bring them into mainstream society. The term 'Adivasi' (meaning original inhabitants) has been self-consciously adopted by the tribal communities in an effort to reclaim their history and a unique place in Indian society.

Histories of Exclusion

The poor educational achievements of Scheduled Castes and Scheduled Tribes can be best understood in the context of deeply embedded caste and social hierarchies that are enacted and expressed in everyday social interactions of community, school and economic life. Functional from pre-colonial times, the system of socially sanctioned discrimination and prejudice against communities designated as outside the caste system has had far-reaching impacts on the self-worth, dignity and economic life of SC and ST groups.

As we enter the twenty-first century, caste is no longer the definitive mode of organizing economic and social relations in India, but it continues to have a lasting impact on the economic, political and social life of communities. Recent studies show that caste-based discrimination continues to be an influential factor in the low educational mobility of both Scheduled Caste and Scheduled Tribe groups, despite government programmes that selectively target aid to children from these Communities (Secada, 1989). Though there are several commonalities in the experience and outcomes of social exclusion for both groups, there are also some critical differences in the ways in which it takes place that have led to somewhat different struggles for equal rights. Although a highly detailed discussion of these differences is beyond the scope of this paper, we will touch upon a few issues that have direct implications for educational equity and inclusion. One critical difference in the nature of discrimination is that in the Hindu caste system some sections of the Scheduled Castes are described as untouchables as or 'less than human', and therefore face extreme discrimination and violence by other caste Hindus. Historically, SC communities were systematically segregated from the rest of the village and were denied access to education, housing and land. Public places such as temples, wells for drinking water, restaurants, toilets, and many other civic facilities were also out of bounds for them (Alexander, 2003). The infringement on their civil rights continues today, especially in rural areas, and instances of violent reprisals against groups who demand equal social status are not uncommon, despite legal prohibitions against caste-based discrimination.

Secondly, the caste-based ideology of hereditary occupations prescribes the most menial and lowly of occupations to SC groups and has determined the socio-economic life of these communities. The majority of SC individuals works as landless agricultural labourers or is engaged in what is considered 'coolie' work. While SCs have traditionally been denied education, even those with education have experienced very limited social mobility due to caste-based opposition to their occupational mobility (Jefferey *et al.*, 2002).

Education: The Way Forward?

The histories of exploitation and marginalisation of Scheduled Caste and Scheduled Tribe communities have produced different engagements with education as a path to social mobility. For Scheduled Castes, access to education has been a focal point in their struggle for equity and social justice. Movements to abolish the caste system and end discrimination have always proposed education as the primary means to overcome caste oppression (Omvedt, 1993). Consequently, the educational status of Scheduled Castes is significantly better in the Southern and Southwestern states of Tamil Nadu and Maharashtra, where strong SC liberation movements and broad based anti-Brahmin movements emerged in the context of the anti-colonial struggle for independence. For a variety of complex reasons, such movements had a comparatively weak presence in North India (Velaskar, 2005). The history of Scheduled Tribe movements is quite different in that basic livelihood needs and the struggle to retain access to forests and natural resources took centre stage in their struggles for dignity and a better life, while access to education remained a secondary issue (Surajit, 2002). Though education was not a critical demand among Scheduled Tribes, government policy focused on education as the main avenue by which to integrate them into 'mainstream' society. The concept of 'ashram schools' – residential schools for ST children – came into vogue in order to overcome structural barriers such as difficult terrain, inaccessible locations and spatially dispersed habitations, and thereby to improve educational access for Scheduled Tribe communities. A centrally-sponsored government scheme of ashram schools exclusively for ST children from elementary to higher secondary levels was initiated in the 1970s and continues to the present (Sujatha, 2002). Ashram schools include vocational training in their curricula in order to provide ST youth with skills and training for jobs in the industrial sector. The poor quality of education in ashram schools, however, has undermined confidence in education as a vehicle for social mobility. The curriculum bears no relation to the economic and social life of Scheduled Tribe communities and instead attempts to wean young people away from it, alienating them in the process. Considering the poor quality of teaching and infrastructure, and the distance of these schools from the community and habitats of the Scheduled Tribes, it is hardly surprising that many families prefer not to send their children to ashram schools and the dropout rate is high among those who do (Sujatha, 2002).

Over the last two decades, the government has increased elementary school provision (grades I-VIII) in and near tribal hamlets, and this has significantly increased rates of enrolment. However, issues of quality and relevance of schooling for ST children have barely received any attention from the national government. The poor quality of infrastructure and teaching, and a curriculum that does not relate to the socio-cultural lives of the Scheduled Tribes nor teach about their history, have all contributed to the communities' disenchantment with schooling. Furthermore, the content of school education devalues their cultures and histories and undermines their sense of self and community identity. Moreover, the poor quality of schooling available to ST children does not prepare them to succeed at higher levels of education nor to compete for jobs, thereby demoralizing young people. Similar issues of self-worth, dignity and livelihoods that school education has failed to address or even acknowledge also arise for Scheduled Caste communities. While SC students have much greater access to elementary education than ST children, they frequently encounter overt and covert acts of discrimination, prejudice and rejection from teachers and fellow students. Commonly reported instances of cruel treatment include being told to sit separately from other students, being called 'untouchable' or stupid, being beaten and caned for presumed infractions and so on (Drèze and Gazdar, 1997). In other words, while elementary schools may appear to be places in which integration can take place, prejudices against Scheduled Castes persist in the classroom, playground and in the micro-practices of schooling. Poor treatment in schools and loss of self-worth and dignity result in drop outs or poor performance in examinations, thus undermining SC and ST students' opportunities to progress to higher levels of education. This, in turn, has a crippling effect on their ability to compete in the job market and increases their sense of alienation from their communities. Concern about this problem has led sections of Scheduled Caste and Scheduled Tribe communities to advocate for separate schools for their children in which they are taught by committed teachers and are able to develop a positive sense of self. Some such schools have been established with support from NGOs and educationists and, in rare cases, on the initiative of the government. For instance, in Andhra Pradesh the government has set up residential schools for SC students that are seen as successful in bypassing the problems encountered in regular government schools.

The understanding that education is a vehicle for integration and assimilation of SC and ST students into the social mainstream is also increasingly being questioned and is seen as having limited usefulness in overcoming prejudice, discrimination and marginalisation. To bring about equity in education for excluded populations such as Scheduled Castes and Scheduled Tribes, scholars and activists advocate a framework of social justice that goes beyond aggregative concerns of equity in the context of access, participation and outcomes, to one which emphasises qualitative aspects of the educational experience and their impact on identity, self-worth and future life chances (Secada, 1989). This, they argue, can only take place in schools that are set up exclusively for Scheduled Caste and Scheduled Tribe students and that are invested in the success of these students (Illiah, 2000). While educators remain divided on how best to provide quality education that will bring about substantial improvements in the lives of SC and ST communities, whether through mainstream or segregated schools, there is consensus that education is a critical resource in addressing the marginalisation of both groups.

History, Economy and Society: Implications for Education of the Scheduled Castes and Scheduled Tribes

While differences between Scheduled Caste and Scheduled Tribe population's make generalisations across these two groups difficult, it is equally problematic to treat SC and ST populations as composite homogenous communities. There are more than 400 major castes among Scheduled Castes and over 500 different tribes among Scheduled Tribes in India. There is therefore a great deal of heterogeneity within each of these populations that calls for a more fine-grained understanding of the specific histories of SC and ST communities in particular places. In the following sections, we first describe the diversity and differences within the Scheduled Tribe community before turning to differences with the Scheduled Caste community. The wide geographical distribution of the Scheduled Tribe community brings along with it wide variation in culture, history and economic conditions. The extent of marginalisation of groups also differs, as do their aspirations, livelihood needs and educational requirements. State programmes are generically targeted at all Scheduled Caste and Scheduled Tribe communities, however, and therefore have tended to benefit the socially and/or economically better off among those populations. Research on these communities has also neglected to explore intra-community inequalities. For primary education policies to succeed, research into the nature of discrimination and marginalization faced by specific Scheduled Caste and Scheduled Tribe communities is needed. With this information, a more precise set of policy and programmatic prescriptions can be generated for different communities.

According to the 2001 Census, the ST population is 84,326,240 and constitutes 8.2 per cent of the total population of India. This population grew by 24.5 per cent during the period 1991-2001 (Census of India, 2002). The SC population, on the other hand, is 166,635,700 and constitutes 16.2 per cent of the total population of India. In certain regions, and particularly the Northeastern states of Arunachal Pradesh, Nagaland, Mizoram and Meghalaya, Scheduled Tribes make up the overwhelming majority of the total population. The overall socio-economic and political status of Scheduled Tribes in these states is significantly better than in other parts of the country, a difference that is also reflected in their educational status and accomplishments. For instance, literacy among the ST population in Mizoram, a state with a ST majority population, is 89.34 per cent, while in Andhra Pradesh, a state with a ST minority population, it is only 37.04 per cent. This unevenness is further complicated when one notes that states with a majority ST population represent only a small percentage of the total Scheduled Tribe population of the country. As Sujatha (2002) points out, the states of Madhya Pradesh, Orissa, Bihar, Maharashtra, Gujarat, Rajasthan, Andhra Pradesh and West Bengal together account for 82 per cent of the total ST population in India, despite the fact that Scheduled Tribes are a minority group in these states.

The Role of Education in Economic Life

The cultural marginalisation and oppression faced by Scheduled Castes and Scheduled Tribes that mainstream education does not tackle is one part of the problem. The second important failing of mainstream education is its inability to deliver the promise of jobs and upward economic mobility. The majority of SC and ST households are engaged in some form of manual labour – cultivation, grazing, mining, scavenging, construction work, or metal, leather or brick work. Mainstream education is singularly focused on building mental skills, however, and so manual skills are generally ignored and devalued. Understandably, SC and ST children internalize the hierarchy of mental skills *vs* manual labour and learn to consider the latter as inferior. Micro-studies show that although Scheduled Caste and Scheduled Tribe populations have a poor rate of success in the job market, individuals do internalize the hidden curriculum of schools that teaches them to devalue and reject manual labour as 'dirty', 'lowly' and a mark of ignorance (Subrahmanian, 2005; Jefferey *et al.*, 2002). In the experience of Scheduled Castes and Scheduled Tribes, therefore, failure to get a job in the modern economy means a double loss, because the 'educated' child is ill-equipped and/or unwilling to participate in the economic activity of the household. Studies also document that caste and political networks are crucial elements for competing successfully in the job market, and that even SC and ST youth who complete high school are often unable to secure jobs due to the lack of such social capital (Subrahmanian, 2005; Jefferey *et al.*, 2002). In such cases, the economic costs to SC and ST households are very high, given that 'schooled' children have lost their ability and inclination to contribute to the household economy, thereby further impoverishing the family (Balagopalan and Subrahmanian, 2003, cited in Subramanian, 2005). Subramanian (2005: 70) cites a Korku (Scheduled Tribe) parent in this regard:

> *"I make my son do both his school work as well as work in the field and look after the cattle. What if he does not do anything with his school work? Then I will be stuck with a son who does not know how to work in the fields. So I teach him both".*

The reluctance of SC and ST parents to keep their children in school can be traced to this disconnection between school education and their prospects in the economy. In their detailed case study on the *Chamar* (leather workers) caste in Bijnor district in Uttar Pradesh, Jeffrey *et al.* (2002) describe how the community's expectation that educated *Chamar* youth will be able to secure government jobs and migrate out of the village have been belied, and as a consequence they are re-evaluating their educational strategies. The research find that these jobs are competitive and that the *Chamar* community does not have the necessary social networks nor are they able to pay the bribes required to secure such jobs. Further, school education is perceived to make people lazy and to reduce their ability to perform agricultural tasks which require physical stamina and a different set of skills and knowledge.

The discontent with schooling as a path towards social and economic mobility is only likely to increase among Scheduled Castes and Scheduled Tribes with the growth in the casualisation of the labour force in urban and rural sectors, a phenomenon that started in the 1990s with economic liberalization reforms. A majority of the labour force is employed in the agricultural sector and the non-agricultural rural economy has also grown in this period. More than three-fourths of the Scheduled Caste population and more than 80 per cent of the Scheduled Tribe population are employed in these sectors (Sundaram and Tendulkar, 2003). Making schooling relevant to the rural economy and the lives of Scheduled Castes and Scheduled Tribes is not only sound pedagogy, but is important for the socio-economic development of these communities.

However, thus far, the focus has been on ensuring initial access to basic education for Scheduled Castes and Scheduled Tribes, while issues of cultural identity and economic productivity have been relegated to the background. The following section will examine the achievements in terms of access to basic education, and the gaps and failures that remain, while paying close attention to regional variations.

Literacy Advancement among Scheduled Castes and Scheduled Tribes

Recent studies show that there is an increased demand for education among the Scheduled Castes and Scheduled Tribes (Drèze and Sen, 2002). The increasing literacy rate among these groups, though at a slower pace, is witness to this trend. According to 2001 Census data, Scheduled Caste children comprise 17.4 per cent of the total youth population and Scheduled Tribes children are 8.97 per cent of the total youth population. In the 6-11 year age cohort, Scheduled Caste children account for 23 million and Scheduled Tribes children for 12 million. In the 11-14 year age cohort, there are 13 million SC children and 6 million ST children. In this section, the development in literacy rates, availability of schools and retention of Scheduled Caste and Scheduled Tribe children in schools is shown.

Literacy and Enrolment: Uneven Progress

Official data reveals that the educational progress of Scheduled Caste and Scheduled Tribe populations are quite remarkable, but only if one remains focused on the quantitative data, and particularly on enrolment. Sadly, the qualitative data reflects quite another picture and merits closer attention as it zeroes in on a particular situation and gives a richer picture. There are many dynamic factors related to this discrepancy, especially the fact that factors related to schooling processes – such as parental education and occupations which are the major determinants in sustaining a child in school – are often neglected in quantitative analysis. A study conducted in Tamil Nadu reveals that there is a significant difference in completing school education among Scheduled Caste and Scheduled Tribe children due to the social disadvantages they face (Duraisamy, 2001). Variations between states are also quite deceptive if one compares the Gross Enrolment Ratio (GER) with the literacy rates among Scheduled Castes and Scheduled Tribes. For instance, in Bihar, the GER for Scheduled Tribes is 79.2 per cent whereas the literacy rate is only 28.2 per cent. The same is the case for Scheduled Tribes in Orissa, Andhra Pradesh, Jammu and Kashmir, and Uttar Pradesh where the literacy rate is below 40 per cent. In general, literacy rates for Scheduled Castes are better than those for Scheduled Tribe populations. However, three states – Uttar Pradesh, Bihar and Jharkhand – have Scheduled Caste literacy rates that are far below the national average, and Andhra Pradesh and Karnataka have also performed poorly. The data shows that SC and ST children are frequently not retained in the educational process for the complete elementary school cycle.

Physical Access to Schools

Access to schooling is no longer a major impediment to ensuring universal education for Scheduled Castes and Scheduled Tribes. The Sixth All India Educational Survey reveals that in 1993,37 per cent of Scheduled Caste habitations and 46 per cent of Scheduled Tribe habitations had schools within them (NCERT, 1998). In that same year, around 45 per cent of Scheduled Caste habitations had a primary school located no more than one kilometer away, while approximately 30 per cent of Scheduled Tribe population habitations had a primary school within one km. Another 11 per cent of Scheduled Tribe populations and 5.5 per cent of Scheduled Caste populations did not have schools located within two km of their habitation. The simple availability of a school, however, does not guarantee that children will enroll or attend.

Retention

The expansion of schools has also been accompanied by an increased demand for education. A good level of provision of primary schools within a reasonable distance (*i.e.*, within 1 km), shows that many of these children drop out of primary school in the higher grades and do not make the transition to secondary schooling. Rapidly expanding enrolments have been accompanied by changing perceptions of the relevance of schooling, the effectiveness of schools, and the benefits of participation in relation to direct and indirect costs. Primary school graduation rates have not increased as rapidly as would be expected from overall enrolment growth. The problems of capturing and retaining the last 20 per cent of non-enrolled or 'at risk' students, and of increasing promotion, completion and transition rates for girls and boys, are inextricably linked to decisions to participate by the poor and other excluded groups.

Economic pressures force a large number of Scheduled Caste children to leave school at an early age. However, this is not the only reason that children leave. Memories of humiliation can also play an important role in the decision to leave, albeit a less visible one (National Commission on Scheduled Castes and Scheduled Tribes, 1998). The poor quality of education is another critical factor that leads to lower retention. Research has found that the majority of students from Scheduled Caste and Scheduled Tribe communities study in government schools that are badly-equipped in terms of the number of teachers, infrastructure and school environment. Discrimination against under-privileged groups is endemic, and takes numerous forms (PROBE, 1999) in Nicobar Islands, Jammu and Kashmir, Nagaland, Sikkim. In recent years, Himachal Pradesh has reversed a previous negative trend and achieved the lowest dropout rates for both Scheduled Castes and Scheduled Tribes. This is due to active state intervention in the educational field, as primary education has remained a consistent priority of the state government, despite different political parties assuming power in the past years. This has provided the necessary conditions for Himachal Pradesh to achieve and sustain an impressive level of success in the primary education sector (see De *et al.*, 2002). The combinations of four main factors help to determine the retention of a child in the school, namely: *(i)* the income of the household, *(ii)* parental education, *(iii)* home environment and *(iv)* school environment. Thus, a boy coming from an affluent upper caste family is almost certain to enter the schooling system and has a high prospect of completing grade VIII. At the other end of the ladder, a girl from a poor Scheduled Caste family has a weaker prospect of entering the schooling system and much less chance of completing grade VIII (Filmer and Pretchett, 1998 cited in Alexander, 2003). In the following section, we focus particularly on how the cost of schooling and the school environment impact on SC and ST students. Classroom processes, where the invisible and visible discrimination against Scheduled Castes and Scheduled Tribes is evident, are discussed.

Apartheid in Times of Equity

Tilak's (2002) analysis of the NCAER survey data states that there is nothing like 'free' education in India. He reports that household expenditure on education is sizeable; households from poor socio-economic backgrounds (*i.e.*, Scheduled Castes/Scheduled Tribes) often spend considerable amounts of their income on education. This includes elementary education, which is supposed to be provided free by the government. Significant expenditure is made on books, uniforms and fees. Scheduled Tribes often spend much more on elementary education than others groups (*i.e.*, Non-Scheduled Caste/Tribe households), even in government schools. For instance, in Himachal Pradesh, Scheduled Tribe households reportedly spend Rs. 966 per child per year in government schools, while Scheduled Caste households spend Rs. 752 and 'others' spend Rs. 760 (see Tilak, 2002). This is similar in Punjab, Tamil Nadu and in the North-Eastern region. In the same way, Scheduled Castes in Kerala and Gujarat spend more than non-Scheduled Castes on elementary education (Tilak, 2002). On the other hand, it has been argued that the case of the states of Kerala, Himachal Pradesh and Tamil Nadu have confirmed that the link between low enrolment in schools and household poverty is only a weak one, and therefore that universal basic education in India is an achievable goal, if implemented with genuine political will (Filmer and Pretchett, 1998, cited in Alexander, 2003).

The demand for schooling by Scheduled Caste and Scheduled Tribe families has not been matched by supply of quality education. On the contrary, the quality of education and environment in government schools has declined over the years and today not just the rich but also those with middle incomes prefer to send their children to private schools. The shift toward private schools is not restricted to the metropolitan cities but is also apparent in smaller towns in India (Kingdon, 1996). To meet the high demand, a variety of private schools, ranging from super-elite to 'budget', have emerged that cater to students from different socio-economic backgrounds. Today, affluent Scheduled Caste families also often prefer to incur additional expenditure and send their children to private rather than government schools. It is ironic, in this case, that government schools by law appoint only qualified teachers whereas private schools, and especially the 'budget' private schools that have mushroomed in the past decade, often hire unqualified teachers and pay them much less than their government school counterparts. As a result, these schools often provide low quality schooling, yet they are typically perceived to offer better quality education and to improve student's chances of progressing through the education system. Studies show that the demand for private schools is also greater for two additional reasons:

1. the extremely poor infrastructure available in most of the government schools, including a lack of proper buildings, toilet facilities, desks and so forth; and

2. the regional language is the medium of instruction and English language is introduced only later in grade III or IV.

Better infrastructure, quality schooling and English language skills have thus become important criteria in shaping school choices for all social classes. Parents who can access private schools opt for them, and the poorest of the poor remain in government schools. It is relevant to note here that 99 per cent of Scheduled Caste children are enrolled in government schools, thus creating a segregated and highly unequal schooling system.

Gender Equity

The education of Scheduled Caste and Scheduled Tribe girls is a serious issue as they are often doubly disadvantaged, due to both their social status and their gender. Gender equity is a major concern, as the drop out rate is higher among Scheduled Caste and Scheduled Tribe girls at the elementary level. In 2004-05, the drop out rate for Scheduled Caste girls was 60 per cent (compared to 55% for SC boys) and for Scheduled Tribe girls it was 67 per cent (compared to 65% for ST boys) at the elementary level. Girls are particularly disadvantaged because family and social roles often do not prioritise their education (see Bandyopadhyay and Subrahmanian, 2008). The age of girls also affects when they drop out. In many states, early marriage and the economic utility of children leads to large scale drop out in the 5-10 year old and 16-20 year old age groups, interrupting the completion of girls' education (Naidu, 1999).

The government has provided special attendance scholarships for girl students in order to keep them in school. A study conducted in Tamil Nadu illustrates that mother's education also plays a significant role in girls' enrolment and grade attainment. It emphasises that girls tend to access public schools within villages, as they are not allowed to travel long distances to attend schools because of social custom and safety concerns (Duraisamy, 2001).

Policies, Programmes and Initiatives

Until 1999, there was a single National Commission to address Scheduled Caste and Scheduled Tribe, the National Commission for Scheduled Castes and Scheduled Tribes. More recently, and in recognition of the different types of assistance required by Scheduled Caste and Scheduled Tribe populations, two separate Ministries have been established to address their concerns: The Ministry of Tribal Affairs was constituted in October 1999, with the objective of providing more focused attention on the integrated socio-economic development of the most under-privileged Scheduled Tribes in a coordinated and planned manner. The National Commission for Scheduled Castes was re-constituted in 2004 under the banner of the Ministry of Social Justice and Empowerment. The Commission has wide powers to protect, safeguard and promote the interests of Scheduled Caste groups.

The government adopted the Special Component Plan (SCP) in 1979 for the socioeconomic and educational development of Scheduled Castes, as well as the improvement to their working and living conditions. The focus of the strategy is on:

(a) economic development through beneficiary-oriented programmes for raising their income and creating assets;

(b) schemes for infrastructure development in the Scheduled areas;

(c) educational development (Ministry of Social Justice and Empowerment, 2005).

For Scheduled Castes in the Northeastern regions, the Planning Commission issued guidelines in September 1998 which require all central government departments to earmark 10 per cent of their gross budgetary support for specific programmes for the development of Scheduled Castes. This is significant, given that the Scheduled Caste population comprises only 2 per cent of the total population in this region. Moreover, the region had been identified as an untouchability and atrocity-free area. The National Annual Plan approved Rs. 1492 crore (Rs. 14.92 billion) for the year 2004-05 including Rs. 65.80 crore (Rs. 658 million) (Ministry of Social Justice and Empowerment, 2005).

At present, states/UTs with sizeable Scheduled Caste populations are implementing the Special Component Plan. The Ministry of Social Justice and Empowerment provides 100 per cent grants in addition to the Special Component Plan under the Central Sector Scheme of the Special Central Assistance to the states/UTs. It is worked out on the basis of the following criteria:

(i) SC Population of the states/UTs: 40 per cent.

(ii) Relative backwardness of the states/UTs: 10 per cent.

(iii) Percentage of Scheduled Castes families in the states/UTs covered by composite economic development programmes in the State Plan to enable them to cross the poverty line: 25 per cent.

(iv) Percentage of SCP to the Annual Plan: 25 per cent. (Ministry of Social Justice and Empowerment, 2005) Similarly, the Constitution of India incorporates several special provisions for the promotion of the educational and economic interests of Scheduled Tribes as well as their protection from social injustice and all forms of exploitation. These objectives are to be achieved through a strategy known as the Tribal Sub-Plan (TSP) strategy, which was adopted at the beginning of the Fifth Five-year Plan (1974-79). The strategy seeks to ensure adequate flow of funds for tribal development from the State Plan allocations, schemes/programmes of central ministries/departments, financial and developmental institutions. The corner-stone of this strategy has been

to ensure that funds are earmarked for TSP by states/UTs in proportion to their Scheduled Tribe populations (Ministry of Tribal Affairs, 2005). To look after the Scheduled Tribe population in a coordinated manner, Integrated Tribal Development Projects were also conceived as part of the Fifth Five-year Plan, and these have continued to be a feature of successive Five-year Plans. During the Sixth Plan (1980-85), the Modified Area Development Approach (MADA) was adopted to cover smaller areas of tribal concentration and during the Seventh Plan (1985-89), the TSP strategy was further extended to cover even smaller areas of Scheduled Tribe concentration. There are now 194 Integrated Tribal Development Projects (ITDPs) in areas of the country where the Scheduled Tribes population is more than 50 per cent of the total population. During the Sixth Plan, pockets outside ITDP areas with a total population of 10,000 and with a ST population of at least 5,000 were covered under the Tribal Sub-Plan and MADA. To date, 252 MADA pockets have been identified in the country as a whole (Ministry of Tribal Affairs, 2005). In the total Tenth Plan outlay, an additional Rs. 1754 crores (Rs. 17.54 billion) was granted for their development in addition to the programmes of Special Central Assistance to the Tribal Sub Plan and Grants under Article 275(1) of the Constitution of India (Ministry of Tribal Affairs, 2005a). The educational development of this group is also targeted through various other schemes, including the establishment of ashram schools.

Incentive Schemes: Ensuring Access and Equity

One way of getting Scheduled Caste and Scheduled Tribe students into school is through the provision of various incentives. Incentives can be categorised in a variety of ways – they can be tangible or intangible, financial or non-financial, direct or indirect. The four major categories are:

1. *Financial Interventions*: Cash transfers directly to a family/child or in a bank (to access later); scholarships/stipends; provision of textbooks, stationery and uniforms; school vouchers and transport assistance (bus passes/cycles).
2. *Provision of Mid-Day Meals:* And other health related interventions: provision of free meals, food distribution to families, provision of Iron and Vitamin A tablets, inoculation and vaccination, separate sanitation facilities and provision of water.
3. *Social Welfare Intervention*: Provision of hostels and interventions for children with special needs.
4. *Additional Incentives:* Aimed at qualitative improvements: improving infrastructure, provision of quality teaching-learning, introduction of computers, sports facilities and remedial teaching, bridge courses, and appointment of Para teachers (Educational Research Unit, 2006). A variety

of these types of incentive schemes have been launched by the central government in order to attract students from Scheduled Caste and Scheduled Tribe communities, including free education at primary level, scholarships, hostel facilities, mid-day meal schemes, free uniforms, free textbooks and attendance-based scholarship for girls. The Mid-day Meal Scheme is the largest and most ambitious programme ever attempted by the Indian Government (or any government in the world) as an attempt to achieve universal elementary education.

State Level Programmes and Policies

At the national level, the Kasturba Gandhi Balika Vidyalaya (KGBV), a special school programme for girl children from Scheduled Castes, Scheduled Tribes, Other Backward Classes (OBC) and other minorities in low female literacy districts, was launched in 2004-05. It aimed to ensure access and quality education to girls through 750 residential schools and boarding facilities at elementary level. Efforts to implement the programme are not uniform at the state level, however, as some states are pro-active in focusing on SC/ST students and some are not.

REFERENCES

Secada, W. G. (1989), Educational Equity *vs.* Equality of Education: An Alternative Conception. In Secada, W.G. (ed.), *Equity in Education.* New York: Falmer Press.

Alexander, J.M. (2003), Inequality, Poverty and Affirmative Action: Contemporary Trends in India. Paper prepared for the WIDER Conference, *Inequality, Poverty and Human Well-being*, 30-31 May, 2003, United Nations University, Helsinki, Finland.

Jeffrey, C., Jeffery, R. and Jeffery, P. (2002), Degrees Without Freedom: The Impact of Formal Education on Dalit Young Men in North India. *Development and Change*, 35(5): pp. 963-986.

Omvedt, G. (1993), *Dalits and the Democratic Revolution: Dr. Ambedkar and the Dalit Movement in Colonial India*. New Delhi: Sage Publications.

Surajit, S. (2002), Tribal Solidarity Movements in India: A Review. In Shah, G. (ed.) *Social Movements and the State: Readings in Indian Government and Politics*. New Delhi: Sage Publications.

Sujatha, K. (2002), Education among Scheduled Tribes. In Govinda, R. (ed.), *India Education Report: A Profile of Basic Education*. New Delhi: Oxford University Press.

Secada, W.G. (1989), Educational Equity *vs* Equality of Education: An Alternative Conception. In Secada, W.G. (ed.), *Equity in Education*. New York: Falmer Press.

Illiah, K. (2000), The State Oppressions and Weaker Sections. In Rao, C. S. and Francis, D. (eds.), *Development of Weaker Sections*. Jaipur and New Delhi: Rawat Publications.

Subrahmanian, R. (2005), Education Exclusion and the Development State. In Chopra, R., and Jeffery, P. (eds.), *Educational Regimes in Contemporary India*. New Delhi: Sage Publications.

Drèze, J. and Sen, A.K. (2002), *India: Development and Participation*. New Delhi: Oxford University Press.

PROBE (1999), *Public Report on Basic Education in India*. New Delhi: Oxford University Press.

Tilak, J. B. G. (2002), Determinants of Household Expenditure on Education in Rural India. National Council of Applied Economic Research Working Paper Series No. 88. Delhi: NCAER.

Naidu, T. S. (1999), *Strategic Planning for the Future Development of the Tribes in India*. Puducherry: Centre for Future Studies, Pondicherry University.

Duraisamy, P. (2001), Effectiveness of Incentives on School Enrolment and Attainment. *Journal of Educational Planning and Administration*. XV (2): pp. 155-177.

Index

Index

J

K

L

M

N

W

X

Y

Z